Marketing Channels

The Advances in Retailing Series

The Institute of Retail Management (IRM) was established to advance the under-standing and practice of retailing by serving as a bridge between the academic community and industry. Two of the principal avenues the IRM uses to achieve this goal are conferences focusing on the latest ideas and research, and publications, including the *Journal of Retailing* and conference proceedings. Thus, the IRM's two most important audiences are academic scholars and practitioners in retailing-related fields.

The Advances in Retailing Series brings together the IRM's conference and publication programs. Initiated with valuable input from both retailers and academics, the series presents an enduring collection of up-to-date studies of problems and issues in retailing theory and practice. It is intended to respond to a variety of pervasive needs by: presenting timely assessments of new developments in the field, bringing fresh perspectives from other industries to critical issues in retailing, stimulating further research on challenging issues raised at conferences, and fostering productive communication and cooperation between retailing executives and academic researchers.

We believe that, as a whole, this series effectively addresses these and other needs. We invite comments and suggestions from our readers on how it can best fulfill its purpose.

The books in the Advances in Retailing Series are:

Personal Selling: Theory, Research and Practice
Edited by Jacob Jacoby and C. Samuel Craig

Managing Human Resources in Retail Organizations
Edited by Arthur P. Brief

Perceived Quality: How Consumers View Stores and Merchandise
Edited by Jacob Jacoby and Jerry C. Olson

The Service Encounter
Edited by John A. Czepiel, Michael R. Solomon, and Carol Surprenant

Marketing Channels: Relationships and Performance
Edited by Luca Pellegrini and Srinivas K. Reddy

 Institute of Retail Management
New York University

Marketing Channels

Relationships and Performance

Luca Pellegrini
CESCOM, Bocconi University, Milan
Srinivas K. Reddy
New York University

Lexington Books
D.C. Heath and Company/Lexington, Massachusetts/Toronto

Library of Congress Cataloging-in-Publication Data

Marketing channels.

(The Advances in retailing series)
"Some of the papers presented at the Third International Conference on Distribution,
held at Angera, Italy, on April 19 and 20, 1985, sponsored by the Centro di Studi Sul
Commercio of the Università Bocconi, Milan, and the Institute of Retail Management,
New York University"—Pref.
Includes index.
1. Marketing channels—Congresses. I. Pellegrini, Luca. II. Reddy, Srinivas K.
III. International Conference on Distribution (3rd : 1985 : Angera, Italy) IV. Università
commerciale Luigi Bocconi. Centro di studi sul commercio. V. New York University.
Institute of Retail Management. VI. Series.
HF5415.129.M37   1986   658.8′7   86-45186
ISBN 0-669-13158-X (alk. paper)

Published simultaneously in Canada
Printed in the United States of America
Casebound International Standard Book Number: 0-669-13158-X
Library of Congress Catalog Card Number: 86-45186

The paper used in this publication meets the minimum requirements of American National
Standard for Information Sciences—Permanence of Paper for Printed Library Materials,
ANSI Z39.48-1984.

The last numbers on the right below indicate the number and date of printing.

10 9 8 7 6 5 4 3 2 1

95 94 93 92 91 90 89 88 87 86

To Ilaria and Haritha

Contents

Preface and Acknowledgments

T his book contains some of the papers presented at the Third International Conference on Distribution, held at Angera, Italy, April 19 and 20, 1985. The conference, sponsored by the Centro di Studi Sul Commercio (CESCOM) of the Università Bocconi (Milan) and the Institute of Retail Management (IRM) of New York University, attracted scholars from economics and marketing disciplines who are researching issues pertaining to distribution. *Marketing Channels* focuses on relationships within marketing channels and their effect on performance.

The chapters in part I deal with vertical agreements in a distribution channel. In chapter 1, Rey and Tirole explore three contractual schemes: (1) the two-part tariff, which the authors portray as the competitive solution, (2) resale price maintenance (RPM), and (3) exclusive territories. The results they obtain throw some new light on established theories. First, in many instances, a competitive policy is shown to be superior to vertical restraints from the manufacturer's point of view when the manufacturer has incomplete information about the retailers' environment. This is true not just for undifferentiated (competitive) retailers, but also when they differ and there is uncertainty about their costs. Basically, this result is a consequence of the superior insurance property of the two-part tariff competitive contract. A second finding is that the well-established conclusions about the equivalence of RPM and exclusive territories under conditions of perfect information are questionable when uncertainty about costs and demand is introduced into the analysis. Cost uncertainty leads to higher manufacturer's profits under RPM, and demand uncertainty has the same result under exclusive territories policies.

In chapter 2, Comanor and Kirkwood view vertical restraints—specifically, RPM—as arising from promotional externalities through free-rider behavior. Like Rey and Tirole, these authors also reach the conclusion that vertical RPM reduces economic efficiency. There is wide agreement that if RPM does not facilitate horizontal collusion, the imposition of RPM to enhance the production of retail services (and the implied price increase) does not harm consumers if sales increase. Also, since the upstream agent would not want to set the price

x • *Marketing Channels*

above the monopoly level, because it would lose sales and profits, there does not seem to be any reason for public intervention. A simple rule of thumb to judge the likely effects of RPM rests, therefore, on its effect on sales: If sales increase, RPM is bound to have positive effects; that is, consumers will evaluate the additional services positively. Comanor and Kirkwood point out that this result stands on the assumption that given an increase in sales, monopolist's profits and consumers' welfare necessarily move in the same direction. But in comparing the two states—with RPM and without RPM—one must consider that although profits are affected only by the behavior of marginal consumers, social welfare is also affected by the impact of RPM on intramarginal consumers. If, for some reason, intramarginal consumers do not evaluate the added services positively, there is no assurance that the overall welfare effect is going to be positive. A case in point is when the additional services consist in providing information about a product's use. Such information is useful to "ignorant" consumers, who will be induced to buy the product, but is of no value to those who already know how to use it. Thus, although an increase in sales and profits can be attributed to the additional purchases of "ignorant" consumers, a change in welfare must be computed by also taking into account the lack of benefit to intramarginal, well-informed customers. Comanor and Kirkwood conclude that this situation may not be uncommon and that it would therefore be unwise to weaken the current regulations against RPM. The only possible exceptions might be the products of new market entrants, since most potential purchasers of such products would be "ignorant" of their specifications.

The first two chapters thus deal with vertical restraints, comparing their outcomes mainly from the point of view of interbrand competition. In the literature, however, more attention has been paid to resale restraints than to restraints that affect interbrand competition, although in practice such restraints are regarded by firms as important tools in shaping their marketing strategies. An explanation of this discrepancy may lie in the more benevolent attitude of antitrust law toward contracts that affect interbrand competition. For example, in the United States, exclusive dealing is not illegal per se. In addition, the issue of market foreclosure, often raised in courts in connection with interbrand effects, has not found a sympathetic reception in the economic analysis literature. In our view, there has been a great need for further research on the incentives and effects—procompetitive or not—of this second type of restraint. Such research is reported in the next two chapters in part I.

In chapter 3, John Chard examines the conditions under which exclusive dealing may have procompetitive effects. He deals with three main issues that may justify exclusive dealing: (1) the provision of information services by the manufacturer, (2) the maintenance of a reputation for quality, and (3) the structure of delivery costs. The first two motives involve some form of opportunistic behavior by retailers with respect to either the sales efforts devoted to a particular product or the provision of specific services needed to guarantee its quality standards. Retailers may exploit the investment made by the manufacturer to establish a reputation for quality, using its product to promote their entire assortment, and then take advantage of the substitutability among competing brands and convince consumers to shift to products that are more profitable because of lower manufacturers' investments. For this to occur, consumers would have to have imperfect information about product specifications, which is a credible assumption for a large number of markets. Such behavior can be particularly resented if the manufacturer is not in a position to protect its investment through patent or copyright—for example, when the design of the product accounts for a large part of its cost. Although exclusive dealing can only partially protect the manufacturer from copying, it at least avoids such behavior within a given shop. The same guarantee is necessary when the manufacturer provides specific services to retailers, such as staff training, and free riding by competitors is possible. Regarding the third incentive to exclusive dealing—the structure of delivery costs—Chard examines instances in which administrative controls are superior to price incentives for reducing transaction costs.

In chapter 4, Luca Pellegrini analyzes the rationale of yet another type of contract—sale or return agreements, whereby manufacturers accept back unsold items, thus taking on the costs related to unsold inventories. Such contracts are less common than those mentioned earlier. However, as they can apply not only to a few goods—typically, magazines and newspapers—but also to services bought or booked through agencies, the practice is less uncommon than may be immediately apparent. The common characteristics of goods or services to which sale or return agreements apply are high perishability and low or zero value of unsold inventories. It may appear, therefore, that the high risk involved in their trade is the reason for such contracts, as producers are forced to assume the cost of this risk to convince retailers to carry their products. Chapter 4 shows that this is not the case and that under certain conditions, a price incentive could be sufficient to convince retailers to hold the amount of product that maximizes producers' profits. The real incentive for sale or return agreements is found in the asymmetries that arise in relation to the penalty cost associated with excess demand accruing to producers and retailers. If the product of a given firm has good substitutes among competing products in the same shop, the retailer is likely to have a low excess demand penalty cost, as it can shift excess demand to other products. This may not be true for the producing firm, as it loses present sales—and possibly future sales—because of consumers' dissatisfaction. If this is the case, sale or return agreements shield the firm from excess demand penalty costs and allocate more efficiently the trading risk involved in marketing its product. In addition, in some instances, the incentive for sale or return agreements is enhanced by the covariant risk advantage that manufacturers have with respect to retailers.

Part II deals with coordination of a marketing channel—a critical and often complex task. Proper management of the complex set of interrelationships in a distribution channel not only affects the morale of the members of the channel but also affects the profitability of all those involved. In chapter 5, Reve and Stern build a political economy model to explore the relationships between interorganizational form, transaction climate, and economic performance in vertical (seller–buyer) interfirm dyads. Their study is based on a unique data base, with data collected from both sides of the dyad. This is a departure from previous research, which relied on data from only one side of the dyad. This chapter indicates the basic direction the research on complex interactions in marketing channels should take to draw valid insights.

Channel managers need diagnostic tools to assess the effectiveness of their channels. It is essential that they classify channel members in order to evaluate them. In chapter 6, Rangan develops a theoretical approach to the classification of channel members by a manufacturing firm. This classification and positioning of channel members on a price/service scale suggests alternative strategies for improving the profitability and length of an account's relationship with a seller.

Distribution is a crucial strategic factor for newspapers and magazines because of their short life span. In chapter 7, Cristini analyzes the distribution choices made by producers of magazines and newspapers and their competitive effects. Based on the results of research conducted in four European countries, he shows that the widely different distribution choices made by publishers are related to channel power considerations. Where wholesalers have a strong bargaining position with respect to producers, producers move to strengthen their direct distribution to consumers. In contrast, where producers have maintained their control of distribution channels, their preferred option is selling through retailers.

In chapter 8 Bamossy and Scammon examine the economic impact of the practice of counterfeiting and related unfair business practices in a variety of industries and countries. They discuss the market factors that contribute to the phenomenon of counterfeiting and assess the roles played by the various channel members in the distribution of counterfeit products. They also present some research questions relating to the costs and benefits of anti-counterfeiting activities and develop a framework to investigate the impact of such activities on the channel members.

The final three chapters (part III) deal with location strategy and forecasting of seasonal demand for retail stores. Choosing where to locate a store outlet is a key strategic decision, as location is an important determinant of the long-term success of a retail store. Whereas most retail location models assume that consumers make single-purpose shopping trips, Ghosh and McLafferty (chapter 9) examine the effect of multipurpose shopping behavior—a more realistic scenario—on the spatial organization of retail stores. They develop a location allocation model that simultaneously determines optimal consumer shopping patterns and retail locations.

What is the impact of changes in the physical environment of a retail store (such as location, layout, and store design) on the store's image? In chapter 10, Dickson examines the dynamics of retail store images over time. In a study of a store that changed location and layout, he finds significant improvement in the image of the store after these changes. However, the image structure, obtained through factor analysis, was unchanged over time. Dickson concludes that the composition of image structure can be considered a stable marketing variable.

In chapter 11, Kelly and Geurts report on a comparison of four methods of forecasting annual sales of seasonal items: (1) an econometric model, (2) a smoothing model, (3) an average of the first two models, and (4) a subjective judgment model. They find that the econometric model performs best across all five product groups.

We gratefully acknowledge the support and contributions of many individuals in organizing the conference and completing this book. The conference would not have been possible without the generous financial contributions of Cassa di Risparimio delle Provincie Lombarde (CARIPLO), the Mediocredito Lombardo, the Chamber of Commerce of Varese, Italy, and the Institute of Retail Management of New York University. We particularly owe our thanks to Professor Antonio Confalonieri, chairman of CARIPLO; Professor Angelo Caloia, chairman of the Mediocredito Lombardo; and Dr. Tino Riganti, chairman of the Chamber of Commerce of Varese for their support in organizing the conference. We also thank Professor Jack Jacoby, director of the IRM, and Professor Aldo Spranzi, director of CESCOM. Linda Nagel and Peggy McKee were extremely helpful during the early stages and were mainly responsible for the excellent response we had from fourteen countries. We also appreciate the help of the reviewers, whose dedicated work is reflected in the high quality of the papers presented at the conference. Finally, we thank the contributors for their patience during the editorial process.

Part I
Vertical Agreements

1

Vertical Restraints from a Principal-Agent Viewpoint

Patrick Rey
Jean Tirole

Much of economic theory is concerned with the study of linear prices, whereby the buyer pays to the seller an amount proportional to the quantity bought. Vertical relationships between manufacturers and retailers (or wholesalers), however, often involve more complex contracting arrangements, broadly named *vertical restraints*. These arrangements range from simple nonlinear price contracts—for instance, those that impose a franchise fee—to instruments that restrict intrabrand or interbrand competition, such as assignments of exclusive territories and exclusive dealing.

The natural theoretical framework for studying these restraints is the principal-agent paradigm. Indeed, we would argue that this is one of the most important fields covered by the principal-agent theory. First, vertical restraint contracts are often more explicit than contracts in other applications of the paradigm, so data can be obtained more easily. Second, vertical restraints are important business strategy instruments; because of this, and because of their observability, they are the object of many policy interventions (for example, antitrust suits). Industrial organization theorists have long recognized this.

We should mention at the outset that principal-agent theory, in its current state, is not a panacea. On the one hand, a number of restraints relate to intrabrand or interbrand competition, whereas most existing applications of principal-agent theory are concerned with a competition-free output. On the other hand, potential arbitrage between retailers, as well as legal constraints, often restricts the set of contracts that a manufacturer can offer to its retailers. Thus, the study of vertical restraints has evolved rather independently of principal-agent theory. (Actually, many of the ideas evoked here were suggested before this theory even existed.) We will try to explain the difference in emphasis between the theory and its application here.

Research support from the Sloan Foundation is gratefully acknowledged. We are grateful to Ralph Winter for helpful comments.

The purpose of this chapter is to survey and classify some ideas associated with vertical restraints.[1] We will discuss their rationale (the issue of private desirability) and their social consequences (social desirability). In the following section, we define the main restraints. Then we look at what we call *control problems*—the subject of most discussions of vertical restraints. It is assumed that there is nothing stochastic in the environment, which is known before the parties sign the contract. Some actions taken by the involved parties (mainly by the retailer) are not observable or verifiable in a court. We first identify the externalities associated with linear prices—between the producer and the retailer, between retailers, or between producers. We then discuss which vertical restraints are especially adequate to correct these externalities.

The next section discusses the new features associated with uncertainty. There, it is assumed that the parties sign contracts under symmetric information but that, after signing, the retailers have superior information about the environment (retail cost or local demand). We note that vertical restraints may not be privately desirable (that is, they are not specified by the contracts), and we show that even when they are privately desirable, they may not be socially desirable. We explain this by the link between uncertainty and the consumer price's average level and flexibility to demand and cost shocks.

We conclude the chapter with a few remarks about cases in which the parties have asymmetric information when signing contracts; this subject has received little attention in the context of vertical restraints.

Linear Prices versus Vertical Restraints

We will start with a basic framework and notation and later enrich the model and the notation.

Basic Framework

The basic framework involves a single supplier, called the *manufacturer*. The manufacturer produces an intermediate good at constant unit cost c, is the only producer of this good, and sells it to a single retailer. The retailer resells the product and, in the simple case, has no retailing cost. (We will introduce a constant unit retail cost γ when we discuss uncertainty.) Formally, after signing the contract, the retailer has a monopoly on a technology that transforms one unit of an intermediate good into one unit of a final good. We use p to denote the wholesale (intermediate) price, q to denote the consumer (final) price, and x to denote the quantity bought by the retailer (x also denotes the final consumption if the retailer does not throw away any intermediate goods). The downward-sloping demand function is $x = D(q)$ (see figure 1–1). We will

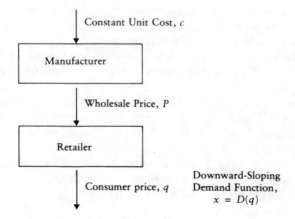

Figure 1–1. Basic Framework

later assume that demand also depends on a promotional effort e exerted by the retailer: $x = D(q, e)$.

We will now define some of the most common contracting forms between manufacturers and retailers:

A *linear price* contract specifies only a payment $T(x) = px$ from the retailer to the manufacturer, where x is the retailer's choice.

A *franchise fee* contract is the simplest example of a nonlinear price (or payment function) contract. The retailer pays $T(x) = A + px$, where A is the franchise fee. We will discuss more general nonlinear prices and their relevance here.

Resale price maintenance (RPM) is a provision in the contract that dictates the choice of the final price q to the retailer. Variants of this restraint are the imposition of a price ceiling, $q \leq \bar{q}$, or a price floor, $q \geq \underline{q}$. (Thus, RPM is a price ceiling plus a price floor, such that $\underline{q} = \bar{q}$).

Quantity fixing specifies the amount x to be bought by the retailer. Variants of this restraint are *quantity forcing*, $x \geq x$, and *quantity rationing*, $x \leq x$. If demand is known and depends on the final price only, and if the retailer cannot throw away the good, quantity forcing is equivalent to a price ceiling, quantity rationing is equivalent to a price floor, and quantity fixing is equivalent to RPM.

Before enlarging the model and further defining common vertical restraints, we will discuss why the theory has focused on such primitive restraints and when these restraints can be imposed. The most obvious cause of the focus is that these restraints are simple and commonly used. But they may not be as primitive as they look in the environments in which they have been studied.

Consider, first, a control, or deterministic, environment (see next section for more details). The manufacturer's concern is to ensure that the retailer picks the "right actions" (for instance, final price or promotional effort). The retailer's decision is generally dictated by the marginal price it pays for the intermediate good. However, in a control environment, the amount of intermediate good consumed and, thus, its marginal price can be foreseen perfectly. Therefore, there is no loss in adopting a two-part tariff—that is, a franchise fee plus a fixed marginal price (at least if the retailer's objective function is concave)—so there is no point in considering more complex nonlinear prices. This vindicates the focus on franchise fees in the literature discussed in the next section.

This justification of two-part tariffs does not hold in a stochastic environment. As is well-known in both adverse selection theory[2] and moral hazard theory,[3] a constant marginal price is generally not desirable, so the manufacturer may wish to use more complex nonlinear prices. However, arbitrage may prevent him from doing so. If there are several retailers (for example, in different markets or geographic areas), some may "bootleg" to prevent total price discrimination. Although it is easy to control the quantity bought directly by a retailer, it is much harder to observe the quantity the retailer actually sells. The usual result is that, with many arbitraging buyers, the upstream unit can only charge linear prices. In the present context, however, the manufacturer can usually observe whether the retailer carries the product and thus can demand the payment of a franchise fee (so long as courts confirm this right). Thus, two-part tariffs can be used despite arbitrage.

This brings us to the following small but important point: the set of vertical restraints that can be used in practice depends on the informational environment—that is, on what can be observed and enforced by the manufacturer. (If the enforcement mechanism is associated with the legal system, the court must also be able to verify the manufacturer's information.) For instance, RPM is not practicable if the retailer can give hidden discounts to its customers.[4] Similarly, quantity fixing is somewhat meaningless in an environment in which the retailers arbitrage. The literature on vertical restraints, like most of the principal-agent theory literature, assumes that relevant variables can be monitored at zero or infinite cost. The zero-one nature of enforceability is a convenient but extreme assumption.

Intrabrand Competition

We will now introduce the possibility of competition among several retailers in the same market. The type of restraint that can be used by the manufacturer in such a case is *exclusive territories*, which divides the final market among the retailers. (See figure 1–2.) A similar restraint is a limit on the density of retailers.

Territories can be understood in a spatial sense but also more broadly in a market segmentation sense (for instance, public versus private markets). The informational requirement is strong for such a restraint to be feasible. For example, in the spatial interpretation of the model, the manufacturer must be able to trace customers and to prove (in case of cheating) that the retailer was aware of their origin (or if not, that obtaining this information would not have been costly). Thus, exclusive territories are more commonly used when the downstream units are wholesalers. Note, however, that allocation of a retail monopoly situation in an isolated territory serves the purpose of the exclusive territories restraint, as do refusals to deal.

Several Inputs

Assume that the downstream unit uses several inputs to produce the final good. Here, the downstream unit can be a manufacturer, or it can be a retailer that sells complementary products to the customer. A restraint specific to this feature is a *tie-in*, whereby the supplier of one of the inputs forces the downstream unit to purchase the other inputs from it (see figure 1–3). (To be precise, we should distinguish between *bundling*, which fixes the quantities of other inputs per unit of manufacturer input, and *requirements contracting*, whereby the manufacturer simply requires that the retailer buy the other inputs from it. The distinction matters under conditions of uncertainty.) All intermediate products are thus tied, and the manufacturer can charge prices for the other inputs that differ from their market prices.

Interbrand Competition

A retailer may sell goods that are close substitutes to the product supplied by the manufacturer. The manufacturer may then impose *exclusive dealing* on

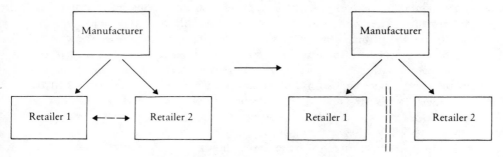

Figure 1–2. Exclusive Territories

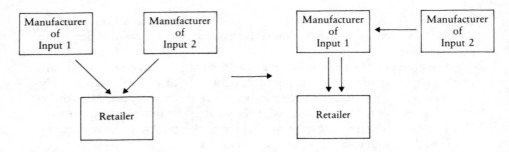

Figure 1–3. Tie-ins

the retailer, which prevents the retailer from selling goods that directly compete with the manufacturer's product.[5]

The foregoing discussion does not exhaust the list of possible contractual provisions. Variations depend on the environment. For instance, if the manufacturer is in charge of national advertising for the product, the contract may include a provision concerning such expenses.

We must conclude this discussion with a few words about the constantly changing legal status of these restraints in the United States. In general, franchise fees are legal, but RPM is currently illegal. Exclusive territories, once forbidden, are now subject to the rule of reason, but tie-ins are illegal.

Control Environments

A *control environment* is a situation in which the contract between the manufacturer and the retailer is signed only when all relevant information about the environment is known and public, so there is no exogenous uncertainty. Whereas the principal-agent theory literature has focused on situations with uncertainty, most of the work on vertical restraints deals with control environments. There are good reasons for this difference. Models that are studied in the principal-agent literature are often so simple that the control problem is trivial.[6] In contrast, the study of somewhat complex control environments with vertical restraints has yielded interesting insights for business strategy. Furthermore, the study of control environments can be considered a first step in the study of more complex problems in which uncertainty does play a role. It thus becomes important to master the control issues.

The problem considered in the control literature is as follows. A number of possibly dependent variables must be chosen by the vertical structure: quantity purchased by the retailer, consumer price, promotional effort, retail location, wholesale price, franchise fee, and so forth. However, only a subset of these variables can be observed and used in the contract. These observable variables are called *instruments*. *Targets* form another subset of choice variables—those that directly affect the aggregate profit (the sum of the manufacturer's and the retailer's profits). Promotional effort and retail price are targets. The franchise fee and the wholesale price are not, because they do not *directly* affect the aggregate profit.[7] The control problem consists in knowing how to use the instruments to reach or come close to the desired values of the targets. (See the following remark for a discussion of what we mean by "desired values.") The literature often considers when there are "enough" instruments to achieve the maximum aggregate profit or vertically integrated profit—that is, the aggregate profit that would obtain if all choice variables were costlessly observable and specified in the contract—what Mathewson and Winter (1982, 1984) call a *sufficient* set of instruments.

Remark on Franchise Fees. If the manufacturer imposes a franchise fee on the retailer, in the absence of uncertainty, only a *constrained-efficient contract* is signed. A constrained-efficient contract is a contract that maximizes the aggregate profit subject to the incentive constraints (decentralization of actions). (See the later discussion of the double marginalization example, in which, because of the absence of a franchise fee, gains from trade between the manufacturer and the retailer are not realized.) This property also holds if the manufacturer and the retailer bargain over the contract; that is, bargaining affects only the level of the lump-sum payment (franchise fee). For our examples, we will assume that the manufacturer chooses the contract. This makes sense if there is a competitive supply of potential retailers.

Franchise fees often have no incentive effects, although they do when the manufacturer cannot control the number of retailers. In such cases, the franchise fee has an effect on entry and is an instrument. Although we may use the term *targets* in other circumstances, we will mainly define it for situations in which a franchise fee is imposed. The basis for the definition of *optimal targets* is then the aggregate profit.[8]

Our control environment is similar to Tinbergen's (1952) economic policy problem, which involved using policy instruments to reach macroeconomic targets.

Consideration of control environments has two small but important consequences. First, risk aversion plays no role, as everything can be foreseen when the contract is signed.[9] Second, in a control environment, most of the restraints that are feasible and costless to enforce are *privately desirable*.[10] The proof is obvious. For any contract, the two parties can foresee the actions they will choose. Fixing them in advance, when feasible, can do no harm to the vertical structure.[11] (Note that this holds even if the set of instruments is not sufficient.)

We will now see how these concepts apply to various environments. For each environment, we start with the choice of actions by a vertically integrated structure, then define the externality associated with linear prices, and finally give various restraints that can be used to correct the externality (contingent on being feasible and effective, of course).

Basic Structure

To study the one manufacturer–one retailer structure, we will begin with a classic issue: *double marginalization* (Spengler, 1950). The vertical structure's only target is the consumer price. The vertically integrated quantity x^m and final price q^m are determined by $x^m = D(q^m)$, and q^m maximizes $\{ (q - c)D(q) \}$.

Consider the decentralized structure and the retailer's choice of the consumer price under a linear wholesale price: $T(x) = px$. The retailer maximizes $\{ (q - p)D(q) \}$. To make a profit, the manufacturer charges $p > c$, which implies that the consumer price chosen by the retailer satisfies $q > q^m$.[12] Because of two successive marginalizations, the consumer price exceeds the vertically integrated price. The externality arises because the retailer does not take the manufacturer's marginal profit $\{ (p - c)D'(q) \}$ into account.

To keep the consumer price (target) down to q^m, the manufacturer may use a franchise fee or RPM. The manufacturer can avoid a distortion at the wholesale level by charging $p = c$ and recovering the retailer's profit by using a franchise fee $(A = (q^m - c)D(q^m))$. The retailer is then the *residual claimant* of the aggregate profit. The marginal cost the retailer faces (c) is the true marginal cost of the vertical structure. Thus, the retailer takes the "right decision." This is a very general principle: in a basic control environment in which all noncontrollable actions are taken by the retailer, making the retailer the residual claimant maximizes aggregate profit and therefore is optimal. Thus, the franchise fee and the wholesale price are sufficient instruments. This simple result also applies in the examples involving promotional effort and multiple inputs. It also holds under uncertainty if the retailer is risk-neutral (see the later section on uncertainty).

Using RPM—that is, fixing the retail price at q^m—clearly solves the double marginalization problem. Actually, a price ceiling $(q \leq q^m)$ or quantity forcing $(x \geq x^m)$ would suffice. To recover the retailer's profit without using a franchise fee, the manufacturer can charge a wholesale price $p = q^m$.

As a second example, we introduce a *promotional effort*, e, exerted by the retailer. The effort costs the retailer a monetary equivalent $\phi(e)$ per unit of output and is not observed by the manufacturer. The demand function is $x = D(q, e)$. Here, e can be considered a presales service.

The vertically integrated consumer price q^m and effort e^m maximize $\{ (q - c - \phi(e)) D(q, e) \}$.

Under linear pricing, the manufacturer charges a wholesale price $p > c$. Thus, for any consumer price q, the retailer's profit margin $(q - p)$ is smaller than the vertical structure's profit margin $(q - c)$. Hence, the retailer's incentive to exert effort is too small. This externality generalizes the double marginalization externality. Here, the retailer also fails to take into account the extra profit for the manufacturer that is associated with an increase in effort: $(p - c)(\partial D/\partial e)$.

To encourge more effort and to obtain the vertically integrated profit, the vertical structure can make the retailer a residual claimant, as noted earlier:

$$p = c$$
$$A = \max_{q,e} \{ (q - c - \phi(e))D(q, e) \}$$

Note that, in this case, addition of one target (effort) does not require more instruments. Quantity forcing is also a sufficient instrument: it suffices that the manufacturer chooses $p = q^m - \phi(e^m)$ and $\underline{x} = x^m$. The retailer obtains a zero profit by charging q^m and exerting effort e^m, and the manufacturer's profit is the monopoly profit (see Mathewson and Winter, 1984).

Remark on Bilateral Effort. Suppose that the manufacturer also chooses some level of effort (brand advertising, for example) at total monetary cost $\phi(E)$. Demand, $x = D(q, e, E)$, increases with the two levels of effort. Let (q^m, e^m, E^m) maximize $\{ (q - c - \phi(e))D(q, e, E) - \phi(E) \}$. If E can be contracted for, no new problem arises. If E cannot be observed and q and e are chosen by the retailer (simultaneously with the manufacturer's choice of E), the two-part tariff that makes the retailer a residual claimant is no longer sufficient. The absence of manufacturer's profit margin leads to a minimal level of effort E (such as zero).

The moral hazard problems associated with the choice of e and E can be solved through two-part tariffs if both are residual claimants—that is, if the retailer's profit margin is equal to $[q - c - \phi(e)]$ and the manufacturer's profit margin is equal to $[q^m - c - \phi(e^m)]$, where q^m and e^m are the vertically integrated price and the retailing effort. But this is feasible only if there is a third party playing the role of a "marginal source," paying the manufacturer $\{ [q^m - \phi(e^m)] x \}$ while the retailer pays the source $\{A + cx\}$, where $A \equiv [q^m - c - \phi(e^m)]D(q^m, e^m, E^m)$.[13] This solution may be difficult to implement: first, side transfers of good x may be hard for the source to observe; second, and more generally, there is scope for a coalition between the manufacturer and the retailer, because the vertical structure's profit margin becomes $\{ [q - c - \phi(e)] + [q^m - c - \phi(e^m)] \}$, thus exceeding the margin without the source. Thus, a coalition between a manufacturer and a retailer leads to "too much" output and to a negative profit for the source.

As a last example, we will take a model with *several inputs*, which resembles much of the previous two cases. Suppose that the retailer uses two inputs, the manufacturer's good and another intermediate good produced competitively at cost (and sold at price) c'. Aside from the final price, the downstream unit (retailer) must choose inputs x and x' to produce output $y = f(x, x')$. The demand function is $y = D(q)$. (Here we distingish between the quantity of the intermediate good and that of the final good.) The two inputs are substitutes in the production function. The vertical structure's maximum profit is given by

$$\max_{x, x'} \{D^{-1}[f(x, x')]f(x, x') - cx - c'x'\}.$$

Let x^m and x'^m denote the solution.

Under linear pricing, again the manufacturer chooses a wholesale price $p > c$. So the relative price of inputs for the retailer $\{p/c'\}$ exceeds the true relative price $\{c/c'\}$ for the vertical structure. The retailer thus substitutes toward the other input and consumes too little of the manufacturer's intermediate good.

To reach the maximum aggregate profit, the retailer again can be made the residual claimant: $p = c$, $A = D^{-1}[f(x^m, x'^m)]f(x^m, x'^m) - cx^m - c'x'^m$. Alternatively, the manufacturer can impose a tie-in, together with RPM. The tie-in allows the manufacturer to impose the true relative price of inputs $p/p' = c/c'$, by charging a price p' for the substitute in excess of its market price c'. (A royalty on output is another means of avoiding input price distortion.) Subject to this condition on relative prices, and adding RPM, $q = q^m$, p, and p' can be chosen so that (1) the vertically integrated profit is realized and (2) the retailer makes no profit, at least if the production function f exhibits constant returns to scale. For further details, see Burstein (1960) Schmalensee (1973), Blair and Kaserman (1978), and Winter (1985). Note that Blair and Kaserman's presentation has no RPM, because perfect competition at the downstream level eliminates the second marginalization.

Remark on Welfare Aspects. These three textbook cases all have the following in common: under a linear price contract, the manufacturer's wholesale price exceeds its marginal cost. Hence, the externality associated with the retailer's decisions goes toward too low a level of effort or too little consumption of the intermediate good and too high a consumer price. Thus, instruments that correct the externality also benefit the consumer.

Intrabrand Competition

We will begin with the simplest case of intrabrand competition. The number of retailers—for example, two—is exogenously given. The retailers cover the same market, and they may or may not be differentiated. With nondifferentiated retailers, the consumer chooses the lowest price or the best price-service combination. With differentiated retailers, other attributes (such as location) matter, and the demand for a retailer's product is not perfectly elastic. We will assume that the retailers are Bertrand-Nash competitors to highlight the competitive aspects of the situation. Forms of (possibly noncooperative) collusion between the retailers would to some extent bring us back to the one-retailer case. Similarly, for the moment we will ignore exclusive territories, which also tend to lead to the one-retailer case.

Let us assume that the retailers are not differentiated. Under linear pricing, if the manufacturer charges p, Bertrand competition between the retailers avoids the second marginalization, so $q = p$. Thus, by charging the linear price $T(x) = q^m x$, the manufacturer obtains the vertically integrated profit (whereas either RPM or a franchise fee would be needed under exclusive territories). If the retailers are differentiated, a second marginalization exists, and RPM can then be used to remedy this.

Next, we will consider the case in which the retailers also *compete through services* (efforts). We will first assume that the service cost is proportional to the number of customers actually served. Let $\phi(e)$ denote this unit service cost. This level of service is a choice variable for each retailer. Consumers consume the product of only one retailer. Let $S(q, e)$ denote the consumer's net surplus at price q and retail service e; note that $\partial S / \partial q = -D(q, e)$. The retailers are not differentiated. (The exposition here follows Caillaud and Rey, unpublished notes.)

The vertically integrated profit is obtained by maximizing $\{[q - c - \phi(e)]D(q, e)\}$ over q and e. Note in particular that, as usual, the choice of effort is dictated by its influence on the *demand* function.

Under a linear price $T(x) = px$, Bertrand competition leads to the maximization of the consumer's net *surplus* $S(q, e)$ under the zero-profit constraint $q = p + \phi(e)$ (consumer price equals wholesale price plus unit service cost). Even though the retailers are nondifferentiated, the vertically integrated profit cannot be reached with a linear price. It is still true that for a given level of effort, the manufacturer, by a judicious choice of p, can lead to the vertically integrated consumer price q^m without leaving a surplus to the retailers. The problem comes from the choice of effort. Competitive retailers choose effort with the consumer's surplus in mind, whereas, for the vertical structure, only the effect of effort on consumer demand matters. Note that introducing a franchise fee does not solve this problem. (Actually, only a zero franchise fee is feasible under Bertrand competition.)

The manufacturer can use a competition-reducing restraint to obtain the vertically integrated profit. One example of such a restraint has already been mentioned: exclusive territories (together with a franchise fee, which helps avoid double marginalization). Another example is RPM, whereby the choice of q and p fixes the service level $\phi(e) = q - p$ under Bertrand competition. Hence, it suffices to impose $q = q^m$ and to pick the wholesale price $p = q^m - \phi(e^m)$.[14]

Thus, we conclude that the manufacturer may want to prevent competition to avoid effort distortion. Also, the two competition-reducing restraints (exclusive territories and RPM) are good substitutes here. (As we will see later, this is not always the case.) However, we must note a difference between the two restraints: exclusive territories isolate retailers from forms of competition other than price; RPM does not.

We will now examine the new features associated with externalities in effort. Mathewson and Winter (1982, 1984) consider a model in which each retailer spends money (on advertising, for example) to increase demand. But this effort cannot be fully appropriated. A fraction of a retailer's expenses turns out to be a spillover on other retailers; that is, it increases their demand. For the retailers to internalize this "horizontal externality," the wholesale price must be lowered somewhat. For instance, if exclusive territories can be granted (together with a franchise fee), the wholesale price must fall under c; that is, the intermediate good must be marginally subsidized.

The externality argument has been invoked repeatedly in the case of discount stores (Telser, 1960; Mathewson and Winter, 1983). It is argued that some high-price retailers supply the necessry information about the product to the customers, who then go to low-service, low-price stores. To encourage an adequate provision of effort (here, information) by the retailers, competition must be reduced or eliminated by imposing either exclusive territories or RPM. The idea is to give the retailers a property right on their services by protecting them from unfair competition.

Next, we will endogenize the number of retailers and their degree of differentiation. Note that if the manufacturer can control the number of outlets and their characteristics (such as location), the problem becomes very much like the preceding one. However, the manufacturer may not legally be allowed to control the location and number of retailers.

So long as a franchise fee belongs to the manufacturer's set of instruments, the number of retailers is determined by the level of this franchise fee plus the zero-profit (free-entry) condition for the retailers. Thus, franchise fees are indirect ways of controlling entry (see Dixit, 1983; Mathewson and Winter, 1982, 1984). The question of control of characteristics (such as location) has not yet been fully studied. The existing models are usually location models in a homogeneous space (for example, a circle with a uniform density of consumers). The principle of maximum differentiation holds for both competing retailers and a vertically integrated structure. Thus, there is no conflict between the manufacturer and a *fixed* number of retailers as to the retailers' locations. This feature does not hold in general (see Bolton and Bonanno, 1985, for a model of vertical quality differentiation with such a conflict; also see the foregoing discussion of the choice of effort by retailers). The resolution of the corresponding conflict will depend on the set of available instruments.

Remark on Patent Licensing. A product or process innovation by a firm that does not want to use the innovation itself but prefers to license it to other producers gives rise to vertical control problems that are similar to the ones we have encountered. Some interesting recent studies have examined the link between patent licensing and downstream competition. Kamien and Tauman (1983) assume that there are several downstream Cournot-Nash competitors. They show that, if the innovation is not drastic (that is, not very important), it is to the innovator's advantage to license the innovation to several firms and to use both a franchise fee and royalties to soften the competition downstream. (In our terminology, $p > c$ is desirable to maintain "collusion" between retailers.) Gallini and Winter (1985) and Katz and Shapiro (1984) also analyze the strategic aspects of patent licensing by one of the downstream firms itself. Although we will not review this literature in detail, some of its features are specific to the patent licensing situation. For instance, as Katz and Shapiro note, it may be hard for the licensor to monitor the licensee's output; thus, after obtaining the technology, the licensee may imitate the innovation and avoid per unit charges. In such a case, a franchise fee is the only instrument available to the licensor. Also, the distinction between horizontal and vertical restraints is somewhat blurred, as the foregoing discussion indicates. (We should also note that this distinction is not so clear-cut as our presentation suggests in the manufacturer-retailer relationship; see later remarks.)

Retail Price Discrimination

This section presents two examples of "textbook" price discrimination through vertical restraints. In both cases, we will assume that several nondifferentiated Bertrand retailers choose prices. This is intended to avoid the well-known problem of double marginalization, thus simplifying the discussion. Also, effort is not a choice variable for the retailers.

The first example is based on the existence of two upstream goods, as illustrated in figure 1–4. The first upstream good is produced by a monopolist, the "manufacturer," at cost c per unit. The other upstream good is produced by a competitive supplier at price c' per unit. A competitive sector distributes these two goods. For consumers, the two goods are complementary, in that they must first buy one unit of the manufacturer's product (fixed consumption), and they can then consume several units of the competitive product (variable consumption). For example, the first good might be a copying machine and the second good paper or ink or maintenance. Consumers are heterogeneous.

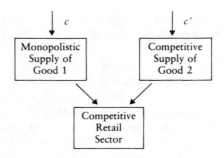

Figure 1–4. Price Discrimination—Two Upstream Goods

"High demand" consumers would consume more units of the second good than "low-demand" consumers would.

We will first consider what the vertically integrated structure (composed of three levels) would do. As shown by the theory of price discrimination,[15] it is optimal to charge a price $p' > c'$ for the variable consumption good. This allows us to have the high-demand consumers pay a bit more without discouraging the low-demand consumers.

We can see immediately that a tie-in allows the decentralized structure to price-discriminate. It suffices that the manufacturer purchases the second good and forces the downstream retailers to buy it at price p'. Thus, we discover a second use for tie-ins: price discrimination. (The issue of input substitution does not arise here, because the consumption of the manufacturer's product is inelastic.) Note that retailers' competition changes the set of instruments required to control the structure. With a single retailer, a franchise fee and a nondistortionary wholesale price ($p = c$) would be sufficient; the retailer would practice price discrimination. The issue, of course, is that perfect competition prevents direct price discrimination by the retailers.

The second example of price discrimination is based on the existence of two distinct consumer markets with different elasticities of demand (see Perry, 1978). The vertically integrated structure would charge two different monopoly prices for the same good (see figure 1–5)—assuming, for instance, that the elasticity of demand is higher in the first market ($\epsilon > \epsilon'$) than $q^m < q'^m$.

In a decentralized structure, the vertically integrated profit can be reached by charging wholesale prices $p = q^m$ or $p' = q'^m$ to retailers serving one market or the other (assuming that they are distinct) if the retailers in each market are competitive. However, this policy is not effective if retailers can arbitrage. The high-elasticity market retailers will resell the good to the low-elasticity market retailers. Then some restraint (such as exclusive territories together with a fixed fee) is required to implement price discrimination. Or else the manufacturer can vertically integrate with one high-elasticity market

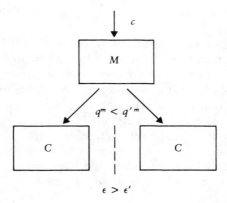

Figure 1–5. Price Discrimination—Two Distinct Markets

retailer, so as to internalize transactions at price q^m, and sell at the unique price q'^m on the intermediate good market.

Interbrand Competition

To conclude, we will briefly discuss interbrand competition. As mentioned earlier, a restraint that is sometimes used to "restrict" interbrand competition is exclusive dealing. When imposing this restraint, a manufacturer must trade off the potential loss of returns to scale[16] and the efficiency gain for the vertical structure. This has been explained as follows: a multibrand retailer may take advantage of the manufacturer's advertising expense to attract consumers and induce them to buy the manufacturer's competitor's products (which presumably do not incur such overall expenses and thus can give a higher profit margin to the retailer). Thus, exclusive dealing is seen as giving the manufacturer a property right in its promotional expenses (see Marvel, 1982).

Other vertical restraints may be used to reduce interbrand competition. Rey and Stiglitz (1985) show, for example, that exclusive territories, by reducing intrabrand competition at the retailers' level, induce a decrease in interbrand competition at the manufacturer's level. The basic idea is that reducing retailers' competition decreases the elasticity of the demand perceived by the manufacturers, whereas in the case of perfectly competitive retailers, the manufacturers directly compete with each other.

It has also been suggested that RPM can help competing manufacturers sustain collusion by reducing the efficacy of secret wholesale price cuts (Telser, 1960; Posner, 1977).

We conclude this section on control problems with three remarks:

1. Despite the very primitive nature of its models (absence of uncertainty), the control literature has been very successful in deriving indications for business strategies and in destroying a number of apparently appealing but fallacious arguments.[17] It has also been very successful (perhaps too successful) in showing that vertical restraints need not hurt the consumer and, *a fortiori*, need not reduce aggregate welfare.

2. This survey of the control literature has been incomplete. Our only goals have been to illustrate the methodology and some basic intuitions. Had we enriched our model further, we would have introduced other types of restraints,[18] and we would have introduced new roles for the vertical restraints we have analyzed.[19]

3. We have not yet mentioned the link between vertical restraints and collusion between retailers. The simplest example of such a phenomenon involves two competing downstream production units that create a trademark in order to obtain exclusive territories or RPM, thus transforming a competitive downstream market into a monopolized market. Vertical agreements are then merely a veil for horizontal collusion.

Uncertainty and Vertical Restraints

In this section, we analyze some new features associated with uncertainty at the retail level. We distinguish two kinds of uncertainties: demand uncertainty and retail cost uncertainty. Demand uncertainty arises when the manufacturer's product is new (or has not yet been introduced in a particular market), or when demand fluctuates over time, or when competitors' strategy—and thus the residual demand for the manufacturer's product—is uncertain. Similarly, retail cost may depend on local conditions (wages, other input prices) or on technological progress. We will assume that the different parties (retailers and manufacturer) have the same information about the environment when they sign contracts. However, the retailers obtain superior information about demand in their market or about retail cost after they sign the contract and before they take actions that affect the vertical structure's targets. We thus emphasize the adjustment of decisions to the environment through delegation.

The asymmetry of information is crucial. If the manufacturer observed (ex-post) the retailers' information, contingent contracts could be signed that would specify the control solution for each state of nature. Under asymmetric information, however, the informed parties' incentive to use their private information to reach their own goals often result in inefficiencies for the vertical structure.

The first point to be made about uncertain environments is that vertical restraints may not be privately desirable any longer. The simplest example of this is obtained from the basic structure: one manufacturer, one retailer. If the retailer is risk-neutral, it is well known that the symmetric information, aggregate profit, and sharing rule can be reached by making the retailer the residual claimant for the aggregate profit; a two-part tariff with $p = c$ will do. Here, RPM would not be redundant but would be deleterious to the aggregate structure, because it would destroy the flexibility of the consumer price or the retailer's effort to cost and demand conditions.

A Simple Framework

In this section, we will present a simplified version of the model analyzed in Rey and Tirole (1985). In this model, a manufacturer produces a single product at constant marginal cost c. The manufacturer supplies a market summarized by a demand function D, which, for the sake of simplicity, is supposed to depend linearly on the difference between a demand parameter d and the retail price q:

$$D(d, q) = d - q$$

There are two retailing sites in this market, each of them occupied by a retailer. The retailers are assumed to be chosen by the manufacturer from among a competitive supply of identical candidates. The manufacturer can propose to each retailer the same two-part tariff (p, A), where p is the wholesale price and A denotes a franchise fee. (We will discuss the different assumptions only briefly here. An extensive discussion of the strong informational requirements that make such contracts optimal can be found in Rey and Tirole, 1985.) Each retailer has a constant marginal cost of distribution γ and accepts the two-part tariff as soon as it obtains a nonnegative expected utility for its profit.

The manufacturer is assumed to have limited information about the environment; in particular, the manufacturer can observe, besides the wholesale price and the franchise fee, only the quantity delivered to each retailer—whether or not this retailer sells the product—and in some cases the retail price and the area of distribution. But the manufacturer cannot observe the actual quantity sold by a retailer in the market, the demand parameter d, or the cost of distribution γ. Note that these assumptions are consistent with the nature of the contracts (two-part tariffs) that are allowed. Because the manufacturer cannot observe the quantity effectively sold by a retailer to consumers, nonlinear pricing is no longer available, as the retailers could then set up a secondary market for the good; the manufacturer can, however, impose a franchise fee when it is informed whether or not the retailers carry its product.

In describing the environmental uncertainty, we now consider only uncertainty that affects the whole market—that is, the two retailers—in the same way. They are therefore still identical once the uncertainty is resolved. (Somewhat similar conclusions hold in the case of independent, idiosyncratic retailer uncertainty. We focus on market uncertainty because it leads to pure Bertrand competition.)

We define the two relevant types of uncertainty:

1. *Demand uncertainty:* The demand parameter d is assumed to be a random variable with support $[\underline{d}, \bar{d}]$, where $\underline{d} \geq c + \gamma$. We note that $d^e \equiv E(d)$ and $\sigma_d^2 \equiv E(d - d^e)^2$.

2. *Retail cost uncertainty:* The constant marginal cost of distribution γ is assumed to be a random variable distributed on $[\underline{\gamma}, \bar{\gamma}]$ where $\underline{d} \geq c + \bar{\gamma}$. Again, $\gamma^e \equiv E(\gamma)$ and $\sigma_\gamma^2 \equiv E(\gamma - \gamma^e)^2$.

The density distributions of d and γ are independent and are known by both the manufacturer and the retailers. The realization of uncertainty (d and γ) is observed by the retailers after their contracts are signed but before they make their pricing decisions.

The manufacturer is assumed to be risk-neutral, which can be justified if it supplies a large number of statistically independent markets. Two alternative, polar assumptions will be made about the retailers' risk aversion: risk neutrality, in which case they care only about the expected value of their profit, or infinite risk aversion, in which case they care only about their profit in the worst possible outcome. (This last assumption could also correspond to the case in which the retailers learn the realization of uncertainty before signing the contract; if the manufacturer then wants to trade with all possible retailers, it must base the contract on the most unlucky of them. Alternatively, one could assume that the retailers might go bankrupt when they realize that they will lose money.) Many of the results can be extended to general utility functions. The consumers' welfare is measured by the expected value of their surplus, defined by

$$S(d - q) = \int_q^{+\infty} D(d - p)dp = \tfrac{1}{2}(d - q)^2$$

The social welfare will be taken to be the sum of the ex-ante manufacturers', retailers', and consumers' welfare:

$$W = E(\Pi_M) + \sum_{i=1}^{i=2} V(\Pi_R^i) + E(S)$$

where $\Pi_M = (p - c)D(d - q) + 2A$, which represents the manufacturer's profit;

Π_R^i = $(q - p - \gamma)D^i - A$, which represents retailer i's ex-post profit $(i = 1, 2)$, and D^i is the demand the retailer faces; Π_R^i is (ex-ante) a random variable;

$V(x)$ = either $E(x)$—the expected value of the variable x (risk neutrality); or Min (x)—the minimal value (extreme risk aversion);

$E(S)$ = $E\{\frac{1}{2}(d - q)^2\}$; that is, the expected surplus is an increasing function of the expected value and the variance of $(d - q)$.

Note that, because there exists, ex-ante, a competitive supply of retailers, the retailers always obtain their reservation utilities. Thus, we need not take them into account in our welfare comparisons.

We now analyze in this framework the respective advantages and drawbacks of three situations: pure competition between retailers, exclusive territories assignments, and resale price maintenance.

Pure Competition between Retailers. We suppose in this case that retailers act as Bertrand price competitors; hence, the retail price is always equal to the constant total marginal retail cost—that is, the sum of the wholesale price p and the constant marginal cost of distribution γ. This implies that the markup is always equal to zero, whatever the state of nature, and thus that the franchise fee must also equal zero, whether or not the retailers are risk-averse.

Exclusive Territories Assignments to Retailers. We suppose in this case that each retailer enjoys full monopolistic power in a part of the market—for example, half of the market. (The exact shares do not matter, unless there is some differentiation between retailers. Assigning half of the market to each retailer is thus the optimal sharing rule if the retailers are symmetric.) Hence, the retailer, given the wholesale price p, chooses a retail price that maximizes $\Pi(d, p, \gamma, q) = (q - p - \gamma)(d - q)$. Let us denote the associated optimal retail price and profit by $q^m(d, p, \gamma)$ and $\Pi^m(d, p, \gamma)$. The maximal franchise fees that can be recovered by the manufacturer are then equal to $2A = 2V[\Pi^m(d, p, \gamma)/2] = Vd[\Pi^m[d, p, \gamma]]$, given the linearity of the function V.

Resale Price Maintenance. In this case, the contracts proposed by the manufacturer impose, besides the wholesale price and the franchise fee, the retail price q. The retailers then have a very passive role; they only have the choice of accepting or rejecting the contract. Given a wholesale price p and a retail price q, the maximal franchise fee F that can be required from each of the retailers, if we suppose that half of the consumers go to each retailer when retail prices are equal, is $A = \frac{1}{2}V[(q - p - \gamma)(d - q)]$.

The Certainty Case

Before going ahead with the analysis of the respective properties of the three aforementioned situations in the presence of uncertainty, we should first note that they are all equivalent in the certainty case, in that the manufacturer's optimal choice always induces the same maximal aggregate profit and the same consumer surplus. In the certainty case, the optimal retail price, from the viewpoint of joint profit maximization, is $q^m(d, c, \gamma)$, and the corresponding integrated profit is $\Pi^m(d, c, \gamma)$.

Actually, the three types of contracts allow the manufacturer to achieve this optimal integrated profit. In the competitive case, it suffices for the manufacturer to quote a wholesale price equal to $p = q^m(d, c, \gamma) - \gamma$ and a zero franchise fee; then the retail price is the monopoly price and all the profits go to the manufacturer. In the exclusive territories case, the manufacturer can sell at marginal cost and impose a franchise fee equal to $\frac{1}{2} \Pi^m(d, c, \gamma)$; the retail price decision is then delegated to the retailer with the "right signal," $p = c$, and the integrated profit is recovered via the franchise fee. Finally, in the resale price maintenance case, the manufacturer can mimic one of the previous two contracts.

Hence, in the absence of uncertainty, vertical restraints induce exactly the same private and social welfares; in particular, the use of franchise fees avoids the double marginalization problem of the exclusive territories restraint. In the sense of Mathewson and Winter's (1984) discussion, two-part tariffs, exclusive territories, and resale price maintenance are sufficient control mechanisms in the absence of uncertainty. Therefore, the properties that we will emphasize now are intimately linked to the uncertainty context. Moreover, as we will show, they depend very much on the nature of uncertainty.

Actually, even when there is some uncertainty, the manufacturer can always implement any desired *expected* value of retail price or final demand; but problems arise with either the adaptation of these variables to modifications of the environment or the provision of insurance. In the next section, we will analyze how vertical restraints deal with these problems.

The Uncertainty Case

We now reintroduce uncertainty about the market (parameter d) and the retail cost (parameter γ). How do such fluctuations affect the agents?

The consumers—who of course prefer a high expected consumption $(d - q)^e$ for a given expected value of demand $(d - q)^e$—prefer a large variance (the net consumer surplus is convex in consumption). Hence, they do not want the retail price to adjust to market (d) fluctuations but want it to respond fully to modifications in retail cost γ.

The retailers' ex-post profit is $\{(d - q)(q - p - \gamma) - A\}$. Minimal variations of this ex-post profit are then obtained for a zero markup, which means that the retail price is fully responsive to the retail cost and not at all responsive to the demand fluctuations.

The manufacturer would like the retail price to adjust to the environment, $q = q^m(d, c, \gamma)$, which responds to a certain extent to both market and retail cost fluctuations, but the manufacturer must also provide insurance to the retailers if they are risk-averse. Insurance requires q not too far from $(p + \gamma)$, which is not consistent with $q = q^m(d, c, \gamma)$, as we will see.

What are the properties of vertical restraints with respect to these objectives? We will take the competitive situation as a reference. We saw that the retailers' markup in all states of nature is equal to zero (perfect insurance of the retailers) so that the retail price fully responds to retail cost fluctuations and not at all to market fluctuations (which is good from the consumers' viewpoint but not too good from the manufacturer's viewpoint).

We will now look at resale price maintenance, whereby the retail price, imposed by the manufacturer, responds neither to market nor to retail cost fluctuations. Thus, RPM has the same properties as competition in the case of pure market fluctuations but behaves much worse in the case of retail cost fluctuations: the demand $(d - q)$ does not adjust at all, while the markup $(q - p - \gamma)$ responds fully.

Exclusive territories assignments have other properties. As in the absence of uncertainty, the manufacturer can sell at marginal cost and so implement the optimal monopolistic retail price relative to the environment. On the other hand, exclusive territories assignments provide little insurance to the retailers and induce a less variable demand, $d - q = \frac{1}{2}(d - p - \gamma)$, than results in the competitive case (or with RPM when there is only market uncertainty).

These considerations will be helpful in understanding the following results:[20]

Proposition 1: Suppose that the retailers have no risk aversion and that there are both market and retail cost uncertainties. Then the manufacturer prefers exclusive territories (ET) to RPM or competition, which are equivalent ($\Pi^{ET} > \Pi^{RPM} = \Pi^C$). By contrast, from the consumers' and the social welfare's point of view, competition dominates RPM and ET ($W^C > W^{RPM}, W^{ET}$).

Proposition 2: Suppose that the retailers are infinitely risk-averse. Then the consumers and the manufacturer agree on the choice of vertical restraints, which depends on the nature of uncertainty: for pure demand uncertainty, competition is equivalent to RPM, and these two arrangements are preferred to ET; for pure cost uncertainty, competition is preferred to ET, which is preferred to RPM.

Most of these results are intuitive in light of the previous discussion.

Consider, first, the case of retailers' risk neutrality. In this case, the manufacturer wants to achieve only two objectives: avoiding double marginalization and adapting the market price as well as possible to environment fluctuations. Competition suppresses the second price distortion, as does RPM in the case of pure market uncertainty; but in each of these two cases, the retail price does not adapt very well to the environmental fluctuations. By contrast, the manufacturer can achieve the two objectives by assigning exclusive territories and selling at marginal cost. By so doing, the manufacturer fully delegates the pricing decision to the retailers, supplying them with the "good" signal (marginal cost of production), and can then recover the expected optimal integrated profit via the franchise fees. Hence, ET clearly dominates RPM and competition from the manufacturer's point of view and permits the manufacturer to realize the vertically integrated profit.

The consumers, on the other hand, prefer a low expected retail price and a highly variable final demand. It can be shown that ET, RPM, and competition lead to the same expected price;[21] as already noted, competition always induces a more variable demand, as does RPM in the case of pure market uncertainty. This explains why they may be more socially desirable. Finally, in the case of pure retail cost uncertainty, RPM generates a very sticky demand and therefore is dominated by ET and competition from both the consumers' and the manufacturer's viewpoints.

Consider, now, the case of retailers' extreme risk aversion. The manufacturer must now trade off the two previous objectives with a third one: providing sufficient insurance to his retailers. Obviously, ET assignments do not score very well on this point, as they induce some profit fluctuations at the retail level. On the contrary, competition—and RPM in the case of pure market uncertainty—provides perfect insurance to retailers. Their profit in the competitive situation in each state of nature is equal to zero; and with RPM, the manufacturer can also force the retailers' markup down to zero if the distribution cost is known. In the case of pure retail cost uncertainty, RPM provides no insurance at all to retailers and hence is still dominated by ET and competition from both the manufacturer's and the consumers' viewpoints.

What is perhaps less immediately intuitive is the reason why, in the trade-off between efficiency (adaption to environment) and insurance, ET is always dominated by competition. The basic idea is that when retailers are extremely risk-averse, the manufacturer cannot recover the benefits of delegating the price decision delegation; the manufacturer can always do better without ET than with it by restoring competition and charging a wholesale price equal to the ET retail price in the worst state of nature, minus the associated distribution cost. Suppose that the wholesale price under ET is p. The maximal franchise fee A that can be required is then characterized by

$$2A = \min_{(d,q)} \{\Pi^m(d, p, \gamma)\} = \Pi^m(\underline{d}, p, \bar{\gamma}) = (\underline{d} - \bar{q})(\bar{q} - p - \bar{\gamma})$$

where $q = q^m(\underline{d} - p - \bar{\gamma})$. The manufacturer's profit is then

$$\begin{aligned}
\Pi^{ET} &= \underset{(d,\gamma)}{E} \{ [d - q^m(d, p, \gamma)](p - c) + (\underline{d} - \bar{q})(\bar{q} - p - \bar{\gamma}) \} \\
&\leq \underset{(d,\gamma)}{E} \{ (d - \bar{q})(p - c) + (d - \bar{q})(q - p - \bar{\gamma}) \} \\
&= \underset{(d,\gamma)}{E} \{ (d - \bar{q})(\bar{q} - c - \bar{\gamma}) \}
\end{aligned}$$

which is the manufacturer's profit associated with competition between retailers at a wholesale price $p = (\bar{q} - \bar{\gamma})$.

Hence, from the manufacturer's point of view, ET is always dominated by competition and sometimes by RPM. This choice is agreed upon by the consumers for the same reasons as before, plus a new reason: because of the insurance motive, the manufacturer is now induced to raise the wholesale price above the marginal cost in the case of ET, in order to lower the retailers' markup and thus their profit fluctuations. Therefore, the expected retail price is now higher under ET.

Conclusion

The simple framework we analyzed shows us that uncertainty about a vertical relationship environment may drastically affect the optimal type of contract used.

It appears that vertical restraints such as resale price maintenance or exclusive territories assignments are not substitutes for one another and that they have specific properties that depend on the nature of uncertainty. It even may be that these vertical restraints are not privately desirable; a manufacturer may prefer its retailers to be Bertrand price competitors rather than assigning them exclusive territories or retail price requirements when these retailers acquire some private information.

It also appears that such vertical restraints may be socially undesirable, even if industrial partners want to use them. In the model we just analyzed, competition between retailers was always socially preferred to exclusive territories and was at least equivalent to resale price maintenance from the consumer and social welfare points of view. Hence, the legal implications of such an analysis are involved. Recently, some authors have suggested that vertical restraints, unless they are used to enforce a dealers' cartel, ought to be legal per se. The analysis here clearly does not support this claim, but rather favors a rule of reason. Of course, such a rule of reason assumes sufficient information for antitrust authorities, which is not always the case; the informational problems we evoked are likely to be even more important for these authorities. Although our discussion may provide some guidelines for application of the rule of reason, a great deal of work remains to be done in this domain to define more precise criteria.

Finally, we should note that, by assuming that the retailers acquire information *before* choosing actions, we emphasized the use of decentralized information to adjust to the environment. Had we assumed that uncertainty occurred *after* the choice of actions (or were not observed by then), the analysis would have been somewhat closer to that of control environments.

Private Information at the Contracting Date

In the preceding section, we assumed that the retailers obtained superior information about demand or cost after signing their contracts and, more generally, that contracts were signed under symmetric information conditions. However, when they sign the contract, the manufacturer may have superior information about aggregate (as opposed to local) demand for its product, for example; and the retailer may have superior information about local demand or about its own efficiency in distributing the product. (Private information on the retailer's side is particularly relevant for renegotiated contracts.)

There is a body of literature on regulation under asymmetric information that analyzes the basic framework studied earlier in this chapter.[22] The manufacturer offers a contract to a single retailer. The retailer has private information—usually about retail costs. The manufacturer tries to induce the retailer to choose the right consumption price or effort without giving the retailer too much money. (That is, the manufacturer trades off the achievement of the vertical structure's targets—which can be obtained by making the retailer the residual claimant but lead to too small a profit for the manufacturer, since the franchise fee cannot discriminate between the potential information of the retailer and the limitation of the retailer's informational rent.) This literature has been developed in a regulatory context and has not yet been extended to include features that are more specific to manufacturer–retailers relationships.

As noted earlier, the manufacturer may also have private information when offering a contract to a retailer. Then the very proposal of the contract reveals information about the manufacturer's state of knowledge. Suppose, for instance, that the manufacturer has private information about the demand a single retailer will face, and offers a two-part tariff (franchise fee A plus wholesale price p); the retail price cannot be monitored and, furthermore, there is arbitrage. Clearly, the manufacturer would like to convince the retailer that demand is high in order to extract a high franchise fee. A credible way to do so when demand is indeed high is to offer a wholesale price p that exceeds the marginal cost c in exchange for a low franchise fee. The manufacturer thus "proves" that it is more interested in variable profits, thus substantiating the claim that demand is high (Maskin and Tirole, unpublished notes). Hence, a distortion at the wholesale price level can be imposed even if the retailer is risk-neutral, but only for signaling purposes.[23]

Conclusion

Much work remains to be done on precontract and postcontract uncertainty to match the well-established and crucial insights of the control literature reviewed in this chapter. We have shown that the introduction of uncertainty yields important new insights for the theory of vertical restraints, which ought to benefit greatly from future interaction with the principal-agent approach.

Another topic worth studying concerns the dynamics of manufacturer–retailer contracts. The static analyses mentioned in this chapter are not adequate to study such issues as the appropriation of quasi-rents on investment in specific assets and the renegotiation of contracts, although these issues sometimes play an important role, for instance, in the decision to attribute territorial protection to retailers.

Notes

1. This chapter is not intended as a comprehensive treatment or list of references; rather, it discusses the methodology and leitmotivs of the literature. For a more complete and clearer overview of the development of the theory of and evidence on vertical restraints, see Caves (1984). See also Blair and Kaserman's (1983) comprehensive treatment.

2. See, for example, Baron and Myerson (1982), Sappington (1982), and Laffont and Tirole (1986) in regulatory contexts.

3. See, for example, Holmström (1979), Shavell (1979), and Grossman and Hart (1983).

4. Discounts may also affect nonmonetary (less observable) dimensions of exchange between retailer and customers. Also, even if discounts can be observed by the manufacturer, such price control may be prohibitively costly. Suppose that one of the

retailer's roles is to analyze customers in order to price-discriminate among them (the manufacturer knowing only the distribution of tastes in the population of customers). A full control of the retailer's pricing policy then requires ex-post knowledge of the entire distribution of prices the retailer charged, which is very costly for the manufacturer and the court to assess. (In other words, they cannot save on monitoring costs by inspecting randomly.)

5. Another (very different) degree-of-freedom factor in interbrand competition is the length of the contract of the level of penalties for breach of contract. See Aghion and Bolton (1985).

6. For instance, the observable variable is output and the unobservable variable is effort. If the production function is deterministic, effort is easily controlled—for example, through a minimum output level requirement.

7. They directly affect only internal transfers. They may indirectly affect targets through incentives, but this is irrelevant to the present classification.

8. In the absence of a franchise fee, the basis for optimal targets is the manufacturer's profit if the manufacturer imposes the contract.

9. Risk aversion may play a role even in the absence of exogenous uncertainty, because the players in the postcontract game, if there is one (for example, between two competing retailers or between the retailer and the manufacturer when both choose effort levels), may choose mixed strategies. In the studies described here, however, this phenomenon does not occur.

10. Exclusive dealing may not be privately desirable, because the fixed cost of having one's own network of retailers may be prohibitive or because of consumer search (see Stahl, 1980).

11. In asymmetric cases (for instance, intrabrand competition with asymmetric retailers), the restraints may be retailer-contingent (for example, RPM specifies different consumer prices for different retailers). However, this does not affect the general proposition.

12. If $(q^m - c)D(q^m) \geq (q - c)D(q)$ and $(q - p)D(q) \geq (q^m - p)D(q^m)$, $(p - c)[D(q^m) - D(q)] \geq 0$ and therefore $q \geq q^m$. The strict inequality is obtained if the monopoly price is unique.

13. On moral hazard in teams and the role of third parties, see Holmström (1982).

14. Quantity forcing is also sufficient; imposing $x \geq D(q^m, e^m)$ together with a wholesale price $p = q^m - \phi(e^m)$ induces the retailers to choose the right effort and price (that is, the ones that maximize aggregate profit).

15. See, for example, Oi (1971), Schmalensee (1980), and Maskin and Riley (1984).

16. For instance, selling several brands or products may increase the retailer's employment, and it saves consumers' search costs.

17. For example, it has been claimed that RPM and exclusive territories prevent intrabrand competition and thus necessarily raise the consumer price.

18. For instance, a multiproduct manufacturer can use "block booking," a practice similar to tie-ins, whereby advantage is taken of the heterogeneous customers' cross-preferences for the manufactured goods (Stigler, 1963).

19. To cite a few arguments (without any judgment regarding their relevance): RPM can be used to promote the manufacturer's product image and to avoid loss-

leader selling by large retailers. Tie-ins can create cost savings in distribution; they can also be used by the manufacturer to control the quality downstream (or can be seen as a way of obtaining information about the retailer's services). Exclusive dealing may similarly allow cost savings (because of larger shipments); but by preventing the exploitation of returns to scale associated with multiproduct retailing, it can serve as a barrier to entry. Also, it can increase the manufacturer's product differentiation.

20. See Rey and Tirole (1985) for a formal proof.

21. This result relies on the linear demand function assumption.

22. See, for example, Baron and Myerson (1982), Sappington (1982), and Laffont and Tirole (1984).

23. Under symmetric information conditions, the manufacturer would make the retailer the residual claimant.

References

Aghion, P., and Bolton, P. (1985). "Entry Prevention through Contracts with Customers." Mimeographed. Massachusetts Institute of Technology.

Baron, D., and Myerson R. (1982). "Regulating a Monopolist with Unknown Costs." *Econometrica, 50* (July):911–30.

Blair, R., and Kaserman, D. (1978). "Vertical Integration, Tying and Antitrust Policy." *American Economic Review, 68* (June):397–402.

——— . (1983). *Law and Economics of Vertical Integration and Control.* New York: Academic Press.

Bolton, P., and Bonanno, G. (1985). "Resale Price Maintenance and Competition in Post-Sales Services." Mimeographed, Oxford University.

Burstein, M. (1960). "A Theory of Full-Line Forcing," *Northwestern University Law Review, 55* (March/April):62–95.

Caves, R. (1984). "Vertical Restraints in Manufacturer-Distributor Relations: Incidence and Economic Effects." Mimeographed. Harvard University.

Dixit, A. (1983). "Vertical Integration in a Monopolistically Competitive Industry." *International Journal of Industrial Organization, 1* (1):63–78.

Gallini, N., and Winter R. (1985). "Licensing in the Theory of Innovation." *Rand Journal of Economics, 16* (Summer):237–252.

Grossman, S., and Hart, O. (1983). "An Analysis of the Principal-Agent Problem." *Econometrica, 51,* (Jan.):7–46.

Holmström, B. (1979). "Moral Hazard and Observability," *Bell Journal of Economics, 10* (Spring):74–91.

——— . (1982). "Moral Hazard in Syndicates," *Bell Journal of Economics, 13* (Autumn):324–40.

Kamien, M., and Tauman, Y. (1983). "The Private Value of a Patent: A Game Theoretic Analysis." Discussion Paper #576, Northwestern University.

Katz, M., and Shapiro, C. (1984). "On the Licensing of Innovations." Woodrow Wilson School Discussion Paper #82, Princeton University.

Laffont, J.-J., and Tirole, J. (1986). "Using Cost Observation to Regulate Firms." *Journal of Political Economy.* Forthcoming.

Marvel, H. (1982). "Exclusive Dealing." *Journal of Law and Economics,* 25 (April): 1–26.

Maskin, E., and Riley, J. (1984). "Monopoly with Incomplete Information." *Rand Journal of Economics,* 15 (Summer):171–96.

Mathewson, G., and Winter, R. (1982). "The Economics of Vertical Restraints in Distribution." In IEA Conference Volume, *New Developments in the Analysis of Market Structures.* New York: Macmillan.

———. (1983). "The Incentives for Resale Price Maintenance under Imperfect Information," *Economic Enquiry,* 15(1):337–48.

———. (1984). "An Economic Theory of Vertical Restraints." *Rand Journal of Economics,* 15 (Spring):27–38.

Oi, W. (1971). "A Disneyland Dilemma: Two-Part Tariffs for a Mickey Mouse Monopoly." *Quarterly Journal of Economics,* 85 (Feb.):77–96.

Perry, M. (1978). "Price Discrimination and Forward Integration." *Bell Journal of Economics,* 9 (Spring):209–17.

Posner, R. (1977). "The Rule of Reason and the Economic Approach: Reflections on the *Sylvania* Decision." *University of Chicago Law Review,* 45 (Fall):1–20.

Rey, P. and Stiglitz, J. (1985). "The Role of Exclusive Territories." Mimeographed. ENSAE.

Rey, P., and Tirole, J. (1985). "The Logic of Vertical Restraints," Mimeographed. Massachusetts Institute of Technology.

Sappington, D. (1982). "Optimal Regulation of Research and Development under Imperfect Information." *Bell Journal of Economics,* 13 (Autumn):354–68.

Schmalensee, R. (1973). "A Note on the Theory of Vertical Integration." *Journal of Political Economy,* 81 (March/April):442–49.

———. (1980). "Monopolistic Two-Part Pricing Arrangements." Working Paper #1105–80, Massachusetts Institute of Technology.

Shavell, S. (1979). "Risk Sharing Incentives in the Principal and Agent Relationship." *Bell Journal of Economics,* 10 (Spring):55–73.

Spengler, J. (1950). "Vertical Integration and Anti-trust Policy." *Journal of Political Economy,* 58 (August):347–52.

Stahl, K. (1980). "Oligopolistic Location under Imperfect Consumer Information." Mimeographed. University of California, Berkeley.

Stigler, G. (1963). "A Note on Block Booking." *Supreme Court Review 1963,* 152–57.

Telser, L. (1960). "Why Should Manufacturers Want Fair Trade?" *Journal of Law and Economics,* 3 (October):86–105.

Tinbergen, J. (1952). *On the Theory of Economic Policy.* Amsterdam: North-Holland.

Winter, R. (1985). "Contracts in Intermediate Markets with Variable Proportions." Mimeographed. University of Toronto.

2
Resale Price Maintenance and Antitrust Policy

William S. Comanor
John B. Kirkwood

A ntitrust law condemns all agreements between manufacturers and dealers that fix resale prices. This rule of per se illegality was first established in the 1911 *Dr. Miles* case and has been reiterated in several recent cases (*Sylvania* 1977, *Midcal* 1980, *Monsanto* 1984). In *Monsanto,* the court struck down certain lower-court attempts to relax the evidentiary standards for proving an agreement to fix resale prices, but refused to depart from its position that such agreements, once properly proved, are per se illegal.

Numerous commentators have criticized this approach. Perhaps the most common position is that a complete ban on resale price maintenance (RPM) is inappropriate, since the practice can be procompetitive. Fixing higher resale prices can stimulate dealer services that otherwise would not be provided. Since RPM can also facilitate collusion, many writers advocate the rule of reason (Williamson 1979, Scherer 1983). Under this standard, courts would examine market power, efficiencies, and other evidence in each case to determine whether RPM was more likely to be procompetitive or anticompetitive.[1]

Some scholars view the rule of reason as a costly and uncertain criterion. They believe that its examination of "all relevant factors" is often expensive, frequently erroneous, and of little guidance to business. Even though RPM can be procompetitive at some times and anticompetitive at others, they conclude that the only acceptable standard is a definite rule. They differ, though, as to whether such a rule should prohibit (Overstreet and Fisher 1985) or permit (Posner 1981) most instances of RPM.[2]

This chapter contributes to the policy debate by reviewing the arguments for legalizing all vertically motivated RPM. It then summarizes recent research showing that such RPM can reduce economic efficiency. Finally, it assesses the implications of these findings for antitrust policy.

Reprinted from *Contemporary Policy Issues* (Huntington Beach, Calif.: Western Economic Association International, Spring 1985).

The Case for Per Se Legality

The best-known advocates of per se legality for purely vertical RPM are Bork (1978) and Posner (1981). Both scholars—now federal judges—rest their endorsement of such a rule largely on three propositions: (1) although RPM can be anticompetitive when it facilitates horizontal collusion among manufacturers or dealers, this result is rare and usually can be attacked as a separate violation of the Sherman Act; (2) purely vertical instances of RPM can enhance efficiency by discouraging free riding on dealer services; and (3) except in unusual cases of manufacturer mistakes, no proven circumstance exists in which purely vertical RPM can harm consumers.

The current ban on RPM proscribes both vertically and horizontally motivated RPM. Because Bork and Posner would repeal this ban and legalize all purely vertical RPM, they must deal with cases in which RPM facilitates horizontal collusion. All commentators agree that these cases can be anticompetitive. Bork and Posner argue that horizontal cases are rare, and in any event, that the underlying collusion can be prosecuted under the Sherman Act. Both arguments raise empirical issues beyond the scope of this paper. While some commentators agree that collusion-facilitating RPM is uncommon (Scherer 1983), others question whether it is so infrequent or the underlying collusion so blatant that antitrust law could abolish RPM as a separate offense (Sharp 1985, Kirkwood 1981).

The second premise of Bork and Posner—that vertical price fixing can increase output and promote dealer services by discouraging free riding—is not controversial. All observers accept the argument, emphasized in Telser's (1960) article, that a manufacturer can profit from limiting price competition among its dealers. At first glance, such a strategy seems counterproductive. Since the manufacturer's sales depend on the price charged to consumers, its output and profits would appear greatest when maximum competition among dealers assures the lowest possible distribution margin. Telser explained that the firm could benefit when vertical price fixing was necessary to stimulate dealer services. By *services,* Telser meant not only delivery, credit, and repair, but also selling, advertising, and promotion. Services include any dealer activities that may increase demand. Having dealers supply these services benefits the manufacturer whenever the resulting stimulative effect on demand exceeds the depressing effect of the higher price charged to consumers.

The manufacturer might contract with its dealers to provide the desired level of services, or consumers might purchase services directly from dealers. Telser suggested, however, that transaction costs frequently make both of these routes impractical. If so, the firm might be unable to generate the desired services without RPM.

Because of the free-rider problem, the manufacturer cannot simply lower its price in the hope that dealers will use the increased revenues to finance desired services. Even if some dealers do so—because they recognize that sales will rise if the services are provided—others may not. Some dealers may offer few services and seek greater sales from a lower retail price. But in this case, Telser writes:

> Sales are diverted from the retailers who do provide the special services at the higher price to the retailers who do not provide the special services and offer to sell the product at the lower price. The mechanism is simple. A customer, because of the special services provided by one retailer, is persuaded to buy the product. But he purchases the product from another, paying the latter the lower price. In this way, the retailers who do not provide the special services get a "free ride" at the expense of those who convince consumers to buy the product (Telser 1960, 91).

Because of the free-rider problem, unrestricted competition discourages dealers from providing desired services, since those who do are rarely recompensed. The solution, according to Telser, is establishing minimum retail prices so that "retailers are forced to compete by providing special services with the product and not by reducing the retail price" (Telser 1960, 92).

Commentators debate the frequency, significance, and generality of the free-rider problem (Scherer 1983, Popofsky 1983, Marvel 1985). There is little debate, however, over its theoretical validity and its importance in some cases. Bork and Posner are correct in asserting that purely vertical RPM can increase output and expand dealer services. But they also assert that aside from rare cases of manufacturer mistakes, purely vertical RPM cannot be anticompetitive.[3] Their principal arguments are worth reviewing, since they provide an illuminating contrast to the findings reported below.

Bork and Posner argue that no single firm in a competitive industry can employ RPM unless the dealer services generated are worth the higher price to consumers. Otherwise, the firm will lose sales to rivals who do not impose RPM. Moreover, no firm using RPM has an advantage; other firms can always duplicate this strategy. Therefore, Bork and Posner conclude that in a competitive industry, purely vertical price fixing cannot harm consumers.

Even if a single firm has monopoly power and thus can exploit consumers, Bork and Posner contend that RPM could not worsen consumers' plight. A manufacturer with this power will set its price at the monopoly level, and the resale price will rise accordingly. This firm has no interest in further price increases, since they would reduce sales and profits. Therefore, a monopolist acting unilaterally would not impose RPM unless the higher resale price generated dealer services that increased consumer demand.

Anticompetitive Effects of Vertically Motivated RPM

Bork and Posner conclude that when a firm has monopoly power, purely vertical RPM is procompetitive because it increases demand and thus generally raises output. In most instances, greater output is a sign of improved consumer welfare since it ordinarily means that a firm has lowered prices, raised quality, or otherwise increased consumer satisfaction.[4] But in some cases, this inference is inappropriate.[5] Spence (1975) showed that under certain conditions, actions that increase output and profits can reduce consumer welfare. Although Spence's work is nearly a decade old, only recently have scholars recognized that it explains how purely vertical RPM can be anticompetitive.

Spence's critical insight was that firm profitability and consumer welfare are governed by different criteria. The profitability of a firm's action depends only on how it affects marginal consumers, those whose purchases would be altered. These consumers determine the impact on output. In contrast, consumer welfare depends on how a firm's action affects all consumers, intramarginal consumers as well as those at the margin.

Accordingly, purely vertical RPM could raise both output and profits and yet reduce efficiency. When deciding whether to employ RPM, a firm would examine the likely impact on marginal consumers. The firm's output and profits would depend on whether these consumers increase purchases when more services are provided (despite the higher price), or curtail purchases because of the higher price (despite the added services).[6] The firm would impose RPM if marginal consumers increased their purchases.

Despite increased output, RPM still could harm consumers as a whole. Although marginal consumers would gain, intramarginal consumers might be hurt. If the latter prefer to purchase the firm's product at a lower price (without additional services), RPM would reduce their welfare.[7] Moreover, the welfare losses to these consumers may outweigh the gains to marginal consumers. When this possibility is recognized, the link between the interests of producers and consumers—presumed by many to hold in a purely vertical context—is effectively broken.[8]

This anticompetitive result is not a mere theoretical artifact. Although no studies of its frequency have been conducted, the following example suggests it is both plausible and potentially important. Suppose that the dealer service promoted through RPM is the provision of information about a product's uses. This information is greatly desired by consumers who are "ignorant" of the product's characteristics, but not valued at all by "knowledgeable" consumers. While ignorant consumers are willing to pay for the information, their knowledgeable counterparts are not.

Assume further that intramarginal consumers are numerous and generally knowledgeable. Many are prior customers who know how the product should be used and have found it useful at the going price. They may have learned of the product from outside sources or from advertising provided by the manufacturer and then gained knowledge through their own experience with the product. Ignorant consumers, however, are largely marginal—perhaps because they understand so little about the product. Their valuations are much lower, since they remain uncertain of the product's utility.

In such circumstances, the profitability of imposing RPM depends entirely on the demand-stimulating effects of the additional information on ignorant, marginal consumers. However, social welfare calculations must also include the adverse effects on knowledgeable, intramarginal consumers, who are forced to pay for information they do not value. If this latter group is large enough, the producer will charge a higher price and provide more information than consumers as a whole desire.

Using this type of analysis, Comanor (1985) and Scherer (1983) have demonstrated that purely vertical price fixing can be anticompetitive. Marvel (1985) reaches the same conclusion in a less-technical exposition. While their models differ, all three show that vertically motivated RPM can increase manufacturer profits and output but reduce consumer welfare.

This result requires four conditions: (1) the manufacturer has some degree of monopoly power; (2) marginal consumers value the services stimulated by RPM and increase purchases despite the higher price; (3) intramarginal consumers do not find the services worth the higher price; and (4) the decreased utility of intramarginal consumers exceeds the increased utility of marginal consumers.

Implications for Antitrust Policy

A thorough evaluation of alternative legal standards for RPM would consider the full range of anticompetitive and procompetitive explanations for RPM. It would assess their detectability, frequency, and significance, as well as such factors as the probability of correct decisions, the clarity of guidance to business, and the cost of litigation under each standard (Overstreet 1983; Fisher and Lande 1983, 1651–91). Such a comprehensive analysis is beyond the scope of this chapter. In this section, we assess only the most significant implications of the findings reported above.

An important issue is whether purely vertical anticompetitive effects would be demonstrable in antitrust litigation. To show such effects, a plaintiff would have to prove that RPM harmed intramarginal consumers more than it benefited marginal consumers. Such proof may be difficult for two reasons. First, no market tests exist to measure RPM's impact on either group of consumers. Their valuations of the services and higher price induced by RPM could be assessed only through indirect evidence or subjective testimony. Second, vertically motivated RPM always benefits marginal consumers. Against this certain benefit, plaintiffs would inevitably present uncertain evidence of a negative overall impact. Although plaintiffs may prevail, their burden would be substantial.[9] How courts would resolve these issues is a matter of some concern. If plaintiffs could never demonstrate that purely vertical RPM was anticompetitive, a legal standard requiring such proof would immunize defendants in all such instances.

This shortcoming would not be serious if anticompetitive instances of vertically motivated RPM were neither frequent nor significant. Indeed, if such instances were a mere thoretical curiosity, the research findings discussed above should have little effect on the choice of a legal rule to govern RPM. On the other hand, if anticompetitive instances were frequent but hard to prove, neither a rule of reason nor a rule of per se legality may be appropriate.

Although no previous studies have examined the prevalence of such instances, this prospect should not be dismissed.[10] It seems quite plausible that substantial quantities of products are bought by knowledgeable intramarginal consumers who would place little value on information services provided by dealers.[11] At the same time, marginal consumers might value these services only slightly more. In addition, such products frequently are differentiated, and their producers possess some degree of monopoly power. Accordingly, until more extensive evidence is available, policymakers should be cautious about proposals to weaken greatly the current rule against RPM.

A limited change, however, might be appropriate. Some commentators have advocated an exception to the per se rule for new entrants (Overstreet and Fisher 1985; Lafferty, Lande, and Kirkwood 1984). Our analysis tends to support such an exception. In the example we discussed, RPM benefited "ignorant" marginal consumers but harmed "knowledgeable" intramarginal consumers. However, few prospective purchasers of a new entrant's product would be knowledgeable; most purchasers are likely to be ignorant. Consequently, purely vertical RPM is more likely to increase efficiency in the case of a new entrant than it would in the case of an established firm. Accordingly, a new-entrant exception to the per se rule against RPM deserves serious consideration.

Notes

1. Many commentators also support the rule of reason because it governs the legality of vertical nonprice restraints (*Sylvania* 1977), and the competitive effects of price and nonprice restraints are similar (Meehan and Larner 1981).

2. Per se rules and the rule of reason are not the only alternatives. Scholars have proposed intermediate standards, such as per se rules with exceptions and presumptions to narrow and structure a rule-of-reason inquiry. These proposals aim to preserve some of the certainty of a per se rule without sacrificing all the flexibility of a rule of reason.

3. Mistakes might not be as rare as Bork and Posner assume. A recent FTC study indicated that in two out of five cases examined, manufacturers used RPM when it was not efficient for them or consumers (Lafferty, Lande, and Kirkwood 1984, 10–13, 16–20.) Even if such instances are more common, Bork would not alter his rule of per se legality: "No court is likely to make a more accurate assessment than does a businessman with both superior information and the depth of insight that only self-

interest can supply" (Bork 1978, 290). Although Bork may be correct that courts cannot reliably identify manufacturer mistakes, such instances may still influence antitrust policy. If they are hard to detect, yet frequent and significant, broad rules against RPM become more desirable.

4. Even if output remains constant, RPM could increase consumer welfare if the new demand curve were sufficiently inelastic. Although price might then rise substantially, consumers may be better off—as reflected in their willingness to pay much higher prices for the product with the added services.

5. Thus, Bork and Posner too readily convert a result in positive economics—that RPM increases dealer services and output—into a conclusion in normative economics—that efficiency is improved.

6. In economic theory, what is strictly relevant is the marginal demand of all consumers, not the total demand of marginal consumers. We have distinguished marginal from intramarginal consumers for ease of exposition. Moreover, to the extent that quantities of the product required by individual consumers are constant or nearly so, the essential distinction *is* between marginal and intramarginal consumers.

7. By definition, intramarginal consumers value the product highly and do not cease purchasing it when its price rises. In addition, since the firm has some monopoly power, these consumers cannot obtain the same product from another firm at a lower price.

8. Bork, for example, asserts: "The manufacturer shares with the consumer the desire to have distribution done at the lowest possible cost consistent with effectiveness. . . . when the manufacturer chooses, he chooses on criteria that also control consumer welfare" (Bork 1978, 290).

9. In other areas of antitrust law, courts and parties find it difficult to determine whether the anticompetitive effects of a practice outweigh its precompetitive effects. When the quantitative issues are especially unyielding, courts and commentators frequently advocate narrowing the scope of inquiry to render the process more tractable. For an excellent discussion of this issue and its application to merger efficiencies, see Fisher and Lande (1983, 1624–50).

10. Marvel (1985) also finds that purely vertical RPM can be anticompetitive. He argues, however, that this result is unlikely for two principal reasons. First, he notes that RPM can increase consumer demand, so that the profit-maximizing retail price remains constant or actually falls. When purely vertical RPM does not raise prices, it ordinarily increases consumer welfare. The vast majority of empirical evidence, however, indicates that RPM raises prices to consumers (Overstreet 1983, 106–63). Marvel's second principal argument is that even when RPM increases prices, "unless the change in demand at the margin is grossly misleading as to conditions for intramarginal consumers, the effect of imposing fair trade will once again be to increase welfare" (Marvel 1985, 21). The point of our anlaysis, however, is that RPM's effect on the demand of marginal consumers may be *very different* from its effect on the demand of intramarginal consumers. Marvel offers no reason why such divergent effects are unlikely.

11. For example, stereo components and personal computers often are purchased by consumers who have gained extensive knowledge of the product through their own experience, discussions with friends, and speciality magazines.

References

Bork, R.H. *The Antitrust Paradox*. Basic Books, New York, 1978, 228–98.

Comanor, W.S. "Vertical Price Fixing and Market Restrictions and the New Antitrust Policy." *Harvard Law Review*, March 1985, 98.

Fisher, A.A., and Lande, R.H. "Efficiency Considerations in Merger Enforcement." *California Law Review*, December 1983, 71, 1580–1696.

Kirkwood, J.B. "The Per Se Rule Against Resale Price Maintenance: A Time for Change?" Remarks before the Antitrust Section of the American Bar Association, 11 August 1981.

Lafferty, R.N.; Lande, R.H.; and Kirkwood, J.B. eds., *Impact Evaluations of Federal Trade Commission Vertical Restraints Cases*. FTC Bureau of Competition and Bureau of Economics Staff Report, Washington, D.C., 1984.

Marvel, H.P. "How Fair Is Fair Trade?" *Contemporary Policy Issues*, Spring 1985, 3, 9–16.

Meehan, J., and Larner, R. "A Proposed Rule of Reason for Vertical Restraints on Competition." *Antitrust Bulletin*, 1981, 26, 195.

Overstreet, T.R., Jr. *Resale Price Maintenance: Economic Theories and Empirical Evidence*. FTC Bureau of Economics Staff Report, Washington, D.C., November 1983.

Overstreet, T.R., Jr., and Fisher, A.A. "Resale Price Maintenance and Distributional Efficiency: Some Lessons From the Past." *Contemporary Policy Issues*, Spring 1985, 3, 43–58.

Popofsky, M.L. "Lawyer's Response." *Antitrust Law Journal*, 1983, 52, 719–29.

Posner, R.A. "The Next Step in the Antitrust Treatment of Restricted Distribution: Per Se Legality." *University of Chicago Law Review*, Winter 1981, 48, 6–26.

Scherer, F.M. "The Economics of Vertical Restraints." *Antitrust Law Journal*, 1983, 52, 687–707.

Sharp, B.S. "Comments on Marvel's 'How Fair is Fair Trade?' " *Contemporary Policy Issues*, Spring 1985, 3, 37–42.

Spence, A.M. "Monopoly, Quality, and Regulation." –Bell Journal of Economics. Autumn 1975, 6, 417–29.

Telser, L.G. "Why Should Manufacturers Want Fair Trade?" *Journal of Law and Economics*, October 1960, 3,86–105.

Williamson, O. "Assessing Vertical Market Restrictions: Antitrust Ramifications of the Transaction Cost Approach." *University of Pennsylvania Law Review*, April 1979, 127, 953–93.

Cases

California Retail Liquor Dealers Association v. Midcal Aluminum, 445 U.S. 97 (1980).

Continental T.V. v. G.T.E. Sylvania, 433 U.S. 36 (1977).

Dr. Miles Medical Co. v. John D. Park and Sons Co., 220 U.S. 373 (1911).

Monsanto Co. v. Spray-Rite Service Corp., 104 S. Ct. 1464 (1984).

3

Economic Effects of Exclusive Purchasing Arrangements in the Distribution of Goods

John S. Chard

Exclusive purchasing (or, as it is also called, exclusive dealing) is a restriction that a supplier imposes on a customer to prevent the customer from purchasing some category of products from any other supplier. It is a vertical restraint, but unlike territorial, customer, or resale price restraints, it limits purchasing rather than resale. It is the converse of a resale restraint, limiting interbrand competition but not intrabrand competition. The nature and effects of exclusive purchasing arrangements are perhaps even less well understood than the nature and effects of resale restraints. By necessarily foreclosing other suppliers from selling a category of products to the customer, exclusive purchasing may conceivably have anticompetitive effects. However, exclusive purchasing may also have procompetitive, efficiency-increasing effects.[1]

This chapter examines the conditions in which exclusive purchasing arrangements involving distributors (especially retailers) may have procompetitive effects. A more detailed analysis of exclusive purchasing than has been available in the past is warranted not least by the fact that regulation of exclusive purchasing arrangements by means of competition rules has become more significant. For example, the European Communities (EC) Commission has recently tried to specify the conditions under which exclusive purchasing agreements (with special conditions applying to beer supply and gasoline service station agreements) can be allowed to operate under European Economic Community (EEC) competition rules. Moreover, exclusive purchasing arrangements do (or potentially can) affect the distribution of a wide range of products. For example, beverages, petroleum products, cars and car parts, agricultural machinery, bicycles, ice cream, spices, frozen foodstuffs, dress patterns, building materials, outboard motors, pets, inclusive tours, shoes, and hearing aids are some of the products that have been the subject of exclusive purchasing arrangements investigated by competition authorities. Thus, it seems worthwhile to develop further the criteria by which businesses can judge the likelihood of success of exclusive purchasing as a marketing strategy.

The following sections analyze three sets of arguments that may be used to justify exclusive purchasing. The arguments relate to the provision of information services by the manufacturer (supplier), the maintenance of a reputation for quality, and the costs of delivery. A final section draws together a few conclusions.

Exclusive Purchasing and the Provision of Information Services by the Manufacturer

A manufacturer may invest in various types of information to improve the distribution and attractiveness of its products. To protect this investment, the manufacturer may negotiate exclusive purchasing arrangements with distributors. Such investments in information include expenditures on advertising, distributor services, and product design.

Advertising

A manufacturer may engage in advertising and other promotional activities to increase demand for its branded product. The simplest way for the manufacturer to cover the cost of advertising is to increase the wholesale price of the product. Implicitly, the manufacturer tries to charge distributors for the additional business generated by the advertising expenditure. Insofar as the advertising is purely brand-specific—in that the additional business that the advertising generates attaches only to the manufacturer's brand—a distributor cannot avoid the implicit charge for advertising services. If, however, a distributor can substitute a similar but unadvertised brand for the advertised product (without completely forgoing the additional business generated by the advertising), it can partly avoid the implicit charge. The distributor will be able to buy the unadvertised substitute brand for a lower wholesale price and yet obtain a similar retail price (the free-rider problem). The distributor's margin is increased at the expense of reduced sales and returns to the advertising manufacturer. In this situation, the manufacturer doing the advertising may require its distributors to buy certain types of products exclusively from that firm. This requirement will prevent distributors from substituting other manufacturers' products and will enable the manufacturer to appropriate the benefits resulting from its advertising expenditure. Thus, exclusive purchasing could encourage higher levels of advertising and, to the extent that advertising expenditure is not wasteful in some sense, more efficient levels of advertising.

The conditions under which exclusive purchasing could be used to protect investments in advertising are worth emphasizing, as they seem fairly precise. First, it appears that advertising and other promotional activities should involve economies of scale of sufficient importance for it to be more efficient for the manufacturer to organize them than for distributors to integrate into these activities. If this were not the case, distributors would bear the costs of the advertising and other promotional activities, and the aforementioned free-rider problem would not exist. Second, for the distributor to be able to free-ride by inducing customers to switch brands, it must be able, relatively costlessly, to convince customers of the substitutability of other products for the brand that persuaded them to buy at the distributor's outlet. Thus, the type of promotional investment that is jeopardized is that which provides more general information about the product. Thus, if highly brand-specific advertising (often associated with "experience" goods) is undertaken, and if it is costly for the distributor to make recommendations that influence customers' choice of brand (perhaps because self-service is used in selling the products concerned), distributors may find it difficult and unprofitable to switch customers from brand to brand, and exclusive purchasing is unlikely to be employed. If, however, advertising of a more directly informational type is undertaken by a manufacturer—perhaps associated with the promotion of a "search" good—there may be more scope for the distributor to influence customer switching. The distributor may choose to display and supply brands alongside the advertised brand that are similar in every respect except that they are not advertised so heavily. If point-of-sale service (for example, demonstration, advice) is usually demanded by the customer, the distributor may be able, relatively cheaply, to persuade the customer to switch brands when this service is given.

Distribution Services

Another possible reason for exclusive purchasing is that it is being used to protect the manufacturer's investment in the development of distributor services. (There are obvious similarities here with so-called business-format franchising. For convenience, I shall use the terms *manufacturer, distributor,* and *distributorship,* but the same arguments would apply if we substituted the terms *franchisor, franchisee,* and *franchise.*) The manufacturer could supply information about management systems, staff training, selling techniques, and after-sales servicing. To the extent that the manufacturer's investment in providing such information can generate customers by increasing the efficiency of a distribution outlet independently of whether that manufacturer's product is sold by the outlet, free-riding possibilities exist unless exclusive purchasing (or a similar restriction, such as a tie-in provision) is employed.

An alternative to exclusive purchasing as a means of preventing free riding might be a royalty on output or sales of all the products sold by the distributor, whether or not the products are supplied by the manufacturer. If the distributor is required to pay royalties, however, it has an incentive to distort the reported amounts of products that are handled. By its very nature, exclusive purchasing prevents substitution of other suppliers' products for the manufacturer's product, and monitoring of such an arrangement may be less costly than monitoring of a royalty system.

To the extent that information designed to improve services at the distribution level is supplied by the manufacturer to a distributor infrequently, it might be argued that efficient charging for the information would require that the distributor pay a fixed fee at the time the information is acquired to reflect the discounted present value of the information. In contrast, other methods of charging, such as exclusive purchasing and royalties on purchases or sales, would result in a charge on business generated at the distribution outlet even when the increased business was a consequence of the distributor's efforts and was unrelated to the manufacturer's investments in developing distributor services. Thus, the distributor's efforts to increase sales would be attenuated, reducing the overall efficiency of the distribution system.

This argument ignores, however, problems associated with transfers of information. The manufacturer may be unwilling to make full disclosure of information before a distributorship agreement is sealed because of the risk of opportunistic behavior by the distributor. In the absence of full information, however, the distributor is unlikely to completely trust the manufacturer's predictions of the profitability of distributorships. The combination of uncertainty and risk aversion will tend to reduce the initial payment the distributor will be willing to make. A manufacturer thus has an incentive to develop a plan under which payments will be made in proportion to the actual profitability of the distributorship. Such a plan will increase the present value of the manufacturer's expected earnings by providing for the more efficient allocation of risk of failure between the two parties. In effect, the manufacturer is insuring the distributor against part of the risk of failure. The manufacturer is better placed to bear part of the risk because, given information impactedness, its subjective assessment of the riskiness of each distributorship is likely to be lower. Moreover, given that even the manufacturer may not be able to estimate the potential profitability of each particular dealership with any accuracy but that, nevertheless, it has information about the general determinants of the profitability of distributorships with certain types of characteristics, the manufacturer may be better placed to bear part of the risk because its investment is likely to be diversified over many distributorships.

For similar reasons, manufacturers may be encouraged to bear part of the risk associated with investments in physical assets that are necessary for the efficient conduct of distributorships and are made on the basis of information about their profitability originating with the manufacturer. This will occur only if the assets concerned have some degree of specificity, as only then does the existence of appropriable quasi-rents and the associated possibility of

opportunistic behavior by the manufacturer increase the riskiness of investment if the investment cost is borne wholly by the distributor rather than shared
with the manufacturer. Thus, for example, investment in a retail site in a major shopping area that requires no special fixtures may present no special risks,
so such investments are likely to be undertaken by distributors rather than
by manufacturers. The assets can easily be converted to alternative uses if their
use in any particular manufacturer's distribution system is found to be unprofitable. However, the problems associated with information impactedness
and the hazards of opportunistic behavior by the manufacturer increase as
the degree of asset specificity associated with investments in the distributorship increases. These problems may be alleviated if the manufacturer bears
part (or all) of the cost of the investments, with the share of the costs being
greater according to the degree of asset specificity regarding the services provided by the asset to the particular distribution system. Thus, it is possible
that the elements often found in distributorship agreements relating to the terms
of financial assistance granted by manufacturers to their distributors and the
provisions in leases of property and equipment may be explained as attempts
to economize on transaction costs.

The problem of inducing appropriate investment at the distributor level
may arise in its most acute form when a rapid expansion or change in the
distribution network for a branded product is getting under way. Uncertainty
and nonconvergence of expectations between manufacturer and distributors
(whether existing or potential) are likely to be very significant. It may be difficult for distributors to perceive the opportunities awaiting them, particularly
when these opportunities depend on changes being made to the arrangements
for the supply of the product to distributors and these changes are not directly
controlled by individual distributors. The manufacturer may be unable to signal
these opportunities without inviting opportunistic behavior by distributors,
which might disclose valuable information about the manufacturer's distribution strategy to rival manufacturers. Even if opportunities are perceived in
a general way, the information may be interpreted in different ways. Thus,
a manufacturer may need to coordinate investments and distribution by means
of various contractual controls and financial assistance or even by outright
vertical integration.

An example of the use of exclusive purchasing to protect manufacturer
investments in developing services at the distributor level is found in gasoline
retailing. In an investigation of gasoline supply by the British Monopolies Commission, it was found that exclusive purchasing had resulted in improvements
in the layout of gasoline stations, in the facilities available, and in the service
given.[2] Arguably, these improvements would not have been realized to the
same extent without capital investment in the retail trade by the oil companies

—in the form of company-owned stations of a high standard, the provision of tied loans, and the lease of tied equipment to retailers—and without the training facilities and advice offered to retailers by the companies.

Product Design

In some situations, it is possible that exclusive purchasing could be used to protect the value of a manufacturer's design investment. Marvel used the example of companies that produce dress patterns.[3] Because successful dress pattern designs could easily be copied by rivals, a rival producer could offer an essentially identical pattern to distributors at a reduced price, reflecting only production costs. Then, if exclusive purchasing were not a requirement, distributors could opportunistically switch customers away from patterns produced by the company that had incurred the design investment costs.

A similar argument was used by Automotive Products to explain its attitude toward "spurious" spares.[4] Automotive Products said that it considered itself entitled to protect what it regarded as its property in the design of its products by not permitting its appointed wholesalers to stock clutches made for replacement only by a manufacturer such as Quinton Hazell, except when no comparable clutches were made by Automotive Products. It took exception to the fact that clutches made by Quinton Hazell could be copies of its own originals and, in the absence of exclusive purchasing requirements, could have been used opportunistically by distributors to switch customers away Automotive Products clutch mechanisms. The validity of this sort of argument as an explanation for exclusive purchasing would appear to depend on at least two conditions:

1. The original design costs are large in relation to the costs of copying.
2. Other means of protecting property rights in information (for example, via patent and copyright laws) are not cheaply available as substitutes for exclusive purchasing.

It is worth noting at this point that *collective* exclusive purchasing, which is often considered to be even less likely to result in procompetitive effects than exclusive purchasing arrangements made by individual suppliers, may also be—in principle and perhaps in practice—a means of protecting investments in information. An example is provided by the case of the Fashion Originators' Guild of America.[5] The original fashion creation designers were not eligible for patent or copyright protection under the law, but Guild members all agreed not to copy the registered designs of other Guild members. To enforce the contract, and to keep other "style pirates" from selling copied designs in direct competition with Guild members, the members of the Guild would sell their merchandise only to retailers that agreed to buy exclusively from Guild members.

Exclusive Purchasing, Reputation, and Quality

It is possible that the quality of a product may vary along several dimensions, including safety, durability, and reliability. The quality characteristics of most importance to the ultimate user of a product depend on the type of product and, possibly, the nature of the user. If users could costlessly identify those quality characteristics that best suited their requirements by inspecting products prior to purchase, suppliers of products (including anyone handling those products before they reach the final user) would have appropriate incentives to supply products with desired characteristics in a cost-efficient manner. Suppliers of a product that did not supply products with desired characteristics or did not supply them at least cost would incur losses and go out of business. Quality characteristics may be difficult (and costly) to identify by inspection and may be revealed only after a product has been purchased and put to use. In these circumstances, suppliers would have appropriate incentives to supply products with desired product characteristics only if they could be penalized after a purchase takes place for selling products that turn out to be poor value for the money. It can be argued that under competitive market conditions, various mechanisms will arise to ensure that the costs of quality faults are borne by the supplier responsible for the faults. These mechanisms include provision of warranties and investment in the advertising of a brand name. Purchasing a product with a warranty enables the buyer to put right, at the expense of the supplier, product defects that may become apparent during use. Heavy promotion of a brand name may indicate to a buyer that the seller is depending on repeat purchases to recoup the costs of advertising. Thus, the buyer may have good reason to believe the quality claims of the supplier; if buyers were dissatisfied with the product in use, so that repeat purchases did not occur on a sufficiently large scale to allow the costs of advertising to be recouped, the seller would incur losses.

A problem arises if there are difficulties and costs in assigning responsiblity for quality faults. This can occur when the quality of a product can be affected by the behavior of more than one economic unit in a chain of supply. For example, the quality characteristics of a manufacturer-branded product may be influenced by a retailer as well as by the manufacturer of the brand. Thus, a final user of the product may find it difficult to know who to blame for any quality faults—the manufacturer or the retailer. A so-called externality problem occurs. A retailer might find it profitable to cut pre- and postsales servicing of a manufacturer-branded product because the retailer's costs would be reduced by more than its revenues. However, it is possible that by debasing the quality of the product, the retailer would injure the reputation of the manufacturer's brand, which would harm the sales of other retailers of the brand. If overall sales of the brand would be reduced by acts of quality debasement resulting from decisions taken independently by retailers, it might be efficient for there to be restraints on retailers' behavior insofar as that behavior could affect the quality of the product. If they were effective in reducing quality debasement, restraints on retailers' behavior would be efficient from the viewpoint of the manufacturer, whose brand reputation would be protected and whose sales and profits would be greater as a result. They would also be efficient from the viewpoint of retailers as a whole, because retailers that debased the quality of a brand in order to cut costs could not free-ride on the efforts of retailers that incurred costs to enhance the quality reputation of the brand. Finally, such restraints would be efficient from the viewpoint of final users, who would not otherwise have the opportunity of purchasing a high-quality brand.

It is conceivable that one way of efficiently controlling retailers' behavior is for the manufacturer to make exclusive pruchasing agreements with them. In its report on liquefied petroleum gas (LPG), for example, the British Monopolies Commission found that exclusive purchasing probably had a beneficial effect on safety because it enabled suppliers to exercise a more effective control over the storage and handling of LPG by their distributors.[6] The safety of their cylinders—and their good reputation for safety—was a matter of importance to Calor, the dominant supplier, and to other suppliers. No supplier wanted its distributors to be associated with cylinders from suppliers whose safety standards might not have been as high as its own.

Before we consider in more detail the use of exclusive purchasing (and other restrictive arrangements) to protect the quality of a product, it is worth noting the following points from the analysis so far.

First, for controls on retailer behavior to be efficient, it must be possible for retailers to influence product quality. If it were not possible for retailers to influence product quality, controls on retailer behavior could not result in higher product quality.

Second, even if retailers can influence product quality, controls on retailers' behavior that are designed to protect product quality will not benefit the manufacturer (in terms of higher sales and higher profits) unless final users reduce their purchases of products that provide poor value for the money and make repeat purchases of products that provide good value for the money. Therefore, final users must be able to perceive differences in the qualities of various products they use and must be willing to pay for qualities that are more expensive to produce.

Third, final users must be unable (or unwilling, because of the costs involved) to ascertain product quality by means of direct inspection before committing themselves to purchase. If it were possible to detect poor quality at point of purchase by simply inspecting the product (and any associated retailer service), it seems reasonable to suppose that the user could make an efficient choice without knowing anything about the name and reputation for quality of the retailer or manufacturer whence the product comes. However, if final users detect quality differences only after committing themselves to purchase, the development of recognizable brand names may be a low-cost way of helping final users make efficient purchasing decisions. Brand names enable final users to identify and distinguish among sources of products with differing qualities so that their purchases can be switched from products (from particular sources) that have not provided good value for the money to those that have.

Fourth, and following from the previous three points, it must be more efficient for the manufacturer's brand name to be used as the indicator of product quality (rather than the retailer's) for external control of retailer behavior to be necessary. If final users relied on retailer brand names to judge product quality and to make purchasing (and repeat purchasing) decisions, there would be no need for manufacturers to control retailer behavior. Each retailer would maintain product qualities at levels desired by final users, because the costs of any quality debasement by a retailer would be fully borne by that retailer in the form of depreciation of its brand name and smaller purchases of products from that retailer. In short, there would be no external effects to control. When retailing is relatively concentrated and manufacturing is relatively unconcentrated (and given the foregoing three points), it may be efficient for the function of developing and promoting brand names to reside with retailers. However, given economies of scale in developing and promoting brand names, it is possible that this function is most efficiently performed by manufacturers if manufacturing is relatively concentrated while retailing is relatively unconcentrated. When it is efficient for the development and promotion of a brand name to be organized by the manufacturer, externality problems may arise in the way suggested earlier—that is, the manufacturer may be blamed for quality faults caused by the retailer. In these circumstances, it may also be efficient for the manufacturer to exert control over retailer behavior.

Now consider the types of control the manufacturer may wish to exert over retailer behavior. The choice of control method will be a function of the retailer behavior that needs to be controlled and the relative costs of alternative control methods. What sorts of retailer behavior may damage the reputation of a manufactuer?

Distributor Mistakes That Affect the Safety and Reliability of the Product

One possibility is that the retailer may make mistakes that affect product safety and that these mistakes are more likely to be made when the retailer sells several manufacturers' products. For example, liquefied petroleum gas suppliers have adopted different valves and regulators for use with their cylinders of gas. It is conceivable that more accidents would occur if retailers distributed more than one supplier's gas cyclinders, because more mistakes might be made in the delivery of cylinders to final customers who might try to fit inappropriate cylinders to their gas appliances. Retailers may expend insufficient resources on quality control (that is, safety) measures, such as strict operating procedures to reduce the risk of accidents occurring, because they do not have as great an interest in maintaining the reputations of manufacturers' brands as the manufacturers themselves do. Manufacturers could pay retailers for undertaking greater quality control and could monitor their efforts, but any one manufacturer might find this method of control costly and might expose itself to free riding by rival manufacturers. Thus, it is possible that exclusive purchasing could be used as a cost-effective method of controlling retailer behavior so as to increase product safety.

Mistakes in handling a number of rival suppliers' products may affect not only the manufacturers' reputations for safety but also their reputations for other dimensions of quality, such as reliability. For example, automotive battery manufacturers used to operate exclusive agency arrangements to retain control, so they argued, over the final "manufacturing" process of filling and charging batteries. This process could not be done until shortly before purchase by the prospective user. Manufacturers argued that if it were not carried out properly, the reputation of their products would be adversely affected. If it were true that the handling of different makes of battery resulted in more mistakes by the distributor, so that incorrect application of charging regimes was more likely than it would be under exclusive agency (exclusive purchasing) arrangements, then these arrangements could be an efficient solution to the distribution problem. At the time of its investigation in the early 1960s, the British Monopolies Commission saw no reason to suppose that the manufacturer would be unable to ensure that the batteries it sold through its distributors were properly filled and charged, even if the distributors were also handling other manufacturers' batteries.[7]

Underinvestment in Distributor Services that Affect the Quality of the Product

Another possibility was intimated earlier, when I referred to the free-rider problem that might arise if a manufacturer pays for quality control by the retailer. Even if retailers do not make more mistakes in the handling of a number of competing brands than they would under exclusive purchasing arrangements, they may still underinvest in pre- and after-sales services that affect the reputation of a brand. Underinvestment may occur in the sense that additional investment in services provided through each retail outlet increases the value of a manufacturer's sales by more than the increase in sales experienced by that retail outlet; that is, there is a positive externality. Some form of restricted distribution arrangement, such as the grant of exclusive territories to distributors or the enforcement of resale price maintenance, could "internalize" the returns (in the form of higher sales of the manufacturer's product) to retailers that invest in additional or better quality service. However, the argument that restricted distribution gives an incentive to retailers to provide the desired services relies on the premise that the manufacturer specifies the services to be provided and then monitors and enforces the arrangements. It seems possible that a manufacturer could ensure that better services (at a lower cost of enforcement) are provided by its retailers by paying for them directly. For example, the manufacturer could invest in the training of retail staff. If it does so, however, it faces the problem of free riding. The manufacturer's investments could be used by distributors to increase the sales of its rivals' products. To prevent this (and to internalize the return on its investment) the manufacturer may find it profitable to set up exclusive purchasing arrangements with its distributors.

This argument is similar to the argument presented earlier in discussing manufacturers' provision of information to their distributors. However, the argument then took a slightly different form. Then, the free-rider problem arose as a result of expenditures by the manufacturer on information services that improved the distribution of its product but that could also have been used by distributors to improve the distribution of rivals' products. Exclusive purchasing arrangements were employed to overcome the difficulties of transferring asymmetrically distributed information from one party (the manufacturer) to another (the distributor). In the present case, the free-rider problem again arises as a result of expenditures by the manufacturer that improve the services associated with the distribution of its product and that could also be used by distributors to improve the services associated with the distribution of rivals' products. However, in this case, the manufacturer's expenditures of concern are those on distribution services (not just information services) provided at the level of individual outlets that are likely to increase the value of the manufacturer's sales through its distribution network as a whole, not just through the distribution points on which the expenditures may be targeted.

Raleigh, a British manufacturer of bicycles, is an example of a firm that has used exclusive purchasing arrangements with its distributors in conjunction with the provision of services to enhance its brand reputation for quality.[8] Raleigh claims that it set up its network of Raleigh 5 Star Dealers to improve standards in the retailing and servicing of its bicycles. Raleigh assists in upgrading premises, provides training for staff, and helps with promotion and advertising. Raleigh 5 Star Dealers are required to sell Raleigh Group bicycles exclusively. In 1980, there were 110 Raleigh 5 Star Dealers, accounting for some 14 percent of the Raleigh's UK bicycle sales, which indicates that an anticompetitive motive for the arrangement was unlikely.

One expenditure incurred by a supplier to maintain the quality of its product and the quality of the services associated with its distribution is not very obvious. This is the expenditure on policing distributors to ensure that they refrain from acts of quality debasement that would otherwise have adverse external effects on the supplier's distribution system as a whole. In this case, too, however, it is possible that exclusive purchasing may be used to internalize the return on such expenditures. This possibility seems most likely to arise if a closely controlled uniform system of distribution for a product is valued by consumers, as may be the case in some franchise networks, in which franchisees are expected to adhere closely to a detailed set of operating instructions. The supplier/franchisor may have an important function in policing the franchise network by monitoring franchisees and enforcing the conditions of the franchise. The supplier/franchisor will have a continuing incentive to carry out quality policing only if it has a continuing share in the business. This share is related to sales rather than profits, as the effectiveness of the policing of franchises is more closely related to sales than to profits.[9] Thus, royalties on franchisees' sales of the supplier's product may be the means of providing this continuous incentive. However, to the extent that franchisees can opportunistically avoid paying the royalty by substituting products obtained elsewhere, exclusive purchasing arrangements may be the preferred method of ensuring that the supplier is rewarded for successful policing effort.

Spare Parts and After-Sales Servicing

Another aspect of retailer behavior that a manufacturer may wish to control in order to maintain its brand reputation is the retailer's use of spare parts in the repair and maintenance of a durable good. The performance of a durable good is likely to depend on the quality of spare parts used to repair and maintain it. If the buyer of the durable good cannot easily ascertain the quality of spare parts by means of direct inspection prior to purchase, he or she may rely on the reputation of the supplier of the durable good to indicate spare parts of a desired quality. So long as spare parts are labeled with the supplier's brand name, it might appear that there is no problem in assigning quality attributes to the supplier responsible for controlling those attributes. On further examination, however, it seems that problems could arise.

First, and perhaps least important, the buyer could be confused by the labeling of the spare part. Such a possibility was mentioned in the aforementioned British Monopolies Commission investigation of Automotive Products' arrangements for the supply of clutch mechanisms. Apart from claiming that it was concerned with protecting its investments in the design of clutch mechanisms, Automotive Products also said it was worried that it could be blamed for product failures for which it was not responsible. Clutches made by Quinton Hazell were supplied under the same part numbers with an additional prefix, so that without realizing it, users might be supplied with nongenuine replacements for clutches installed as original equipment by Automotive Products. Moroever, in rebuilt clutches, the cover assembly used might be the Borg and Beck original, with Borg and Beck's name still stamped on it, although it would be supplied in a package that made it clear that it was rebuilt by Quinton-Hazell. (Borg and Beck is a trademark used by Automotive Products.) Automotive Products argued that once such a clutch was installed in a car, or if a "spurious" driven plate was put in a Borg and Beck clutch, its identity would not be apparent, Automotive Products would likely be blamed for failures for which it was not responsible, and its reputation might therefore suffer. (The Monopolies Commission was not impressed by this argument.) Exclusive purchasing arrangements could conceivably be used to reduce the possibility of customer confusion and to maintain the reputation of a supplier. However, an alternative (perhaps more costly) arrangement would be for the supplier to make it a condition of its distributors that they not sell similar products bearing marks that might identify the product with the supplier concerned.

A second problem could arise when a supplier sells a durable good through a franchise system of distribution in which its name is heavily identified with its franchised distribution outlets. Customers might expect that the quality of the spares used in after-sales servicing on the durable good by franchised distributors would be maintained at a particular standard. Indeed, customers might gain from being able to rely on this expectation if they want to save themselves the trouble of specifying and checking the source of the spare parts used. If customers should perceive that servicing falls below an expected standard (resulting, perhaps, from the use of poor-quality spares), the reputation of the supplier would suffer, and customers could suffer from being unable to rely on the quality of spares supplied through franchised outlets. Thus, the supplier/franchisor might use exclusive purchasing arrangements that require franchised distributors to buy spare parts exclusively from it or sources approved by it in order to protect its reputation and ensure customer satisfaction. This argument, like the earlier ones, relies on the idea that reputation effects (in the present case, those associated with the quality of spare parts) adhere to the supplier rather than to the distributor and that alternative methods of defending the supplier's reputation are more costly.

An obvious example of this argument is the case made by car manufacturers in defense of their exclusive purchasing arrangements with franchised distributors covering the acquisition of spare parts. It is interesting to note that in a report on motor parts, the British Monopolies Commission believed that customers' interests would be protected in the absence of exclusive purchasing arrangements because franchisees would have their own interest in ensuring that they did not supply their customers with inferior parts.[10] However, in a case involving Volkswagen, a judgment by the German Federal Supreme Court implied that the interest of parts manufacturers and distributors in maintaining the quality of parts was less than that of the car manufacturer.[11] The British Monopolies Commission did not discuss the extent to which car manufacturers could defend their reputations by using alternative means to exclusive purchasing arrangements—presumably because the commission believed that reputation effects adhered primarily to the distributor. In contrast, the German Federal Supreme Court examined this question in some detail. It concluded that there was no cheaper way of ensuring that parallel delivery parts were maintained at as high a quality level as genuine parts. Parallel delivery parts were spare parts that were made by a component manufacturer also making original equipment and genuine parts for Volkswagen but that were supplied directly to distributors, as opposed to the genuine parts indirectly supplied via Volkswagen. The court said that, even if it were legally possible, it would be more costly for Volkswagen to extend its examination of spare parts supplied by a component manufacturer to Volkswagen (which the court seemed satisfied did increase the quality of deliveries) to parts supplied directly to franchised distributors than for exclusive purchasing arrangements to continue. The court also said that it would not be a more moderate means of avoiding false expectations of customers and defending its reputation for Volkswagen to instruct franchised distributors to obtain the customer's prior consent or to inform the customer subsequently if parallel delivery parts were used. This would be precisely contrary to Volkswagen's interests, which the court believed did merit protection. The court considered that the exclusive purchasing arrangements were part of a marketing policy whereby Volkswagen aimed to advertise the availability of a uniform range of spare parts of the best quality for maintenance and repair work in any VAG enterprise (franchised distributor) and to create corresponding confidence in the minds of its customers. The court thought this policy could not be criticized under the rules of competition.

Thus, whereas the British Monopolies Commission found that the use of exclusive purchasing arrangements for car parts by car manufacturers and importers in Britain were not in the public interest, the German Federal Supreme Court found that Volkswagen's arrangements in Germany were not unfair. In context, both conclusions may have been correct. Nevertheless, the contrast suggests that the argument concerning the efficiency of exclusive purchasing arrangements vis-à-vis possible alternative arrangements in signaling and achieving an assured level of quality of spare parts must be very carefully assessed in such cases.

Car parts also provide us with another aspect of behavior by distribution outlets that a supplier may wish to control—namely, the *pricing* of spare parts. The reputation of a durable good supplier could be based on a marketing strategy that emphasizes that its products have a long life and remain economical even after a long period of use. Car manufacturers have argued that to carry out such a strategy effectively, a combined costing of parts, or price averaging, is necessary; the prices of parts for which there is greater demand are set to earn a higher profit margin so that the prices of the less sought-after parts for older car models can be set at "reasonable" levels. Without further elaboration, this argument seems rather unsatisfying. It is not clear how the customer (and the reputation of the supplier) would benefit from such price averaging. A buyer of a durable good is presumably more interested in the (discounted) total cost of buying and maintaining the good over its economic life (which is unaffected by price averaging) than in the distribution of that cost over time.

It is clear from the foregoing analysis that the protection-of-reputation argument in favor of exclusive purchasing arrangements is hydra-headed and chameleon-featured. However, although it is difficult to pin down and assess, the protection-of-reputation argument must be taken seriously, and it appears that competition authorities should analyze it more closely in the future than they seem to have done in the past.

Exclusive Purchasing and the Costs of Delivery

It can be argued that exclusive purchasing may enable a supplier to reduce the costs of delivering its product to distributors. Although this argument has not been developed in the academic literature, it has been used in defense of exclusive purchasing by some firms involved in investigations by the British Monopolies Commission. For example, the argument has appeared in reports on gasoline supply, ice cream, and liquefied petroleum gas, and a similar argument was expounded in a report on frozen foodstuffs in defense of discounts for reserving space in refrigerated cabinets. The argument seems to rely on the idea that financial incentives for delivery in larger quantities cannot operate flexibly enough to ensure that delivery costs (and distribution costs as a whole) are as low as they would be under exclusive purchasing arrangements (perhaps together with minimum drop requirements). Thus, the validity of the argument appears to depend on whether a transaction cost rationale can be found for choosing a delivery system that relies on administrative controls in preference to one that relies on direct price incentives. If such a rationale exists, it would tie in with the transaction cost–based explanations for exclusive purchasing already discussed. No such rationale (nor any other) has been fully developed in the British Monopolies Commission reports when the issue of delivery cost savings has been discussed.

The British Monopolies Commission's report on ice cream and water ices can be taken as an example of the state of thinking about the delivery cost argument.[12] Glacier (Lyons Maid) argued that the practice of exclusive purchasing in respect to the static sites it supplied with ice cream avoided undue fragmentation of distribution and therefore was likely to lower delivery costs. Glacier contended that, given the need and the special circumstances of the industry to provide direct distribution to customers, the most economic method was to operate a preorder system by "tele-selling" from the depot, with trucks going on predetermined selling routes with predetermined orders. Unduly small

deliveries to retailers were avoided by the restriction on the sale of other suppliers' products, combined with a system of minimum delivery quantities. It
would not be possible to maintain the latter at an effective level if retailers
were free to deal in competitors' products, as pressures from those competitors
would cause the retailer to take the opportunity to "top up" with smaller
deliveries from them. On the other hand, financial incentives for delivery in
larger quantities would militate against a steady off-take from the depots and
would tend to result in serious depletion of the retailer's stock, with a conse-
quent loss in sales, as it delayed the next order to qualify for a bigger drop
discount. This might occur precisely when the retailer should be in a position
to take advantage of the market at a time of sudden improvement in the
weather. Thus, the burden at the depots, instead of being spread reasonably
evenly, would increase to an even greater extent at such times than it did under
existing arrangements. In the absence of the tie, Glacier believed that it would
distribute no greater quantity of products but would distribute to a larger
number of outlets and in a much greater number of deliveries of a much smaller
average size, thus requiring more depot facilities—particularly a bigger vehicle establishment. Journey planning would be more liable to disruption (and
point-of-sale advertising costs and the costs of sales material would be greater),
but with no increase in overall sales volume, unit costs would rise. Glacier
also partly justified its "cabinet tie" (whereby retailers supplied with a
refrigerated cabinet by an ice cream manufacturer agreed to stock in the cabinet
only ice cream supplied by that manufacturer) on the grounds that it contained
the costs of distribution.

Another ice cream manufacturer, Walls, argued that the cabinet tie increased predictability in delivery and so reduced costs, because the company
knew how much refrigerated space was available for storage on the premises
of retailers it had the exclusive right to supply. The retailer was under an obliga-
tion to purchase from Walls in such times and such quantities as were
reasonable with regard to the refrigerator hired to it. Walls was therefore enabled to achieve the maximum drop size per delivery from the lowest vehicle
rate mileage while ensuring that stock levels in retail outlets were sufficient
to meet sudden surges in demand. Thus, potential sales were not lost and the
number of supplementary deliveries required (and the resources to provide
them) was reduced, ensuring that the retailer was neither underserviced nor
overserviced. Given the dependence of demand on weather conditions, planning uncertainties were unavoidable, but they would be increased markedly
in the absence of cabinet exclusivity; achieving the same sales volume would
call for an increase in the distribution resources required (with greater
underutilization of them) because of greater unpredictability of consumer identity, location, size, and frequency of order and, thus, higher costs. Walls carried out a study of the extent to which variations in the costs of delivery to
retailers of comparable turnover depended on whether they had a company-

supplied refrigerated cabinet or their own. The results of the study showed that, for each £100 of sales, own-cabinet retailers required 11 percent more deliveries and contacts than retailers with company-supplied cabinets. The results implied that Walls' total costs would increase by about 0.8 percent if all cabinets were owned by the retailers.

Walls stated that it had never found it practicable to relate discounts directly to drop size (other than in bulk deals) and hence indirectly to variable distribution costs. Except for customers with large storage space, the effect of granting discounts for large drops conflicted with the need to keep cabinets fully stocked (as the failure of its 1969 experiment demonstrated), a need that was fundamental to the ice cream business because of extreme fluctuations in consumer demand. Peaking of demand and deliveries on good weather days would become an even more serious problem than usual, because customers would wait until the last minute before ordering in order to obtain a bigger drop size—by which time everyone wanted supplies.

Similar arguments can be found in other British Monopolies Commission reports. They seem plausible, and they certainly appeared to satisfy the commission in the three cases discussed here—gasoline, ice cream, and liquefied petroleum gas supply. Yet the arguments also remain rather imprecise and relatively untested. They must be developed if they are to be properly tested.

Work on case studies of ice cream, gasoline, and liquefied petroleum gas supply suggests that the advantages of administrative/contractual controls (including, perhaps, exclusive purchasing) relative to financial incentives (such as order-related quantity discounts) increase under the following circumstances:

1. As the number of drops per delivery round increases, the problem of identifying the costs of handling particular sizes of orders becomes greater. Hence, it becomes more difficult (and costly) to produce an order-related quantity discount structure that gives appropriate incentives to retailers to order their products in optimum quantities.

2. As the methods of delivery and storage become more specialized to the products of the supplier, the tendency for the supplier to integrate forward into the delivery and storage of the products becomes greater. This enables the supplier to gain the advantages of flexible control of interrelated stages in a distribution process by means of greater reliance on management organization, rather than by means of greater reliance on more detailed and hence more complex structures of financial incentives.

3. As the unpredictability and magnitude of fluctuations in demand increase, the more important become the problems of planning reserves of products and allocation of products in available storage throughout the distribution system, rationing supplies, and dealing with emergency demands, relative to the problem of ensuring—other things being equal—that drop quantities are of maximum feasible size.

Casual empiricism suggests that two or more of these sets of circumstances were more important in the trades mentioned earlier than they are in delivery conditions in many other trades. If these sets of circumstances change significantly over time, we should expect the changes to be reflected in alterations in delivery systems and in the use of contractual controls relative to financial incentives. The introduction by oil companies of surcharges for loads of small size seems to be associated with the increased importance of one-drop deliveries, an increase in the cost advantages of delivering larger loads, and a less marked peaking of demand. It appears that the justification for exclusive purchasing arrangements in the supply of gasoline can no longer rely (if it ever could) on the argument that it results in delivery cost savings.

Conclusions

This chapter has analyzed the conditions under which exclusive purchasing can be a procompetitive marketing strategy, as when it is used to safeguard incentives for suppliers to underwrite the competitive efforts of their distributors. The chapter has extended earlier work[13] by suggesting that exclusive purchasing may encourage supplier investments not only in information services but also in other services that improve distribution, including the maintenance of a reputation for quality and, possibly, the organization of efficient delivery systems. Thus, the justification for exclusive purchasing arrangements may be wider than is sometimes suggested by public policy pronouncements, which by their nature usually emphasize the possible anticompetitive effects of exclusive purchasing.

Leaving aside possible anticompetitive effects, it is clear that any possible advantages of exclusive purchasing will vary according to the nature of the product. The advantages become greater as the importance of relevant supplier investments increases and as free-rider problems become more acute. Against any advantages must be weighed any increases in distribution costs that result because exclusive purchasing prevents distributors from offering a wider range of competing brands.

Notes

1. See, for example, Richard A. Posner, *Antitrust: An Economic Perspective* (Chicago: University of Chicago Press, 1976), 201–5; Robert H. Bork, *The Antitrust Paradox: A Policy at War with Itself* (New York: Basic Books, 1978), 199–309; and Howard P. Marvel, "Exclusive Dealing," *Journal of Law and Economics*, 25 (April 1982):1–25.

2. Monopolies Commission, *Supply of Petrol to Retailers in the United Kingdom*, HC 264 (London: HMSO, 1965).

3. Marvel, "Exclusive Dealing."

4. Monopolies Commission, *Supply of Clutch Mechanisms for Road Vehicles,* HC 32 (London: HMSO, 1986).

5. Fashion Originators' Guild of America v. Federal Trade Commission, 312 U.S. 457 (1941). The analysis in the text is based on R.G. Holcombe and R.E. Meiners, "The Contractual Alternative to Patents," *International Review of Law and Economics* 1 (December 1981):228–30.

6. Monopolies Commission, *Supply of Liquefied Petroleum Gas,* HC 147 (London: HMSO, 1981).

7. Monopolies Commission, *Supply of Electrical Equipment for Mechanically Propelled Land Vehicles,* HC 21 (London: HMSO, 1963).

8. Monopolies Commission, *Bicycles,* HC 67 (London: HMSO, 1981).

9. P.H. Rubin, "The Theory of the Firm and the Structure of the Franchise Contract," *Journal of Law and Economics,* 21 (April 1978):223–33.

10. Monopolies Commission, *Supply of Motor Parts in the United Kingdom,* HC 318 (London: HMSO, 1982).

11. Case KVR 8/80 before the German Federal Supreme Court, reported in *European Commercial Cases,* 1982, 295–313.

12. Monoplies Commission, *Supply in the United Kingdom of Ice Cream and Water Ices,* Cmnd 7632 (London: HMSO, 1979).

13. See references in note 1, especially Marvel.

4
Sale or Return Agreements versus Outright Sales

Luca Pellegrini

This chapter investigates the rationale of sale or return agreements (SR) as an alternative to outright sales (OS). Under SR, producers take back unsold items and therefore assume the commercial risk involved in selling the goods they produce. The analysis focuses on SR that constitutes a permanent selling policy. It is not concerned with SR that is tied to new goods and meant to convince retailers to accept them in their assortments until the goods have established themselves in the market. Nor is it concerned with cases in which SR is granted to retailers in conjunction with changes of packaging or withdrawal from the market of luxury goods to avoid discounted sales by retailers. (In such cases, SR is normally a consequence of retail price maintenance.)

The kind of SR to be dealt with here implies the permanent reduction in status of retailers to that of simple agents of producers. In the distribution of goods, this is an uncommon practice; to my knowledge, it is the rule only for newspaper and magazine distribution. It is much more widespread in selling services—for example, sales or bookings of airline tickets and hotel rooms through travel agencies, which do not bear any risk related to unsold inventories. In all of these cases, the common feature is the high perishability of the goods and services sold and the very low or zero value of unsold inventories—that is, the high commercial risk involved in the trade of these goods and services. I shall try to show that this is not, in itself, a reason to prefer SR to OS. Incentives for SR lie, instead, in the different penalty cost associated with excess demand for retailers and producers and in the covariant risk advantage that producers might have with respect to retailers. I shall first describe a simple model to determine optimal inventories under uncertainty, and then I will use the model to analyze SR versus OS.

The Proposed Framework

A number of simplifying assumptions must be made so that the model is easy to handle, as the main interest will be not in technical details but in developing as simple a framework as possible to enlighten the problem at hand. There is always a trade-off between what is lost by simplifying reality to obtain definite analytical results and the benefits of using more realistic and complex settings, which, however, lead to less definite findings and might confuse rather than clarify the problem one is trying to solve. I hope I have struck the right balance.

Both producers and retailers must be characterized. The market we shall deal with is assumed to consist of a number of producers that have some market power and therefore face a downward-sloping demand curve for their products. This is due to product differentiation that makes the different products, though of the same type, substitutable for one another only to a certain extent. The products are sold through a large number of identical retailers that sell their services in a perfectly competitive market or in a market where monopolistic competition prevails. There are no excess profits, and the income earned by retailers is just enough to keep them in business. This implies that the price of retail services, the retail margin, is the same to all sellers.

The demand is uncertain, and whoever bears the commercial risk has to solve an optimal inventory holding problem. If the demand exceeds the availability of one of the goods, either the producer of that good or the retailer incurs a penalty cost. Both producers and retailers are assumed to be risk-neutral.

The model developed in the following pages will involve a one-stage maximization exercise; all intertemporal considerations will be avoided. The simple model obtained should be useful for addressing the issue at hand.[1] This one-stage inventory problem will be specified along the lines originally drawn by Karlin (1958) and Mills (1962), and more recently proposed by Irvine (1981).[2] I shall formulate the profit maximization for a producer under SR and then compare the results with those under OS. The discussion will first involve a single producer and a single seller, then a single producer and many sellers. Under SR, the producer directly faces an uncertain demand. Following Mills, it is convenient to imagine demand as consisting of two elements, a "riskless" one and a stochastic one:

$$X = f(p, u) = x(p) + u \qquad (4.1)$$

where $x(p)$ is the forecast made by the firm as a function of the retail price p and u is the forecast error. The distribution function of u, $f(u)$, is assumed independent of p[3], and $E(u)$ is set equal to zero. Moreover, for the time being, the retail price is assumed to be exogenously given and set to a constant value. Under these assumptions, the expected revenue of the firm is

$$E[R^p(z)] = (p - m) \int^{z-x} (x + u) f(u) du + (p - m) \int_{z-x} z f(u) du \qquad (4.2)$$

where m is the per unit margin given to retailers and z is the amount of the good available for sale in the period under consideration. The first term in equation 4.2 represents the revenue of the firm when $z > (x + u)$, excess supply; the second term is the revenue when $z \leq (x + u)$, excess demand. Equation 4.2 can be rewritten as[4]

$$
\begin{aligned}
E[R^p(z)] \;=\;& (p - m)x - (p - m) \int_{z-x} xf(u)du \\
&+ (p - m) \int^{z-x} uf(u)du + (p - m) \int_{z-x} zf(u)du \quad (4.3)
\end{aligned}
$$

Using $E(u) = 0$, equation 4.3 can be further simplified as

$$
E[R^p(z)] \;=\; (p - m)x - (p - m) \int_{z-x} (x + u - z)f(u)du \quad (4.4)
$$

To obtain expected profits, costs must be subtracted from equation 4.4. Three elements should be considered: production costs, costs associated with excess demand, and inventory carrying costs. Over the relevant production range, marginal costs will be assumed constant.[5] Thus, total variable costs are simply c times z. The penalty cost associated with excess demand stands for the firm's evaluation of expected losses arising from customers' dissatisfaction. Customers react to stockouts in different ways: they might buy a substitute in the same shop, postpone the purchase, try to find the desired product in a different store, and so on. These different reactions by customers imply different costs, and costs are also likely to differ between producers and retailers. The main problem with excess demand penalty costs is that they are intertemporal and that they are not proportional to the level of shortage but most likely an increasing function of it. Here again, to keep the model as simple as possible, I shall formalize this class of costs as proportional to excess demand—that is, $a(X - z)$ for $X > z$, where a is the per unit penalty cost.[6] A second cost suffered when end-of-period inventories are positive is an interest cost, possibly including a storage cost, that is proportional to the value of items unsold. Since this type of cost is not central to the analysis, it will be assumed to be equal to zero. In a one-stage model it is also necessary to consider the residual value of the inventories at the end of the period considered and available for the next selling period. In practice, because goods with very high perishability and services will be considered here, this salvage value is best viewed as the scrap value of unsold items. In this way, we need not consider the amount of inventories existing at the beginning of the selling period, and all available products can be thought to be newly produced. The salvage value will be set equal to $b(z - X)$ for $z > X$. The expected profit of the producer is then

$$
\begin{aligned}
E[\Pi^p(z)] \;=\;& (p - m)x - (p - m) \int_{z-x} (x + u - z)f(u)du \\
&- cz - a \int_{z-x} (x + u - z)f(u)du \\
&+ b \int^{z-x} (z - x - u)f(u)du \\
\;=\;& (p - m)x - cz - (p - m + a) \int_{z-x} (x + u - z)f(u)du \\
&+ b \int^{z-x} (z - x - u)f(u)du \quad\quad\quad (4.5)
\end{aligned}
$$

The first-order condition for optimal output is easily found by partially differentiating equation 4.5, as follows:

$$\frac{\partial E[\Pi^p(z)]}{\partial z} = -c + (p - m + a) \int_{z-x} f(u)du + b \int^{z-x} f(u)du$$

$$= 0 \tag{4.6}$$

Denoting the cumulative density function of u as $F(u)$, equation 4.6 can be rewritten in the usual marginal revenue/equal marginal cost form:

$$(p - m)[1 - F(z - x)] = c - a[1 - F(z - x)] - bF(z - x) \tag{4.7}$$

Equation 4.7 simply states that the firm should produce extra units of output until marginal revenue (the price net of retailer's margin times the probability of excess demand—that is, of selling the extra units produced) equals marginal cost (the cost of producing the extra unit minus the saved penalty cost times the probability of selling the unit minus the salvage gain times the probability of not selling the unit. Collecting the probability of not selling the marginal unit produced, we obtain

$$F(z - x) = \frac{(p - m) - c + a}{(p - m) - b + a} \tag{4.8}$$

Equation 4.8 can be written explicitly in terms of the optimal output for the producer under SR:

$$z^p = x + F^{-1}\left(\frac{(p - m) - c + a}{(p - m) - b + a}\right) \tag{4.9}$$

Hence, z^p is always greater than expected demand x by a buffer of inventories if $F^{-1}(.) \neq 1$.[7]

To compare SR and OS, we must perform the same exercise used to compute z^p under the alternative selling policy. Under OS, retailers bear the commercial risk, and the amount of product to be held for resale is their own decision, given the wholesale price q. Retailers will compute the optimal amount of goods to purchase exactly as producers do under SR. The only difference is that their marginal cost is q, not c, and they will likely have a different excess demand penalty cost, which we shall call d. Although this might not be always true, it will be assumed that the salvage cost is the same for producers and retailers. The expected profit for any given retailer is then[8]

$$E[\Pi^r(z)] = px - qz - (p + d) \int_{z-x} z(x + u - z)f(u)du$$

$$+ b \int^{z-x} (z - x - u)f(u)du \tag{4.10}$$

Partially differentiating with respect to z and performing the same manipulations as for the producer case under SR, we obtain

$$z^r = x + F^{-1} \left(\frac{p - q + d}{p + b + d} \right) \tag{4.11}$$

SR versus OS

It might appear that SR is preferable to OS when the salvage value of unsold inventories is very low or, in the case of services, zero. Since retailers pay q, for each unit to be sold, while producers have a cost per unit of c, and $c < q$, the cost of unsold items falls more heavily on retailers than on producers. Quite obviously this is not the case, since producers will allow a higher margin to retailers under OS to compensate for the risk retailers bear. In fact, it is easy to show that SR and OS are equivalent selling policies if demand forecasts by retailers and producers are the same and if $a = d$. Suppose, for convenience, that $a = d = b = 0$, so that equations 4.9 and 4.11 reduce to

$$z^p = x + F^{-1} \left(\frac{(p - m) - c}{(p - m)} \right) \tag{4.12}$$

$$z^r = x + F^{-1} \left(\frac{p - q}{p} \right) \tag{4.13}$$

Since gathering information to make demand forecasts presumably has a nonzero cost, producers will be better off under OS than under SR if in the former case they attain profits at least equal to those attained in the latter. Because we know that the highest producers' profits under SR are associated with optimal output z^p and that retailers' profits are determined by market forces, independently of the selling policy chosen by producers, it is enough to show that given the stated conditions, there exists a value of r , q such that $z^p = z^r = \hat{z}$ and that both producers and retailers make the same profits under the two selling regimes.

Letting $z^p = z^r = \hat{z}$, we need only equate the producer and seller profits under SR and OS and show that they are the same in correspondence of a single value of q, q. For the retailer, profits under SR and OS are, respectively:

$$m^1\hat{z} = m^1(x - \textstyle\int_{z-x}^{\hat{}} (x + u - \hat{z})f(u)du) = m^1H \tag{4.14}$$

$$m^2\hat{z} = m^2H - q^2 \textstyle\int^{\hat{z}-x} (\hat{z} - x - u)f(u)du \tag{4.14a}$$

where m^1 and q^1 stand for margin and wholesale price under SR and m^2 and q^2 stand for the corresponding variables under OR. Because market forces make retailers' profits equal, whatever the selling regime, and also because

$$p - q^1 = m^1 \quad \text{and} \quad p - q^2 = m^2 \tag{4.15}$$

the left-hand sides of equations 4.14 and 4.14a can be equated and rewritten as

$$q^1 H = q^2 H + q^2 \int^{\hat{z}-x} (\hat{z} - x - u) f(u) du \qquad (4.16)$$

and

$$q^2 = q^1 [H/(H + \int^{\hat{z}-x} (\hat{z} - x - u) f(u) du)] \qquad (4.17)$$

But the denominator of equation 4.17 is just equal to $\hat{z}$.[9] Hence:

$$q^2 = q^1 (H/z). \qquad (4.18)$$

Thus, q^2 is equal to q^1 times the ratio of expected demand H and $\hat{z}$. If inventories are positive, $\hat{z} > H$ and therefore $q^2 < q^1$—that is, $m^2 > m^1$. The wider retail margin under OS is a function of the degree of uncertainty concerning demand.

Is this value of the wholesale price compatible with the equality of producers' profits under the two selling regimes? Producers' profits under SR are given by equation 4.5, substituting for $\hat{z}$ and positing $b = a = 0$:

$$
\begin{aligned}
E\left[\Pi^{1p}(z)\right] &= (p - m^1)x - cz - (p - m^1) \int_{z-x} (x + u - z) f(u) du \\
&= q^1 x - cz - q^1 \int_{z-x} (x + u - z) f(u) du \\
&= q^1 H - cz \qquad (4.19)
\end{aligned}
$$

whereas under OS they are

$$\Pi^{2p}(z) = q^2 z - cz \qquad (4.20)$$

If the left-hand sides of equations 4.19 and 4.20 have to be equal:

$$q^2 z - cz = q^1 H - cz, \qquad q^2 = q^1 (H/z) \qquad (4.21)$$

and q^2 satisfies the condition that producer's profits under OS be at least equal to those made under SR; therefore, $q^2 = \hat{q}$.

Excess Demand Penalty Cost and Choice of Selling Policy

The result reached in the preceding section indicates that the choice of the optimal selling policy of producers is not determined by the high commercial risk involved in the trade of products with very low or zero salvage value of end-of-period inventories. This is not to say that the nature of salvage costs is unimportant. It is apparent that the commercial risk related to uncertain demand diminishes as the salvage value approaches the production cost or, under OS, the wholesale price. If the interest cost is not too high, this implies that the probability of shortages will be made very low by increasing the beginning-of-period stock of products. With a zero interest cost, as under the foregoing assumption, it will in fact be driven to zero whichever agent bears the commercial risk (equation 4.8). If this is the case, there is no point in using SR. A low salvage cost is therefore a necessary precondition to make the choice of selling policy a relevant issue, but it is not in itself a sufficient condition to choose SR over OS.

The choice is determined by other sources of asymmetries between producers and retailers. Two obvious reasons to prefer one or the other selling policy could be a different behavior toward risk or differences in the cost of information. If retailers are risk-averse and producers are risk-neutral, or less risk-averse then retailers, it becomes convenient for producers to choose SR, although I do not see any obvious reason why this should happen. Instead, it is much more likely that retailers have access to better information about their own specific markets at a lower cost than producers. As already suggested, this would make OS more convenient, ceteris paribus—and more so as the number of retailers increases. The crucial assumption appears to be the one concerning the excess demand penalty cost. Consumers' reactions to stockouts differ, and the implications of those reactions are not the same for producers and retailers. The main question here is the degree of substitutability among goods or services of the same class. If the products within a class sold by a given retailer have a high degree of substitutability with one another, the retailer has a fairly high probability of convincing its customers to shift from an unavailable good or service to other similar products from a different producer that are still in stock. For the retailer, stockouts do not imply a penalty cost, and the retailer will not have a strong incentive to hold inventories. The opposite happens to individual producers that lose potential buyers. Moreover, if customers buy what is offered by a competitor, the efforts toward product differentiation might be stifled by a reduction of brand loyalty, so SR therefore becomes a viable alternative. This asymmetry between producers and retailers points to a well-known area of potential conflict between them; that is, under standard OS policies, retailers have an incentive to try to increase product substitutability, whereas this goes against the efforts made by producers to render the demand curve they face less elastic.

The opposite happens when the degree of substitutability is small. Here, it is the retailer that not only loses revenue but, because the customer might try to find what he wants in a different shop, incurs the risk of losing the customer for future purchases. Shop loyalty is at stake. Low substitutability therefore implies high excess demand penalty costs for retailers and an incentive for producers to favor OS. Finally, when substitution effects involve a different class of products or products that are not present in the types of shops concerned, the penalty cost is likely to be similar, and OS is also likely to be preferred, as in the foregoing example with a zero penalty cost for both retailer and producer.

Some examples will help clarify the point check the hypotheses made. The case of services that are sold or booked through agents is the easiest to fit into the proposed framework. For example, for airline tickets or hotel rooms, customers are not likely to have strong preferences for a particular carrier or for a particular hotel within a given category of establishments. Consequently, travel agencies do not have strong incentives to bear the risk of unsold inventories under OS for any particular firm, and SR becomes a sensible alternative to a possible price war. Note that, at least in the airline case, there are instances when OS is chosen. Charter flights are sold in advance by carriers to travel agencies, which have then to find customers to fill the places they have bought. The high cost of the information network needed by the booking system opens a space for firms that enter the market to undercut the market of carriers that sell under SR.

Among goods, SR is a common practice for newspapers and magazines. Newspapers are sold in most countries with full sale or return policies. This can be justified along the lines proposed earlier, considering that different newspapers are good substitutes for one another. When SR is limited to a given percentage of the amount of product delivered, as in the case of U.K. quality newspapers, this is probably because of their lower degree of substitutability.

The same kind of reasoning applies to magazines. Full SR is granted to magazines with small circulation, whereas those that enjoy a large readership sometimes grant only limited SR. Again, this is because of the lower substitutability of the large-circulation magazines; frequent stockouts discourage customers from visiting the shop. For small-circulation magazines—those that are not market leaders, the substitution effect is larger, and potential buyers are more easily convinced to shift to a competing product. Small-circulation magazines also suffer an additional disadvantage: customers might not expect to find them if they are late in asking for the new issue in their usual shop. Thus, no blame is put on the retailer. Finally, small-circulation magazines, of which each retailer sells only a few copies, are at the margin of assortments, and it is unlikely that retailers would devote much effort to forecasting their demand accurately, since inventory decisions affect sales at the margin of such marginal products. Thus, there are several reasons for the producer to grant full SR.

Interdependence of Demands at Different Points of Sale

Thus far, the comparison of SR and OS has taken into account the relative profits of a single producer and a single retailer. If the comparison is made between a single producer and all its distributors, a new and different asymmetry, potentially relevant for the choice of selling policy, has to be considered: whereas each retailer maximizes profits with respect to its own sales, each producer maximizes profits with respect to its own sales, each producer maximizes profits with respect to sales of all its distributors. If there is some interdependence of the demands at different points of sale, producers can take advantage of the lower variability of total demand. To clarify this point, consider the possible sources of demand uncertainty. The first is related to variation in the amount of product sold per unit of time, since customers do not buy regularly; for example, newspapers are not bought every day, even by regular readers. This affects both overall demand and the demand at each point of sale. But a second important source of demand uncertainty affects demand at each point of sale although it does not alter total demand. This uncertainty arises when customers purchase a given good irregularly in two or more shops. The larger the number of sellers of the good—that is, the easier it is for customers to purchase it without making a special shopping trip—the more important this source of demand variations becomes. Demands at each point of sale are no longer independent of one another.

When customers shift randomly from shop to shop, profit maximization entails evaluation of the demand at any given shop over the joint probability of demand at that and all other related shops. This in itself does not alter the problem as formalized earlier. In fact, expected demand for any given retailer is[10].

$$E(X_i) = \int \ldots \int X_i f(X_1, \ldots, X_n) dX_1 \ldots dX_n = \int X_i f(X_i) dX_i \quad (4.22)$$

and expected total demand for any given producers is

$$E(\Sigma X_i) = \int \ldots \int (\Sigma X_i) f(X_i, \ldots, X_n) dX_i \ldots dX_n$$
$$= \Sigma \int X_i f(X_i) dX_i \quad (4.23)$$

Thus, taking into account a single producer and all its distributors does not alter the problem; the objective function for producers is separable with respect to each retailer. What really matters is the assumption of risk neutrality. This is, in fact, why the two situations—independence versus dependence of point-of-sale demands—lead to the same result. The cost of risk is, by assumption, made equal to zero. But risk neutrality is only a convenient assumption that simplifies exposition. It is much more plausible that agents, be they retailers or producers, have some degree of risk aversion (and this without any need to argue for a different relative degree of risk aversion). If this is the case, and if agents give some weight not only to the mean of their expected profits but also to their variance, then when demands are negatively correlated, producers can exploit the advantage of a covariant risk. Whereas the variance of the demand in equation 4.22 remains var(X_i) for each retailer i, for producers it becomes

$$\text{var}(\Sigma \ X_i) = \Sigma(\text{var } X_i) - 2 \sum_i \sum_j \text{cov}(X_i X_j), \qquad i \neq j$$

Under these conditions, risk aversion and correlated demands, SR allows for the exploitations of a covariant risk. Note that this is true both when substitutability among goods of the same type is high and when it is low. In the first case, it is an additional incentive for favoring SR. In the second case, it is an option for producers to expand sales and profits, since retailers will hold smaller inventories than producers would hold under SR because of their lower cost of commercial risk.

Endogenous Prices and Resale Price Maintenance

Throughout the preceding discussion, retail prices were set to some constant value, assuming that they were exogenously given. The assumption is a very unrealistic simplification, but it was made to free the analysis from an added difficulty—namely, the fact that SR is normally observed together with resale price maintenance (RPM). Since RPM is much more common and better understood than SR,[11] considering the two selling policies together might have led us to view SR as a corollary of RPM. But this is not the case when the choice is between SR and OS. The causality runs the other way around: given SR, RPM is an obvious compliment to it when retailers can exploit some market power. Moreover, considering endogenous prices in the model would have made the analysis much more complex without adding much to it.[12] I shall therefore limit myself to a few remarks concerning price policy to justify why, within the assumptions made, setting prices equal to some exogenously given value is not too serious a limitation—or, from a different point of view, why RPM is a secondary issue when considering the choice of SR versus OS.

What has to be shown is that the same retail price is compatible with both SR and OS; that is, whichever agents set the prices, retailers or producers, the equilibrium price is the same—a result long ago established by McClelland (1966) for a world without uncertainty. The framework used by McClelland can be slightly modified to fit the set of assumptions made here. This modification is done in figure 4–1, where the demand (D) for a given good and marginal revenues (MR) and marginal costs (MC) for both retailers and producers are portrayed. The retailers' average cost curve (AC^q) is constructed under the assumption that variable costs are zero. The only variable cost element is the wholesale price q. Moreover retailers do not make any profit; monopolistic competition prevails. The producers' marginal costs

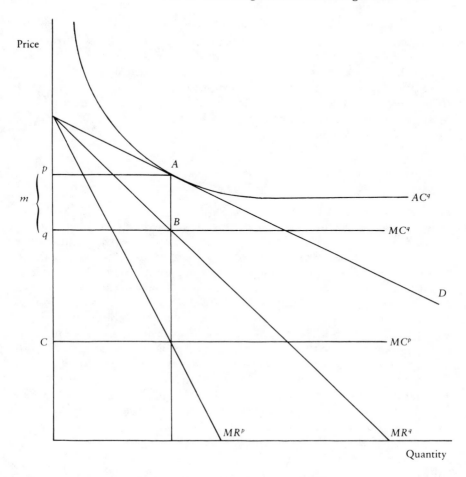

Figure 4–1. Vertical Price Formation

(MC^p) are, as before, constant. Under OS, the retailers' marginal revenue curve (MR^q) is the demand curve for producers. Given q, retailers fix a price p that is consistent with the producers' profit maximization. Under SR, producers have to forecast the demand D, but their demand curve remains MR^r, since retailers will sell their goods so long as $MR^r = q$ because at that price their revenues, $pq\,AB$, are consistent with market equlibrium. The optimal equilibrium price remains p.

If uncertainty about demand is introduced under the foregoing assumptions (identical demand forecasts by producers and retailers, behavior toward risk, no intertemporal considerations, and so forth), the essence of price policy does not change identically unless asymmetries about excess demand penalty costs and producers' advantage under covariant risk are introduced. It seems possible to conclude, therefore, that price policy, particularly RPM, is logically a distinct issue from the choice of SR versus OS and that the assumption of exogenous prices is not distorting the perception of the relative advantages of the two selling policies. Obviously, RPM might be needed in conjunction with SR when retailers could exploit some market power or would pursue price policies that go against producers' interests.

Conclusions

The rationale for sale or return agreements has been investigated in an attempt to isolate the elements that make it a worthwhile policy for firms to adopt. It was shown that, under conditions that appear to be sufficiently general, the choice of SR is not caused by the high commercial risk related to goods or services for which the salvage value of unsold inventories is very low or zero. This is a necessary but by no means sufficient condition for SR. Asymmetries related to the excess demand penalty costs by retailers and producers must be added to a low salvage value to obtain conditions that might lead to the adoption of SR. This happens when substitutability among competing goods is high, so that the excess demand penalty cost is higher for producers than for retailers. Moreover, incentives for favoring SR are increased if, under risk aversion, producers can exploit the covarient risk originated by the interdependence of demands at different points of sales. Finally, it was argued that resale price maintenance, though often observed together with SR, is logically a corollary to it.

Notes

1. Although this assumption is very demanding, it is symmetric for both producers and retailers. Since the aim of the chapter is to focus on the asymmetries that might lead to the assumption of commercial risk by producers, some of the simplifications made, such as avoiding intertemporal considerations, do not alter the nature of the comparison between the behaviors of producers and retailers facing an uncertain demand.

2. See authors cited for details. The model used here follows closely their specification of a one-stage maximization problem under uncertainty. The exposition of the model is therefore concise. Interested readers are referred to Karlin (1958) and Mills (1962), in particular, for technical details.

3. This implies that firms can forecast demand at different prices with the same accuracy—a plausible assumption for price variations within a range related to firms' common experience.

4. In fact, note that

$$x = \int^{z-x} xf(u)du + \int_{z-x} xf(u)du$$

5. Assuming constant marginal costs does not alter the nature of the comparison of the behavior toward risk of producers and sellers. For details about optimality conditions under variable marginal costs, see Karlin (1958).

6. Again, the approximation is symmetric to both producers and retailers.

7. If an interest plus storage cost term h, proportional to inventories held, were included in equation 4.8, the right-hand side would become

$$\frac{(p - m) - c + a}{(p - m) - b + a + h}$$

In this case, even if the salvage value b were equal to c, inventories would not be enough to always satisfy demand.

8. Equation 4.10 portrays retailers' revenues, not retailers' profits, but I shall assume that retailers have only fixed costs, so that maximizing revenue is equivalent to maximizing profits.

9. In fact:

$$
\begin{aligned}
H + \int^{\hat{z}-x} (\hat{z} - x - u)f(u)du &= x - \int_{\hat{z}-x} (x + u - \hat{z})f(u)du \\
&+ \int^{\hat{z}-x} (\hat{z} - x - u)f(u)du \\
&= x - \int_{\hat{z}-x} (x + u)f(u)du \\
&- \int^{\hat{z}-x} (x + u)f(u)du + \hat{z}\int f(u)du \\
&= \hat{z}
\end{aligned}
$$

10. See, for example, Mood, Graybill, and Boes (1974).

11. See, for example, Mathewson and Winter (1983) and references cited therein.

12. See Zabel (1970), Irvine (1981), and Amihud and Mendelson (1983) for explicit consideration of price policy under uncertain demand and positive inventories.

References

Amihud, Y., and Mendelson, H. (1983). "Price smoothing and inventory." *Review of Economic Studies, 50,* 87–98.

Irvine, F.O. (1981). "An optimal middleman firm price adjustment policy: The short-run inventory-based pricing policy." *Economic Inquiry, 19,* 245–69.

Karlin, S. (1958). "One stage inventory models with uncertainty," in *Studies in the Mathematical Theory of Inventory and Production*, ed. K.J. Arrow, S. Karlin, and H. Scarf. Stanford, Calif.: Stanford University Press.

Mathewson, G.F., and Winter, R.A. (1983). "The incentives for resale price maintenance under imperfect information." *Economic Inquiry, 21,* 337–48.

McClelland, W.G. (1966). *Costs and Competition in Retailing.* London: Macmillan.

Mills, E.S. (1962). *Price, Output and Inventory Policy.* New York: Wiley.

Mood, A.M.; Graybill, F.A.; and Boes, D.C. (1974). *Introduction to the Theory of Statistics.* London: McGraw-Hill.

Zabel, E. (1970). "Monopoly and uncertainty." *Review of Economic Studies, 37,* 205–19.

Part II
Issues in Channel Coordination

5
The Relationship between Interorganizational Form, Transaction Climate, and Economic Performance in Vertical Interfirm Dyads

Torger Reve
Louis W. Stern

The political economy perspective of interorganizational relations, as formulated by Wamsley and Zald (1973), Benson (1975), and Stern and Reve (1980), advocates the division of an interorganizational dyad into an internal economy and an internal polity. The structure of the *economy* is defined by the extent of vertical[1] (buyer-seller) coordination between the pair of interacting organizations, running along a continuum with pure market transactions at one end and hierarchical (within-the-firm) transactions at the other (cf. Williamson 1975). The structure of the *polity* is defined by the power-dependence relations between the two organizations, running along a continuum with atomized, minimal power at one end and maximal, centralized power at the other (cf. Perrow 1970; Pfeffer and Salancik 1978). Combining elements of both the economy and the polity results in a picture of the structure of the interfirm dyad's *political economy.* In this chapter, attention is focused on how the structure of vertical interfirm dyads, viewed as political economies, is related to the climate within dyads and the performance of the various institutions comprising them.

Interorganizational relations can be analyzed in terms of structural arrangements or interorganizational forms, which pattern the dyadic linkages, and in terms of the quality of the dyadic exchange taking place—here referred to as the *transaction climate.* Interorganizational form, it is argued, is likely to affect transaction climate, and both interact with economic performance. In this chapter, the basic argument is explored empirically in the context of vertical relations between business organizations engaged in distribution of consumer goods and services.

Interorganizational form in vertical interfirm relations can be defined in terms of at least three major dimensions: (1) vertical interactions, (2) formalization, and (3) centralization. Vertical interfirm interactions are the flows of activities, resources, and information that take place between two organizations linked together in a distribution channel (cf. Van de Ven and Ferry 1979). Formalization of interfirm transactions refers to the degree to which rules, fixed policies, and procedures govern interorganizational flows. And centralization of interfirm decision making refers to the extent to which power to make and implement interorganizational decisions is concentrated in one of the two interacting organizations. Both formalization and centralization are analogous to the corresponding structural variables commonly used in intraorganizational studies (e.g., Hall 1975, Hage 1980) and their extensions in interorganizational analyses (Marrett 1971, Aldrich 1976, Van de Ven and Ferry 1979).

Transaction climate in interorganizational relations can be described along a cooperative-conflictual continuum. The exact spot on the continuum that any interfirm dyad occupies at any given point in time can be defined by describing the sentiments that exist between the parties to the transactions. Relying on the organizational literature on conflict and trust, these sentiments or antecedents to a specific cooperative-conflictual state are defined here in terms of goal compatibility, domain consensus, evaluation of accomplishment, and norms of exchange (cf. Benson 1975, Bonoma 1976).

In large measure, our substantive attention focuses on what industrial organizational economists have termed the structure-conduct-performance relationship. However, instead of using the traditional economic form of analysis, with its emphasis on such market structure variables as concentration ratios and entry barriers, we are adopting a behavioral perspective. In other words, we believe that there is an underlying stream of causation, with structure (interorganizational form) affecting conduct (transaction climate). Both of these variables, in turn, affect the performance of dyad members. Although there are numerous feedback loops among these variables, our main concern is with the traditional direction postulated by industrial economists and adopted in much of the work in macro organizational behavior. However, given the exploratory nature of our work, attention here is focused only on uncovering significant associations between and among the variables, not on establishing causal linkages.

Theoretical Background and Hypotheses

Two sets of hypotheses regarding the relationship between interorganizational form and transaction climate were developed to provide a preliminary test of two competing theories related to these variables. The first set of hypotheses was derived from institutional theories of interorganizational relations, especially as articulated by Williamson (1975, 1979, 1981), Arrow (1971, 1974), and Chandler (1977). The second set of hypotheses was derived from sociopolitical theories of interorganizational relations that focus on power relationships (for an overview, see Pfeffer and Salancik 1978, Stern and El-Ansary 1982).

Contemporary institutional theories of interorganizational relations focus on transaction costs. For example, one of Williamson's (1975) main propositions is that hierarchy-mediated transactions are often superior to market-mediated transactions from a transactional effectiveness and information cost point of view. Williamson's major thesis is that market transactions may become very costly because of human factors, such as bounded rationality and opportunistic behavior, coupled with environmental factors, such as uncertainty and economically concentrated input and output markets (that is, small-numbers bargaining). When information is unequally possessed, opportunistic behavior is likely to prevail, and exchange may become commercially hazardous. Instead of completing market exchange through extensive contracts and lengthy specifications of rights and obligations—accounting for all possible contingencies of an uncertain future—the market institution itself is often replaced by internal organization or heirarchy. Although transacting business across markets and transacting across hierarchies are often viewed as alternative means for organizing economic activity, it is possible to conceive of a continuum ranging from predominantly market-mediated transactions to predominantly hierarchy-mediated transactions (Williamson 1979). In our terminology here, such a continuum is represented by the interorganizational form or degree of vertical coordination, as operationalized by vertical interactions, formalization, and centralization.

The transaction costs argument that underlies the choice of interorganizational form rests primarily on behavioral factors. Each interorganizational form is closely associated with a specific transaction climate, which is a set of sentiments and behaviors that characterize the exchange taking place. As indicated earlier, transaction climate can be described by the following variables:

Goal compatibility: the extent to which both organizations in a vertical interfirm dyad perceive that they can both attain their goals concerning the joint tasks facing them (cf. March and Simon 1958, Schmidt and Kochan 1972, Kochan et al. 1976).

Domain consensus: the degree of mutual agreement regarding the proper assignment of products, populations, territories, functions, and technologies in a vertical interfirm dyad (cf. Levine and White 1961, Warren et al. 1974, Cadotte and Stern 1979).

Evaluation of accomplishment: the degree of approval or disapproval by one member of the dyad concerning the extent of accomplishment of the interorganizational tasks by the other member of the dyad (cf. Benson 1975).

Norms of exchange: the extent to which interfirm transactions are based on mutual trust, whereby the parties share a unit bonding or belongingness (cf. Bonoma 1976).

According to Williamson (1975), hierarchical transactions permit "convergent expectations" and more satisfactory "trading atmospheres" than market transactions do, all other things being equal. Therefore, our first hypothesis (H1) is a logical extension of Williamson's thinking, expanded to include a richer set of behavioral variables.

> **H1:** The tighter the interorganizational form (defined in terms of increased vertical interactions, greater formalization, and greater centralization), the more favorable the transaction climate will be (defined in terms of greater goal compatibility, greater domain consensus, higher evaluation of accomplishment, and more positive norms of exchange).

The second and competing set of hypotheses linking interorganizational form and transaction climate is based on theories that emphasize the role of power dependence in interorganizational exchange and focus on the prevalence of conflicts in the relations between organizations. Contributors include sociological theories of power dependence and exchange (Emerson 1962, Cook 1977), social-psychological theories of power and conflict (Raven and Kruglanski 1970), and sociopolitical theories of distribution channels (Stern and El-Ansary 1982). Common to this literature is the notion that the use of power that culminates in centralized coordination and control strategies will often create negative sentiments, conflicts, resistance, opposition, and retaliation behavior within a social action system. Empirical studies of power-conflict relations in social psychology and in marketing (Reve and Stern 1979; John and Stern 1982) as well as organization theory studies of the relations between organization structure and organizational behavior (for reviews, see Hall 1975, Hage 1980) have provided some support for this notion. Thus, a competing hypothesis to hypothesis H1 can be advanced:

> **H2:** The tighter the interorganizational form (defined in terms of increased vertical interaction, greater formalization, and greater centralization), the less favorable the transaction climate will be (defined in terms of lower goal compatibility, lower domain consensus, lower evaluation of accomplishment, and more negative norms of exchange).

The two hypotheses, H1 and H2, are positioned as strong, competing alternatives to emphasize the contrasts in thinking that can be found in the interorganizational literature. Clearly, the relationships postulated are mediated by situational and environmental factors. In other words, neither of these sets of propositions realistically represents a general law. At the present stage of theory development, however, we are more interested in broad covariation between key variables than in precise propositions that account for all mediating variables.

The two competing sets of hypotheses, H1 and H2, thus provide the base for empirical testing of the relationship between interorganizational form and transaction climate as independent and dependent variables, respectively. Support for either hypothesis should have implications for interorganization design and management generally. Regardless of the findings, however, the critical issue is not climate but performance. In other words, it is possible that support could be found for hypothesis H2, indicating that the greater the vertical coordination in vertical interfirm dyads, the more negative the sentiments are between the dyad members. Yet even though the sentiments are negative, performance of the interacting organizations could be high, indicating—superficially, at least—that the conflictive climate is functional rather than dysfunctional. Indeed, the constructive role of social conflict has been addressed many times in the sociological and organizational literatures (e.g., Coser 1956, Pfeffer 1981). Given the importance of performance, it is imperative that we attempt to measure its relationship to both interorganizational form and transaction climate.

Theories of vertical integration, vertical control, and joint decision making all include analyses that indicate that reduction of suboptimization and internalization of externalities, scale economies, and efficiency gains are all achievable through increased programming of a relationship (see Etgar 1976, Warren-Boulton 1978). Even though there is recognition in the literature of the considerable trade-offs in terms of flexibility and innovativeness, increased programming is generally held to lead to increased performance. This belief leads to the third hypothesis:

H3: The tighter the interorganizational form (defined in terms of increased vertical interaction, greater formalization, and greater centralization), the higher the economic performance of the members of the vertical interfirm dyad will be (defined in terms of standard accounting measures such as gross profits, productivity, and return on assets).

With regard to the relationship between transaction climate and performance, it appears that most scholars would argue that the less conflictive the climate is, the higher performance is likely to be, despite discussion in the literature about the functionality of conflict. One of the reasons for this belief is that no one is certain where the boundary line is between functional and dysfunctional conflict (cf. Boulding 1965). Therefore, less conflict would seem to be a safer bet than more conflict. A more cogent theoretical rationale has been provided, however, by Williamson's (1975) discussion of transaction climate in hierarchies as compared with markets. Hierarchical transactions (that is, transactions within the firm) supposedly permit the achievement of higher goal compatibility and domain consensus, more positive evaluations of accomplishment, and more trustful norms of exchange than do transactions that take place across a market composed of independently owned and operated institutions or agencies. Indeed, the positive sentiments generated by moving to hierarchical transactions from market transactions permit, according to Williamson's theory, a reduction in the transaction costs of search, haggling, disputes, and auditing. When exchanges take place in an atmosphere of trust and commonality of purpose, transactions are less costly to complete. Potential savings in transaction costs can be translated into economic performance benefits, which gives rise to the fourth hypothesis:

> H4: The more favorable the transaction climate (defined in terms of higher goal compatibility, higher domain consensus, more positive evaluation of accomplishment, and more positive norms of exchange), the higher the economic performance of the members of the vertical interfirm dyad will be (defined in terms of standard accounting measures such as gross profits, productivity, and return on assets).

Research Design and Methodology

The overall research design chosen for testing the hypotheses was a cross-sectional field study, using data from a sample of distribution channel dyads of wholesale and retail firms located in Norway. Different industries, product categories, and distribution systems are represented, the only requirement being that both a wholesale and a retail level exist. A field study design was selected because of the limited theoretical understanding of vertical interfirm relations in distribution and because the emphasis in the study was on theory construction and theory development. To document the potency of the theoretical approach taken, the phenomena of interest should be empirically observable in a natural field setting. The empirical setting, Norway, can be described as a highly stable, developed, and affluent economy. Norwegian wholesaling and retailing are characterized by a decentralized structure with relatively small units. The firms operate in a fairly homogeneous environment, minimizing the effects of external variation that are thought to be important for distribution channel functioning (Achrol et al. 1982).

The unit of analysis for studying distribution channel structuring and functioning in this study was the organizational *dyad,* consisting of a wholesale and a retail organization linked together in an ongoing trade relationship. The focus on vertical interfirm dyads is consistent with the dyadic interaction approach for studying transactions (Bonoma et al. 1978). The dyadic interaction approach takes the two-party exchange relationship as its fundamental subject matter or phenomenon to be explained. Any interorganizational network is made up of dyads, and any complex relationship in the marketplace can be modeled as sequences, systems, or networks of dyadic exchanges (cf. Aldrich and Whitten 1981; Achrol et al. 1982).

In previous studies of interorganizational relations, data have almost always been collected from only one side of interorganizational dyads. In the very few cases where data have been collected from both sides of such dyads, convergence of the data has been largely lacking (e.g., El-Ansary and Stern 1972, Provan et al. 1980). The present study diverted from the modal approach to interorganizational research by deliberately measuring interorganizational variables from both sides of the dyad. In this research, data from vertical interfirm dyads were collected through approximately parallel forms presented to both the wholesaler and the retailer organizations. Each observation obtained was independent of the other observations, in that only unique wholesaler-retailer dyads were included and no single wholesaler or retailer organization was registered more than once. The collection of data was based on a key informant approach, in that key personnel of an organization gave relatively objective accounts of the phenomena explored as seen from the viewpoint of the total organization.[2] The key informants selected were typically the top executives of the wholesale and retail firms, and both reported on the interfirm transactions linking the two organizations.

Three phases of sampling and data collection were needed to obtain dyadic data. In phase 1, the *total* population of Norwegian wholesale firms (with ten or more employees), according to official records of the National Bureau of Statistics, was contacted by an initial mail questionnaire. Of the 735 firms contacted, 378 firms responded; 238 responses were usable in the subsequent analysis.

In phase 2, one retail customer for each of the wholesalers that completed phase 1 was randomly drawn from lists of six retail customers reported by the wholesalers in the phase 1 questionnaire. Of the 238 retailers that received the extensive mail questionnaire of phase 2, 170 responded; 140 responses were usable for analysis. In phase 3, an approximately parallel mail questionnaire was sent out to the corresponding wholesalers. Of the 140 wholesalers contacted in phase 3, 104 responded; 99 responses were usable for analysis. The final data set then consisted of 99 vertical interfirm dyads, with complete information from both the wholesale and the retail firms.

Representativeness of the firms included was checked by comparing the data collected with statistics on the total population of wholesale and retail firms in Norway, broken down by SIC codes. A slight overrepresentation of large firms was found at both the wholesale and retail levels. Primitive tests for nonresponse bias were also performed by comparing data for organizations included in the final set with data collected for organizations not included; no systematic response biases could be detected.

Operational Definitions and Measures

As indicated earlier, interorganizational form, or the extent of vertical coordination within a vertical interfirm dyad, is defined in terms of three major dimensions: (1) vertical interfirm interactions, (2) formalization of interfirm transactions, and (3) centralization of interfirm decision making. Vertical interactions were operationalized in terms of perceptions of joint activities, assistances, and programs established to facilitate distributive tasks between a wholesaler and a retailer. The relevant activities, assistances, and programs were generated from trade sources via numerous personal interviews. Formalization of transactions was defined as the perceived degree to which rules, fixed policies, and procedures governed the relationship between a wholesaler and a retailer. Centralization of interfirm decision making was defined as the perceived degree of influence on dyadic actions as measured over the distributive flows linking a wholesaler and a retailer.

Transaction climate was defined, as previously noted, in terms of four major dimensions: (1) goal compatibility, (2) domain consensus, (3) evaluation of accomplishment, and (4) norms of exchange. Operationally, the degree of goal compatibility was defined as the extent to which key informants from each wholesaler and retailer organization perceived that their organization was presently attaining its goals or aspiration levels in terms of basic distributive flows in the dyad, given the actions of the opposite organization. The degree of domain consensus was defined as the level of agreement with the present allocation of roles, distributive tasks, and functions in the dyad. Evaluation of accomplishment was specified as (1) the evaluation of the task performance and competence of personnel of the other organization, and (2) the satisfaction with the services rendered by the other organization (see Lusch 1976). Finally, norms of exchange in wholesaler-retailer dyads were defined as the extent to which each wholesaler and retailer felt confident that the other would adhere to dyadic decisions and by the openness and sharing of information by the two parties (cf. Williamson 1975). A large pool of items was generated for each of the aforementioned variables, and the items were then subjected to expert screening and pilot testing. Samples of the items actually used in the study, along with the scales employed, are reproduced in table 5–1. (Copies of the actual instruments used are available from the senior author.)

The reliance on perceptual measures for interorganizational form and transaction climate clearly weakens the measurement qualities of the study. Perceptual measures always contain more measurement error than unobtrusive or "objective" measures, and perceptions of organizational phenomena are likely to vary considerably according to whose perceptions are recorded, especially when complex social judgments have to be made (see Phillips 1981). A limitation of the present study is that it only accounts for perceptual discrepancies between key informants *across* dyadic levels.

In addition to the sets of independent and dependent variables already discussed, three categories of economic performance indicators were included in

Study Measures

Variables	Initial Number of Items	Typical Items	Scales	Final Number of Items	Cronbach's Coefficient Alpha
Interorganizational Form					
1. Vertical interactions	12	"The supplier offers us a complete marketing plan for for his products" (R); "We offer the retailer a complete marketing plan for our products" (W)	8-category ratings scale: (0) "not at all," (1) "to an extremely small extent," to (7) "to an extremely large extent"	8 (R); 7 (W)	.856 (R); .876 (W)
2. Formalization	6	"The relations between the supplier and our firm are governed by written contract" (R); "Complaints and returns from the retailer to us are handled through standard procedures" (W)	8-category true-false scale: (1) "erroneous description," (2) "very poor description," to (7) "completely correct description," plus "nonrelevant" category	5 (R); 4 (W)	.701 (R); .635 (W)
3. Centralization	10	"Our advertising campaigns for the supplier's products are determined in deatil by the supplier" (R); "The retailer determines which ordering procedures he is going to use" (W)	8- category true-false scale, as above	4 (R); 3 (W)	.685 (R); .578 (W)
Transaction Climate					
1. Goal compatibility	7	"High economic profitability at the supplier level is often obtained at the cost of our own profitability" (R); "The retailer often wants us to carry a broader assortment of products than what we are presently doing" (W)	7- category Likert-type scale: (1) "very strongly disagree" to (7) "very strongly agree"	5 (R); 4 (W)	.719 (R); .675 (W)
2. Domain consensus	8	"There are often disagreements between our firm and the supplier as to whom has responsibility for inferior or defective products delivered" (R); "The present relationship between our firm and the retailer is based on a very clear division of labor" (W)	7-category Likert-type scale, as above	4 (R); 6 (W)	.597 (R); .733 (W)
3. Evaluation of accomplishment	9	"The supplier has poor knowledge of the special needs and wants of our customers" (R); "The reatiler's personnel are very competent in their work" (W)	7-category true-false scale, as above	4 (R); 7 (W)	.769 (R); .780 (W)
4. Norms of exchange	9	"When an agreement is made we can always rely on the supplier fulfilling all the requirements" (R); "We have the feeling that the retailer sometimes hides important information from us" (W)	7-category Likert-type scale, as above	4 (R); 6 (W)	.714 (R); .797 (W)

R = retail level form; W = wholesale level form.

the study: (1) gross profits, (2) productivity, and (3) return on assets. Data were collected from both wholesale and retail firms. Gross profits were computed before taxes, value added tax excluded. Productivity measures were (1) gross profits per employee, and (2) total sales per employee. A rudimentary return on assets measure was gross profits/average inventory level. To obtain measures that applied directly to the specific channel dyads studied, total profits measures were weighted by the proportion of total sales (or purchases) accounted for by the dyad.

Purifying the Measures

Various checks were performed to purify the measures obtained. First, there was a check for missing values in the data collected, and items with a high proportion of missing values were deleted from further analysis. Second, there was a check for normality, and items with a highly skewed distribution were deleted because of the requirements of the analytical methods used. Third, there was a check for internal consistency reliability by computing Cronbach's coefficient alpha. Items with low item-to-total-scale correlations were deleted to reduce error and unreliability. The underlying rationale is a domain sampling model (Nunnally 1978), which holds that the purpose of any measurement is to estimate the score that would be obtained if all the items in the construct's domain were included. Low item-to-total-scale correlations indicate that some items are not drawn from the appropriate domain and, consequently, that such items should be deleted.

Finally, each multi-item construct was subjected to common factor analysis to obtain undiminsional representations of the constructs. The requirement of unidimensionality comes from the theory from which the constructs are derived. Items were deleted until a stable single-factor solution resulted. Separate factor analyses were performed for the wholesaler and retailer versions of the instrument.

When the item scale analysis and the factor analysis are compared, the unidimensionality requirement imposed by the factor analysis turns out to be a stricter requirement, since items deleted because of low item-to-total-scale correlations are almost always deleted in the final single-factor solutions. Both methods seem to conform to the requirements of the domain sampling model. One example of a final scale will illustrate the procedure used to purify measures. Variable 1—vertical interactions—in the wholesaler versions initially contained twelve items. Two items were deleted because of a high proportion of missing data and high skewness. One item was deleted because of relatively low item-to-total-scale correlation (.3), and two additional items were deleted in the factor analyses. The final one-factor solution showed an eigenvalue of 4.1, 58.1 percent of total variance accounted for, high loading on seven items, and factor loadings ranging from .49 to .83.

The factor-analytical procedure used results in a violation of a strict parallel form measurement across dyadic levels, as the scales for wholesale and retail levels may not always contain identical items or the same number of items. The violation is permissible, it can be argued, given the different roles wholesale and retail organizations perform. Thus, *identical* operational measures of organizational variables may be too strict a requirement. Some care should be taken, however, when interpreting analyses that use data for the same variable across dyadic levels.[3]

After constructing unidimensional scales for each construct, simple aggregation of item scores into a construct score was performed. Any remaining missing values were taken into account to obtain comparable aggregate scores.

Several problems may be noted with the method used for purifying the measures. Ideally, measurement development should be based on a separate sample, and measures should be validated on a different sample. Given the number of observations needed and the population of relevant organizations already exhausted, measurement development was limited to a second-best procedure. Furthermore, the procedure introduces potential problems of sequential measurement error and capitalization on chance.

Reliability of the Constructs Measured

Internal consistency reliability, as computed by Cronbach's alpha, ranged from .578 to .876 for the wholesaler version of the instrument and from .597 to .856 for the retailer version of the instrument, referring to the multi-item revised scales of the three independent variables and the four dependent variables of the main hypotheses, H1 and H2. The results are reported in detail in the last column of table 5–1. Data on firm characteristics showed a very high test-retest reliability (range: .87–.98) as assessed for wholesale firms responding to both phase 1 and phase 3.

Convergent and Discriminant Validity of the Constructs Measured

Convergent and discriminant validity of the constructs measured were assessed by simple correlation analysis and by common factor anlaysis, taking multi-item measurements as a substitute for multiple methods. Items measuring a specific construct were expected to show high intercorrelations and low correlations with items measuring other constructs. When common factor anlaysis was run on items representing different constructs, items measuring a single construct were expected to load on the same factor (evidence of convergent validity). Items measuring different constructs were expected to load on different factors, and the same item was not expected to load on several factors (evidence of discriminant validity).

When common factor analysis was run for the items constituting the independent variables of interorganizational form, four and three factors were extracted for the wholesaler and retailer versions of the instruments, respectively, using the elbow rule for eigenvalues exceeding 1.0 as the cutoff rule. The varimax rotated factor loadings matrices are presented in table 5–2. Factor 1 in both

Table 5–2
Factor Analysis, Independent Variables

Wholesaler Version of Instrument, Varimax Rotated Factor Loadings Matrix

	Factor 1	Factor 2	Factor 3	Factor 4
I 1	.52	.44	−.26	.28
I 2	.53	.31	.15	.11
I 3	.75	.29	.20	.17
I 4	.68	.44	−.04	.13
I 7	.71	.34	.24	.12
I 9	.60	.37	−.07	.36
I12	.63	−.06	−.04	−.10
C 3	.19	.56	.25	.10
C 4	.30	.36	.05	.13
C 9	.16	.74	−.12	−.12
F 2	.13	.20	.43	.43
F 4	−.05	.02	.15	.77
F 5	.25	.41	.28	.23
F 6	.14	.00	.79	.01
Eigenvalue	5.31	1.86	1.19	1.14

Retailer Version of Instrument, Varimax Rotated Factor Loadings Matrix

	Factor 1	Factor 2	Factor 3
IR 1	.71	.49	.00
IR 2	.69	.16	.02
IR 3	.47	.31	.31
IR 4	.58	.44	−.07
IR 9	.71	.33	.14
IR10	.36	−.02	.16
IR11	.62	.19	.04
IR12	.70	−.01	.21
CR 1	.13	.33	.09
CR 4	.07	.58	.40
CR 9	.05	.59	.07
CR10	.17	.77	.00
FR 1	.27	.55	.10
FR 2	.10	.29	.60
FR 3	.11	.12	.64
FR 4	.23	−.12	.55
FR 6	−.01	.14	.77
Eigenvalue	5.45	2.15	1.76

versions concerned vertical interactions, loading highly on all interactions items. Factor 2 in both versions reflected the centralization variable and also included one formalization item ("written contracts") for the retailer version. The factor referred to as "centralization" also includes some relativley high loadings on vertical interaction items ("cooperative advertising program" and "training program"). The last factors contained formalization items. The anlaysis shows some not entirely satisfactory evidence of convergent and discriminant validity for the three independent variables.

When common factor analysis was run for the items constituting the dependent variables of transaction climate, four factors with eigenvalues exceeding 1.0 were extracted for both the wholesaler and retailer versions of the instrument. The varimax rotated factor loadings matrices are reported in table 5–3. Evaluation of accomplishment came out as a separate factor in both cases also and included one evaluation item from the domain consensus measure. Goal compatibility and domain consensus loaded on two factors in both cases, but with some overlap of items. Finally, norms of exchange loaded on a separate factor in both cases, one or two items grouping with goal compatibility.

The evidence of convergent and discriminant validity presented in tables 5–2 and 5–3 shows that problems remain. For the hypotheses to be tested, low convergent and discriminant validity of the measures of interorganizational form is considered to be the most critical. The centralization measures, especially, have poorer measurement qualities than we would like to see. The need to distinguish clearly among all four aspects of transaction climate is less urgent at this stage, so long as a cooperative-conflictual continuum can be assumed.

An alternative test for convergent and discriminant validity of the construct measures is a comparison of scores for wholesalers and retailers linked in vertical interfirm dyads. Although it is not a perfect measure, a comparison of scores provides some indication of the amount of informant bias in the data. Both wholesalers and retailers were responding to questions about the collective properties of their interactions with one another. Although substantial perceptual discrepancies should be expected because of differences in roles, functions, and orientation, the intercorrelations of corresponding variables should be higher than the correlations between different variables. In the total correlation matrix (see table 5–4), such a pattern seems to hold for the three independent variables. When the retailer and wholesaler scales were correlated, intercorrelations were .60, .50, and .26 for interactions, centralization, and formalization, respectively.[4] Similar evidence of convergent and discriminant validity cannot be observed for the four dependent variables. The intercorrelations are as low as .17, .10, .15, and .16 for goal compatibility, domain consensus, evaluation of accomplishment, and norms of exchange, respectively. Clearly, the transaction climate in the vertical interfirm dyad is perceived differently by the two parties (John and Reve 1982). This should be taken as a serious warning for organizational researchers looking at data from only one side of interorganizational dyads.

Table 5–3
Factor Analysis, Dependent Variables

Wholesaler Version of Instrument, Varimax Rotated Factor Loadings Matrix

	Factor 1	Factor 2	Factor 3	Factor 4
GC 1	.65	.10	−.06	−.08
GC 3	.36	.05	.50	.26
GC 6	.52	.04	.37	.20
GC 7	.60	−.07	.22	.12
DC 1	.34	.09	.26	.15
DC 2	.63	.04	.25	.08
DC 3	.00	.45	.49	.17
DC 5	.65	−.03	.38	.05
DC 6	.17	−.01	.63	−.05
DC 7	.20	.00	.79	.12
EV 1	.03	.82	−.10	.15
EV 2	.08	.22	.47	.20
EV 4	.06	.88	.02	−.02
EV 5	.39	.30	.26	.20
EV 6	.01	.46	.13	.01
EV 8	−.01	.43	.06	.25
EV 9	.04	.84	.08	.07
NE 1	.29	.38	.04	.45
NE 2	.22	.12	.22	.91
NE 3	.34	.14	.20	.64
NE 5	.70	−.05	.07	.25
NE 7	.66	.09	−.01	.21
NE 9	.06	.35	.08	.34
Eigenvalue	6.45	3.29	1.80	1.41

Retailer Version of Instrument, Varimax Rotated Factor Loadings Matrix

	Factor 1	Factor 2	Factor 3	Factor 4
GCR 1	.02	−.15	.10	.71
GCR 2	.16	.01	.01	.52
GCR 3	.26	.21	.45	.49
GCR 4	−.06	.29	.29	.59
GCR 7	−.04	.00	.50	.34
DCR 1	−.01	.25	.44	.13
DCR 3	.29	.57	.19	.08
DCR 6	.31	−.19	.67	.06
DCR 7	.23	.12	.65	.10
EVR 1	.32	.55	.05	.16
EVR 5	.59	.38	.10	.20
EVR 7	.27	.71	−.12	.03
EVR 8	.24	.55	.14	−.04
NER 1	.64	.24	.23	.03
NER 2	.74	.37	.17	.03
NER 3	.69	.21	.03	.06
NER 7	.01	.22	.25	.42
Eigenvalue	5.07	2.43	1.45	1.21

When item means across dyad levels are compared, systematic discrepancies can be observed. Wholesalers tend to report higher scores for vertical coordination. Retailers are less positive in their evaluation of accomplishment than wholesalers are, and retailers often also perceive more issues of conflict than wholesalers do. These discrepancies in perceptions may be due to the differences in their roles, because wholesalers are suppliers, and retailers are their customers. One might expect suppliers to effect more coordinative efforts, while customers tend to find fault with their sources of supply, regardless of reality. In any case, such discrepancies demonstrate the importance of dyadic data in interorganizational research and point to some potential problems for interorganizational management when assessing transaction climate.

What is especially important to note from the foregoing results and discussion is that the conclusions one draws in interorganizational research critically depend on the sets of measures to which one attends. This will be clearly illustrated in the following discussion of hypotheses testing.

Hypotheses Testing: Empirical Results

The hypotheses testing reported here relied on the unidimensional scales for each construct of the perceptual data. Simple aggregation and averaging of scores were used to obtain construct scores. Separate analyses were performed for the wholesaler and retailer data, as well as for combinations of wholesaler and retailer data. The empirical methods used were correlation analyses, multiple regression analyses, and canonical correlation analyses.

Empirical Testing: Hypotheses H1 and H2

The first hypotheses tested in the present study concerned the relationship between interorganizational form and transaction climate. Hypothesis H1 stated that vertical coordination was expected to be positively associated with favorable transaction climate. This hypothesis was countered by hypothesis H2, which stated that vertical coordination was expected to be negatively associated with favorable transaction climate. The corresponding subhypotheses of H1 and H2 specified empirical associations between the sets of independent and dependent variables. The competing subhypotheses were tested using a simple correlation analysis, whereas the competing hypotheses H1 and H2 were tested by canonical correlation analysis. The empirical results of the correlation analyses are presented in table 5–4, and the results of the canonical correlation analysis are reported in table 5–5.

Hypothesis H1, postulating a positive association between vertical coordination and transaction climate, gains some empirical support for two of the three independent variables. Vertical interfirm interactions correlate positively with goal compatibility (.34, .21) and domain consensus (.21, .11), and formalization correlates positively with domain consensus (.22, .30), evaluation

Table 5–4
Total Correlation Matrix

	I_w	C_w	F_w	GC_w	DC_w	EV_w	ME_w	I_r	C_r	F_r	GC_r
(1.1)											
I_w	1.00										
C_w	.54***	1.00									
F_w	.26***	.05	1.00								
(1.2)			**(2.2)**								
GC_w	.34***	.16*	-.04	1.00							
DC_w	.21**	-.05	.22**	.44***	1.00						
EV_w	.07	-.26***	.32***	.27***	.50***	1.00					
ME_w	.06	-.17**	.22**	.40***	.56***	.60***	1.00				
(1.3)				**(2.3)**				**(3.3)**			
I_r	.60***	.35***	.14*	.17**	.11	.00	.04	1.00			
C_r	.23**	.50***	.15*	-.08	-.08	-.22**-	-.01	.27***	1.00		
F_r	.29***	.24**	.26***	.08	.04	.02	.11	.22**	.30***	1.00	
(1.4)				**(2.4)**				**(3.4)**			**(4.4)**
GC_r	.06	-.06	.03	.17**	.01	.14*	.18**	.21**	.03	.17**	1.00
DC_r	-.03	-.17**	.07	.16*	.10	.21**	.20**	.11	-.16*	.30***	.50***
EV_r	-.16*	-.28***	.05	-.01	.05	.15*	.07	-.06	-.31***	.12	.35***
ME_r	-.11	-.17**	-.07	.12	-.04	.11	.16*	.07	-.15*	.15*	.47***
(1.5)				**(2.5)**				**(3.5)**			**(4.5)**
SE_w	.26***	.16*	.00	.26***	.21**	.22**	.05	.16*	-.01	.13*	-.32***
$P1_w$	.34***	.21**	.15*	.25***	.26***	.08	.05	.20**	.11	.15*	-.38***
$P2_w$	.25***	.06	.14*	.10	.09	.02	-.03	-.16*	-.12	.00	-.27***
$P3_w$	.18**	.03	.15*	.25***	.24***	.26***	.08	.10	-.16*	.04	-.30***
$P4_w$	.19**	.00	.15*	.20**	.10	.07	.13*	.15	.04	.13*	-.04
(1.6)				**(2.6)**				**(3.6)**			**(4.6)**
SE_r	.04	.25***	.04	.07	.13*	.05	-.12	.07	.09	.03	-.17**
$P1_r$	.22***	.29***	.14*	.15*	.02	-.09	.10	.11	.42***	.19**	-.05
$P2_r$	.09	.15*	-.01	-.01	-.11	-.13	.06	.17**	.29***	.11	.15*
$P3_r$	.17**	.21**	-.05	.07	-.01	-.12	.05	.14*	.33***	.21**	.00
$P4_r$	.13	.24***	.04	.02	-.09	.00	.02	.04	.22***	.09	.07
Scale											
Mean	4.57	3.74	4.77	4.66	5.17	5.09	5.46	3.78	3.81	4.88	4.56
SD	1.56	1.53	1.25	1.05	.81	.71	.85	1.57	1.58	1.34	1.06

$n = 99$

    * $p = \leq .10$

  ** $p = \leq .05$

*** $p = \leq .01$

DC$_r$	EV$_r$	ME$_r$	SE$_w$	P1$_w$	P2$_w$	P3$_w$	P4$_w$	SE$_r$	P1$_r$	P2$_r$	P3$_r$	P4$_r$
1.00												
.41***	1.00											
.62***	.50***	1.00										
			(5.5)									
.07	−.08	−.04	1.00									
−.05	−.17**	−.13	.74***	1.00								
−.03	−.16*	−.21*	.27***	.61***	1.00							
−.07	−.03	−.07	.91***	.78***	.44***	1.00						
−.06	−.27***	−.21*	.10	.30***	.43***	.16*	1.00					
			(5.6)					(6.6)				
.00	−.13	−.05	.14*	.02	−.06	.00	−.08	1.00				
.07	−.12	.01	.12	.37***	.15*	.02	.08	.01	1.00			
.14*	−.12	.14*	.06	.10	−.04	−.01	−.15*	−.11	.35***	1.00		
.10	−.22**	.10	.20**	.13	.00	−.01	.10	.22**	.39***	.81***	1.00	
.14*	−.26***	.02	−.01	.05	.09	−.03	−.01	.01	.24***	.66***	.57***	1.00
5.06	4.95	5.11										
1.06	1.11	1.18										

Table 5–4 continued

List of Variables

	Wholesaler Level	Retailer Level
Interorganizational form		
1. Vertical interactions	I_w	I_r
2. Centralization	C_w	C_r
3. Formalization	F_w	F_r
Transaction climate		
1. Goal compatibility	GC_w	GC_r
2. Domain consensus	DC_w	DC_r
3. Evaluation of accomplishment	EV_w	EV_r
4. Norms of exchange	NE_w	NE_r
Indicators of economic performance		
1. Gross profits	$P1_w$	$P1_r$
2. Percent gross profits	$P2_w$	$P2_r$
3. Gross profits per employee	$P3_w$	$P3_r$
4. Gross profits/inventory level	$P4_w$	$P4_r$
5. Sales per employee	SE_w	SE_r

Note: Gross profits figures are weighted by proportion of sales (or purchases) accounted for by the channel dyad studied.

of accomplishment (.32, .12), and norms of exchange (.22, .15) for both the wholesale and the retail levels. The other correlation coefficients for vertical interactions and formalization with dimensions of transaction climate were not significantly different from zero (the only exception being a positive correlation between formalization and goal compatibility at the retail level).

Hypotheses H2, postulating a negative association between vertical coordination and transaction climate, gains some empirical support only for the centralization dimension of interorganizational form. Centralization correlates negatively with evaluation of accomplishment ($-.26$, $-.31$) and norms of exchange ($-.17$, $-.15$) for both the wholesaler and the retailer levels. The findings were further supported by results of a similar correlation analysis on the extended sample of retailers ($n = 140$), wherein centralization correlated negatively with all four dimensions of transaction climate.

Only one correlation, centralization and goal compatibility at the wholesale level, points in a different direction. However, some caution is needed in interpreting the results for the centralization variable, given the measurement limitations noted earlier.

Correlating interorganizational form as perceived by the wholesalers with transaction climate as perceived by the retailers renders additional support for the finding of a negative association between centralization and transaction climate variables. All four correlation coefficients were negative; centralization correlated $-.17$, $-.28$, and $-.17$ with domain consensus, evaluation of accomplishment, and norms of exchange, respectively.

A similar cross-level correlation for vertical interactions and formalization with the four dimensions of transaction climate considerably weakens the aforementioned empirical support for hypotheses H1

In summary, the results of the testing of hypotheses H1 and H2 using simple correlation analysis give partial, though relatively weak, support to both hypotheses. For vertical interactions and formalization of operations, hypothesis H1—derived from institutional theories of interorganizational relations and predicting a positive association with favorable transaction climate—has received some empirical support. For centralization of interfirm decision making, on the other hand, hypothesis H1 has to be rejected, thereby giving the competing hypothesis H2 some empirical support. The negative association between centralization and channel sentiments was most pronounced at the retailer level. Limitations in the data, however, should caution us against drawing strong conclusions based on these results.

An additional test of hypotheses H1 and H2 was done by means of canonical correlation analysis (for some precautions, see Meredith 1964, Alpert and Peterson 1972, Lambert and Durand 1975). The three independent variables—interactions, formalization, and centralization—were related to the four dependent variables—goal compatibility, domain consensus, evaluation of accomplishment, and norms of exchange—to determine the overall significance and magnitude of the relationships between the two sets of variables. The results of the canonical correlations analyses are reported in table 5–5 for both the wholesale and the retail levels. Only one canonical pair was found to be significant in each analysis performed. The canonical correlations between

Table 5–5
Results of Canonical Correlation Analysis

	Wholesale Level		Retail Level	
	Canonical Loadings	Canonical Weights	Canonical Loadings	Canonical Weights
Interorganizational form (X_1)				
Vertical interactions	−.24	−.07	.00	−.01
Formalization	.69	.76	.04	.77
Centralization	−.69	−.71	−.29	−.91
Transaction climate (Y_1)				
Goal compatibility	−.30	−.64	.18	−.44
Domain consensus	.39	.17	.06	.67
Evaluation of accomplishment	.82	.80	.14	.77
Norms of exchange	.46	.13	.05	.11
Canonical correlation (R_{c_2})	.504		.502	
Canonical root (R_c)	.254		.252	
Wilks' lambda (λ)	.632		.696	
Significance	$p < .001$		$p < .002$	

$n = 99$

interorganizational form (X_1) and transaction climate (Y_1) was about .50 $(p < .001, p < .002)$ for both the wholesale and retail levels. This gives a canonical root exceeding .25, which is the total amount of variance accounted for.

When interpreting the canonical loadings for the wholesaler level, table 5–5 shows centralization and formalization entering the X-set with the highest loadings and evaluation of accomplishment, norms of exchange, and domain consensus entering the Y-set with the highest loadings. It should be noted that centralization exhibits a negative canonical loading, whereas the other loadings interpreted are positive. For the retailer level, table 5–5 shows relativley low canonical loadings, but the same pattern of loadings emerges. An intuitive interpretation of the results presented in the table is that linear composite X_1, consisting of low centralization and high formalization, is positively associated with linear composite Y_1, consisting of positive evaluation of accomplishment, trustful norms of exchange, and relatively high domain consensus.

Formalization and centralization appear as two key dimensions of interfirm coordinative arrangements, entering with opposite signs when related to interfirm sentiments. Evaluation of accomplishment, domain consensus, and norms of exchange all appear as dimensions of transaction climate, whereas goal compatibility seemed to behave somewhat differently.

All of the foregoing results, taken together, imply partial empirical support for both hypotheses H1 and H2. Hypothesis H1 received some support for interactions and formalization being positively associated with favorable transaction climate. Hypothesis H2 received some support for centralization being negatively associated with a favorable transaction climate. Centralization has a power component that fits the theoretical rationale underlying hypothesis H2, and vertical interactions and formalization have a logistics component that fits the routinization of transaction argument that underlies hypothesis H1.

Empirical Testing: Hypotheses H3 and H4

Hypothesis H3 explored the linkages between interorganizational form and economic performance, and hypothesis H4 explored the linkages between transaction climate and economic performance. Five crude indicators of economic performance were included—gross profits, percent gross profits, gross profits per employee, gross profits/average inventory level, and total sales per employee—for both wholesaler and retailer levels and for the two levels combined. As mentioned earlier, profits figures were weighted according to the proportion of sales or purchases accounted for by the particular dyad studied. The hypotheses were tested using simple correlation analysis and multiple regression analysis. The results of the correlation analysis are reported in table 5–4.

Hypothesis H3, postulating a positive association between dimensions of interorganizational form and indicators of economic performance, obtained considerable empirical support, given the limitations in the data. Vertical interactions as reported by wholesalers were found to correlate positively with all five indicators of economic performance at the wholesale level, with correlation coefficients ranging from .18 to .34 ($p < .05$), as well as correlating positively with three indicators of economic performance at the retail level. A similar pattern holds also for vertical interactions as perceived by retailers, although the correlations are somewhat lower. Centralization, as reported by both wholesale and retail levels, correlates positively with all indicators of economic performance at the retail level, with correlation coefficients in the range of .22 to .42 ($p < .01$), excluding retail sales per employee. These results were not confirmed for economic performance at the wholesale level.

Hypothesis H4, postulating a positive association between a favorable transaction climate and indicators of economic performance, obtained minimal empirical support. Correlations between transaction climate and indicators of economic performance for the wholesale level were in the right direction, with ten of twenty correlation coefficients significantly positive at the .05 level or better. Goal compatibility and domain consensus conformed to the hypothesis, with positive correlations as high as .26 ($p < .01$), whereas norms of exchange failed to confirm the hypothesis. The data for the retail level showed even less empirical support for hypothesis H4 than the wholesale data did. Only six of twenty correlation coefficients were significantly positive, and eight correlation coefficients turned out to be negative, three of them significant at the .05 level. The negative correlations refer to evaluation of accomplishment, and this may speculatively be interpreted as an indication of functional conflict in the dyad. Alternatively, the negative correlations may be explained as a confounding with centralization, which was found to be positively associated with economic performance and highly negatively associated with evaluation of accomplishment at retail level.

Overall, a relatively low total variance in economic performance was accounted for by interorganizational form (H3) and transaction climate (H4), as evidenced by multiple regressions run for each performance indicator. The empirical support was strongest for hypothesis H3, whereas hypothesis H4 received little or no empirical support. This indicates that vertical coordination may, in fact, have a small positive effect on economic performance, whereas the effects on economic performance of transaction climate variables may be difficult to observe in the short run. Better and more sensitive measures of economic performance and a more highly specified model of interorganizational performance are needed before more conclusive evidence on the critical economic performance linkage can be generated. Given the dismal state of research on organizational effectiveness, however, any significant empirical results should be considered a small victory.

Discussion

The study reported here has several key limiations that must be acknowledged. In trying to overcome the biases associated with sampling only one side of interorganizational dyads, other biases were introduced when collecting dyadic data. Error or bias may have been introduced by the sequential character of the sampling design, by the overrepresentation of relatively large organizations, and by the selection of key informants. Also the problem of response bias cannot be ruled out. In securing sufficiently large variation in the variables studied, heterogeneous organizations across various product categories and SIC groups were included. Thus, measurement error was introduced by the cross-sectional nature of the study and the lack of tailoring of measures to specific categories of distribution-type organizations. In spite of substantial pilot testing of measures, further screening of items was needed to construct scales. The sequential procedure used in selecting items for the scales and the lack of a hold-out or validation sample for scale construction may have produced scales that did not have all the desired psychometric properties. This is evidenced by some problems of item scale discrimination, even within a particular level of the interfirm dyads. An alternative procedure, relying on the holistic construal methodology suggested by Bagozzi and Phillips (1982), may have permitted the modeling of the extent of random and systematic error in the measures and may have allowed better control over these sources of error when testing substantive hypotheses. The correlational analysis used, assuming no errors of measurement, should be questioned, given the measures obtained; thus, caution is needed when interpreting the results.

Limitations also arise from the research design selected relative to the model tested. Because of the initial stage of theory development, two theories of interorganizational relations were posed as competing. If both hypothesized effects were present simultaneously, the two effects might have canceled each other, producing zero or near-zero empirical associations. In future studies investigating the relations between institutional and sociopolitical theories of interorganizational relations, deliberate efforts should be made to separate the two effects. Also, generalizability of the findings is limited by the empirical setting chosen and the types of organizations included.

Finally, there is a lack of convergence when constructs referring to interorganizational transactions are considered from the perspective of different sides of the interfirm dyads. The lack of dyadic convergence of measures was particularly pronounced for dimensions of transaction climate, whereas some convergence was observed for dimensions of interorganizational form (John and Reve 1982). Assessments of interfirm sentiments differed substantially across dyadic levels, with wholesalers—initiating much of the vertical coordination in the dyads—reporting more cooperative sentiments than retailers did.

The issue of discrepant perceptions across dyadic levels is an important one, not only in terms of the research implications but for the whole issue of managing interfirm relations. The harsh reality in many interorganizational settings is that the interacting organizations simply do not understand one another's needs and practices very well. Suppliers and customers interpret one another's actions and strategies from very idiosyncratic points of view. There is rarely a systematic effort on the part of managers or boundary personnel at one level of a distribution channel to empathize fully with the implications of their actions on managers at other levels.

To the extent that the substantive findings of the study can be relied upon, the results have tentative implications for theories of vertical interfirm relations in distribution settings. Hypothesis H1, arguing the position of institutional theories of interorganizational relations, obtained only partial support. Hypothesis H2, taking an extreme position of sociopolitical theories of interorganizational relations, was only partially supported for centralization of decision making within interorganizational dyads and received little or no empirical support for other aspects of coordinative arrangements. Organized vertical relationship—in the form of joint programs, assistances, and formalized routines of operations—were positively associated with favorable interorganizational sentiments, partially supporting hypothesis H1. Probably, such programs were seen as facilitating interfirm activities and possibly also as resulting in gains in economic performance (cf. hypothesis H3). The negative effects on transaction climate, partially supporting hypothesis H2, seemed to arise when decisions were centralized—that is, when the autonomy of the other party was constrained. Vertical coordination through programming had a weak positive effect on transaction climate (H1), whereas centralization of power affected evaluations and trust negatively (H2). Hierachical coordination and control through the simultaneous use of programming and centralization had mixed effects on interorganizational sentiments and behavior. The findings are consistent with Child's (1973) findings of centralization and formalization as alternative means of coordination is an intraorganizational setting.

Williamson's notion that a favorable transaction climate is positively associated with increased means of vertical coordination received only modest empirical support. The modifications of the Williamsonian view concerned the centralization of power and the perceived use of power. On this point, Williamson may have too optimistic a view of organizational functioning, because opportunistic behavior likely exists within systems approaching hierarchies. When Williamson (1975) suggests that decisions by fiat facilitate transactions within hierarchies, the negative effects of the power component on transaction climate have not been fully accounted for. Centralization of decision making is likely to give rise to conflictual sentiments in interorganizational relations. The power element seems to be the discriminating factor between the two competing theories of interorganizational relations.

An important implication of the findings, however weak, is that the two theories advanced are complementary rather than competing. Institutional theories of interorganizational relations may best apply to the programming aspects of coordinative arrangements, and sociopolitical theories may best apply to the power aspects of coordinative arrangements. Further studies will be needed to spell out the relationships between the two sets of theories in more detail—for example, by studying the effects of various bases of power (cf. John and Stern 1982).

The findings of a positive linkage between dimensions of vertical inter-firm coordination and rudimentary indicators of economic performance point to the importance of including "objective" measures of organizational effectiveness in organizational research. Despite a largely underspecified performance model and primitive measures of economic performance relative to the dyadic perspective taken, significant empirical associations were detected for several of the structural constructs. Adding covariates such as firm size, duration of interfirm relationship, and asymmetry of dependence did not significantly alter the findings. However, the specific implications of the findings of a performance linkage are impossible to derive from the present study, because the empirical results differed depending on which reported measures were included in the various analyses.

Summary

Interorganizational relations in vertical interfirm dyads consisting of wholesaler and retailer organizations were studied in a cross-sectional survey design. The objectives of the study were to investigate the association between interorganizational form and transaction climate, as well as the empirical linkages with economic performance. Interorganizational form was conceptualized in terms of vertical interactions, formalization, and centralization; transaction climate was conceptualized in terms of goal compatibility, domain consensus, evaluation of accomplishment, and norms of exchange. Two competing theories of interoganizational relations hypothesized opposite empirical associations between the two sets of variables.

The results of this exploratory study indicated that vertical programming and centralization had differential relationships with transaction climate. Joint programs and formalization of interorganizational activities were found to correlate positively with favorable transaction climate, whereas centralization of interfirm decision making correlated negatively with favorable transaction climate. A theoretical implication is that institutional and sociopolitical theories of interorganizational relations are complementary rather than competing, with centralization of power as a discriminating element. The study also indicated a weak, positive empirical association between vertical coordination and rudimentary indicators of economic performance.

As we have continually pointed out, the results of this study must be accepted with considerable caution. The foremost contribution of the study is its emphasis on methodological issues. Studies that rely on only single-level data of interorganizational relations may present a distorted view of interorganizational functions. Despite all of the limitations in this preliminary research effort, the study underscores the need to collect data from both sides of interorganizational dyads. The study also indicates a direction for studying the underlying structure and processes of interorganizational relations in business settings and examining their implications for economic performance.

Notes

1. In the specific context of this study, which is marketing channels, the term *vertical* refers to relationships and activities that take place between different levels of distribution—for example, between manufacturers and wholesalers or between wholesalers and retailers (cf. Stern and El-Ansary 1982). In this sense, it refers to seller-buyer or supplier-customer interactions, which is consistent with the terminology in industrial organization economics (cf. Scherer 1980). It should not be confused with the typical usage in much of the organizational behavior literature, where the term *vertical* generally refers to superior-subordinate relations within a chain of command.

2. For shortcomings of the key informant approach using single or multiple informants from the *same* organizations, see Phillips (1981) and Silk and Kalwani (1982).

3. In a specific analysis focusing on the reliability and validity of key informant data from vertical interorganizational dyads (John and Reve 1982), a subset of the present data was used to obtain identical measures across dyadic levels. This refinement did not alter the findings reported in this chapter.

4. Note, though, that the correlation between the retailer formalization construct and the retailer centralization construct is slightly higher than that between the formalization measures across dyadic levels. Similarly, the correlation between vetical interactions and centralization at the wholesale level is almost as high as that between the centralization measures across dyadic levels. This observation corresponds to the factor loadings pattern presented in table 5–2.

References

Achrol, Ravi Singh; Reve, Torger; and Stern, Louis W. 1982. "The Environment of Marketing Channel Dyads: A Framework for Comparative Analysis." *Journal of Marketing* 47 (4):55–67.

Aldrich, Howard E. 1976. "Resource Dependence and Interorganizational Relations: Local Employment Service Offices and Social Services Sectors Organizations." *Administration and Society* 7:419–54.

Aldrich, Howard E., and Whitten, David A. 1981. "Organization Sets, Action Sets, and Networks: Making the Most of Simplicity." In P. Nystrom and W. Starbuck (eds.), *Handbook of Organizational Design,* Vol. 1, 385–408. New York: Oxford University Press.

Alpert, M.I., and Peterson, R.A. 1972. "On the Interpretation of Canonical Analysis." *Journal of Marketing Research* 9:187–92.

Arrow, Kenneth J. 1971. *Essays in the Theory of Risk Bearing.* Chicago: Markham.

———. 1974. *Limits of Organizations.* New York: Wiley.

Bagozzi, Richard P., and Phillips, Lynn W. 1982. "Representing and Testing Organizational Theories: A Holistic Construal." *Administrative Science Quarterly* 27:459–89.

Benson, J. Kenneth. 1975. "The Interorganizational Network as a Political Economy." *Administrative Science Quarterly* 20:229–49.

Bonoma, Thomas V. 1976. "Conflict, Cooperation and Trust in Three Power Systems." *Behavioral Science* 21:499–514.

Bonoma, Thomas V.; Bagozzi, Richard P.; and Zaltman, Gerald. 1978. "The Dyadic Paradigm in Marketing Thought." In Thomas V. Bonoma and Gerald Zaltman (eds.), *Organization Buying Behavior.* Chicago: American Marketing Association.

Boulding, Kenneth E. 1965. "Economics of Human Conflict." In E.B. McNeil (ed.), *The Nature of Human Conflict.* Englewood Cliffs, N.J.: Prentice-Hall.

Cadotte, Ernst R., and Stern, Louis W. 1979. "A Process Model of Dyadic Interorganizational Relations in Marketing." In Jagdish N. Sheth (ed.), *Research in Marketing,* Vol. 2. Greenwich, Conn.: JAE Press.

Chandler, Alfred D., Jr. 1977. *The Visible Hand.* Cambridge, Mass.: Harvard University Press.

Child, John. 1973. "Predicting and Understanding Organization Structure." *Administrative Science Quarterly* 18:168–85.

Cook, Karen. 1977. "Exchange and Power in Interorganizational Relations." *Sociological Quarterly* 18:62–82.

Coser, Lewis A. 1956. *The Functions of Social Conflict.* London: Free Press.

El-Ansary, Adel I., and Stern, Louis W. 1972. "Power Measurement in the Distribution Channel." *Journal of Marketing Research* 9:47–52.

Emerson, Richard M. 1962. "Power-Dependence Relations." *American Sociological Review* 27:31–41.

———. 1972. "Exchange Theory, Part II: Exchange Relations, Exchange Networks, and Groups as Exchange Systems." In Joseph Berger, Morris Zelditch, and Bo Anderson (eds.), *Sociological Theories in Progress,* Vol. II, 58–87. Boston: Houghton Mifflin.

Etgar, Michael. 1976. "The Effect of Administrative Control on Efficiency of Vertical Marketing Systems." *Journal of Marketing Research* 13:12–24.

Hage, Jerald. 1980. *Theories of Organizations.* New York: Wiley.

Hall, Richard H. 1975. *Organizations: Structure and Process,* 2d ed. Englewood Cliffs, N.J.: Prentice-Hall.

John, George, and Reve, Torger. 1982. "The Reliability and Validity of Key Informant Data from Dyadic Relationships in Marketing Channels." *Journal of Marketing Research* 19 (November):517–24.

John, George, and Stern, Louis W. 1982. "Opportunism in Vertical Marketing Systems: A Transaction Cost Approach." Working paper 3-82-12, University of Wisconsin—Madison.

Kochan, Thomas A.; Cummings, L.L.; and Huber, George P. 1976. "Operationalizing the Concepts of Goals and Goal Incompatibilities in Organizational Behavior Research." *Human Relations* 29:527–44.

Lambert, Z.V., and Durand, R.M. 1975. "Some Precautions in Using Canonical Analysis." *Journal of Marketing Research* 12:468–75.

Levine, Sol, and White, Paul E. 1961. "Exchange as a Conceptual Framework for the Study of Interorganizational Relationships." *Administrative Science Quarterly* 5:583–601.

Lusch, Robert F. 1976. "Sources of Power: Their Impact on Intrachannel Conflict." *Journal of Marketing Research* 13:382–90.

March, James G., and Simon, Herbert A. 1958. *Organizations.* New York: Wiley.

Marrett, Cora Bagley. 1971. "On the Specification of Interorganizational Dimensions." *Sociology and Social Research* 56:83–99.

Meredith, W. 1964. "Canonical Correlations with Fallible Data." *Psychometrika* 29:55–56.

Nunnally, J.C. 1978. *Psychometric Theory.* New York: McGraw-Hill.

Perrow, Charles. 1970. *Organizational Analysis: A Sociological View.* Belmont, Calif.: Wadsworth.

Pfeffer, Jeffrey. 1981. *Power in Organizations.* Boston: Pitman.

Pfeffer, Jeffrey, and Salancik, Gerald R. 1978. *The External Control of Organizations: A Resource Dependence Perspective.* New York: Harper & Row.

Phillips. Lynn W. 1981. "Assessing Measurement Error in Key Informant Reports: A Methodological Note on Organizational Analysis in Marketing." *Journal of Marketing Research* 18:395–415.

Provan, Keith G.; Beyer, Janice M.; and Kruytbosch, Carolos. 1980. "Environmental Linkages and Power in Resource-Dependence Relations between Organizations." *Administrative Science Quarterly* 25:200–223.

Raven, Bertram H., and Kruglanski, Arie W. 1970. "Conflict and Power." In Paul Swingle (ed.), *The Structure of Conflict,* 69–100. New York: Academic Press.

Reve, Torger, and Stern, Louis W. 1979. "Interorganizational Relations in Marketing Channels." *Academy of Management Review* 4:405–16.

Scherer, Frederick M. 1980. *Industrial Market Structure and Economic Performance,* 2d ed. Chicago: Rand McNally.

Schmidt, Stuart M., and Kochan, Thomas A. 1972. "Conflict: Toward Conceptual Clarity." *Administrative Science Quarterly* 17:359–70.

Silk, Alvin J., and Kalwani, Manohar U. 1982. "Measuring Influence in Organizational Purchase Decisions." *Journal of Marketing Research* 19:165–81.

Stern, Louis W., and El-Ansary, Adel I. 1982. *Marketing Channels,* 2d ed. Englewood Cliffs, N.J.: Prentice-Hall.

Stern, Louis W., and Reve, Torger. 1980. "Distribution Channels as Political Economies: A Framework for Comparative Analysis." *Journal of Marketing* 44:52–64.

Van de Ven, Andrew H., and Ferry, Diana L. 1979. *Measuring and Assessing Organizations.* New York: Wiley Interscience.

Wamsley, Gary, and Zald, Mayer. 1973. *The Political Economy of Public Organizations.* Lexington, Mass.: Lexington Books.

Warren, Roland L.; Rose, S.; and Bergunder, A. 1974. *The Structure of Urban Reform.* Lexington, Mass.: Lexington Books.

Warren-Boulton, Frederick R. 1978. *Vertical Control of Markets: Business and Labor Practices.* Cambridge, Mass.: Ballinger.

Williamson, Oliver E. 1975. *Markets and Hierarchies.* New York: Free Press.

———. 1979. "Transaction-Cost Economics: The Governance of Contractual Relations." *Journal of Law and Economics* 22:233–61.

———. 1981. "The Economics of Organization: The Transaction Cost Approach." *American Journal of Sociology* 87:548–77.

6
Relationship Management of Distributors: A Proposed Framework

V. Kasturi Rangan

F undamentally, channel managers need diagnostic frameworks to assess
how effectively they are managing their channels. They need a classification scheme for evaluating their current distribution channel members and guidelines for improving the effectiveness of their channel management practices. Here, effectiveness is a measure of deviation from the
company's prescribed norms: the less the underachievement from the norm,
the greater the effectiveness. Given the product-market environment, is the
company managing its channels as well as it can? If the company's channel
management is not as effective as it should be, what can the managers do to
improve its effectiveness? For example, a large firm with a distinctive competence (expert power) may be expected to lead and effectively control its
distribution channels. Thus, IBM, with its vast resources and technological
leadership, may be expected to pretty much dictate its distribution policies;
and McDonalds, with its strong consumer preferences and store management knowledge, may be expected to administer a tight franchise system. In
contrast, a smaller firm would not expect to dominate and control its channels as some of its larger competitors do. The amount of power a manufacturer exercises over its distributors is a function of the firm's internal
strengths, the nature of the product and its market, and most important, the
channel environment and the intensity of competition. Moreover, effectiveness is a relative phenomenon. What is considered effective distributor management from the point of view of one manufacturer may not be so for
another manufacturer. Also, what is considered effective distributor management at one point in time may not be so at a later time. For instance,
many foreign firms have made inroads into North American markets by initially offering very flexible and attractive distribution arrangements. These
arrangements have been considerably streamlined and tightened, however,
after the products have attained a strong consumer demand. Clearly, different criteria are used to evaluate effectiveness at different stages of a firm's
growth.

Unfortunately, the existing literature on channel management does not directly provide insights into these issues, for two primary reasons: first, the implications of the research are not directly useful for practicing managers; second, the focus of the research is more descriptive than decision-oriented. The following brief review of the literature explains the rationale for making the foregoing inferences.

A Brief Review of Past Research and Its Usefulness for the Present Study

The literature on channel management is as diverse as it is vast. Some of the better-researched constructs include power (Hunt and Nevin, 1974; Wilkinson, 1974; Lusch, 1976; Etgar, 1978), conflict (Rosenberg and Stern, 1971; Brown and Frazier, 1978), and satisfaction (Hunt and Nevin, 1974; Lusch, 1976; Dwyer, 1980). Also, a number of theories and integrative frameworks have been developed (Williamson, 1975; Porter, 1974; Stern and Reve, 1980; Gaski, 1984). Most of these studies have been executed with great sophistication and attention to research design and methodology. Yet very few guidelines have emerged that a channel manager of a manufacturing firm could use and exploit. In the 1980s, many manufacturers acknowledge their interdependence with their distributors. Management of the relationship is considered important for mutual profits. Given manufacturers' and distributors' better level of appreciation of the channel system, some of the conclusions that may be drawn from the cited studies are not particularly enlightening—for example:

Use of coercive power leads to more conflict.

Use of noncoercive power leads to greater satisfaction.

Economic power has a larger weight in the overall power construct.

Channel systems have economic as well as political goals.

Although managers of businesses do not use the same construct labels that researchers use, they are in general agreement with the sentiments underlying the foregoing conclusions and find them to be straightforward and obvious.

The general thrust in the literature has been on developing theories and hypotheses at an aggregate level. The findings of the research apply to the entire industry or the channel system, whereas decision makers need guidelines at an individual firm level. Their immediate concern is focused on the first level of distribution—the transaction from the seller to the buyer. (The term *seller* will be used here in a generic sense to refer to manufacturers of goods and services, and the term *buyer* will be used in a generic sense to refer to the distributor at the first level of transaction, be it a wholesaler, a retailer, an agent, or an end user.) In the short term, very few managers worry about the entire channel system, from the seller to the end user. Most of their concerns are about their primary buyer and how they can be better managed to reach the ultimate user effectively.

Wilkinson (1974) gathered data from all manufacturers and distributors of a consumer durable involving heavy installation costs. The data were used to draw conclusions on the power dimension in distribution channels. Hunt and Nevin (1974), researching the sources of power, gathered data from a number of fast-food franchise outlets. In a similar study, Lusch (1976) used auto dealers for his data base. Etgar (1978) used distributors of beer, liquor, gasoline, boats, cars, motorcycles, organs, and swimming pools to form his data base for examining the components of an overall power construct. These and many other studies have all focused on an aggregate data base consisting of a number of buyers and sellers. This methodology is appropriate for deriving statistically supportable theories and hypotheses of distribution channels in general. However, from the point of view of a practicing manager of a selling firm, the conclusions are hardly useful.

The primary problem is aggregation of dissimilar data. For example, it is well known that different firms in the same industry often adopt different distribution practices that reflect their own corporate goals and strengths. McDonalds and Burger King, two important participants in the fast-food industry, have different franchising policies for their retail outlets. Avon and Revlon, two important participants in the cosmetics industry, approach their consumers through vastly different channels. Another drawback of aggregate data is its implicit disregard for heterogeneity. Buyers come in different sizes and grades, and sellers are conscious of this variation. Although restrictive trade practices are prohibited by law, functional discounts, quantity discounts, and special management attention and administrative support are not. Clearly, the overall package of distribution policies and practices a seller offers would differ across major groups of buyers. Thus, theories and hypotheses developed from aggregate data are not appropriate at an individual firm level, because they ignore the variation in buyer's behavior and the sellers' marketing policies.

There appears to be sufficient motivation to examine the seller-buyer interaction from the point of view of a single manufacturing firm, and there is clearly a case for acknowledging the heterogeneity among buyers in the analysis. Although the notion of individual member behavior has not been the focus of channel management research, a completely different research stream on "national account management" has acknowledged and explored this facet. Shapiro and Moriarty (1982) have suggested different management approaches for the different groupings of a manufacturer's direct accounts. In a sense, this is channel management with the manufacturer integrated downstream. In related research in the field of buyer-based segmentation, Moriarty and Reibstein (1982) and Bonoma and Shapiro (1983) have suggested that buyer behavior-based segments offer the best opportunity for a manufacturer to deliver a consistent and responsive marketing mix to the end user.

This chapter attempts to build on the available research in channel management by combining it with the account-level perspective of national account management. The purpose of the research is to develop measurable indicators for classifying buyers. The classification scheme will also attempt to explain the variation in the seller's profitability across various buyers. Finally, the patterns of behavior governing each relationship will be assessed in the specific context of the decisions the seller has to make. The fundamental thrust of this chapter will be to examine the seller-buyer interaction from the perspective of the seller and to recommend models of behavior that will improve the seller's management of the buyers. The following sections present the classification scheme, its intuitive rationale, the mathematical equations underlying the scheme, and the methodology of measurement. The concluding section examines the decision implications of the resulting analyses.

Framework for Analysis

Buyers can be classified on two dimensions: price intensity and service intensity. *Price intensity* is measured in terms of an overall price advantage or disadvantage with respect to the other buyers of the same seller (for the same product). Although the Robinson-Patman act prohibits price discrimination by the seller, some buyers are able to take advantage of differential discounts mainly because of their size and the kinds of channel functions they perform. Moreover, some buyers take better advantage of "offers on deal" and "trade promotions" than others. Often, the advantage can be traced to expertise or access in terms of the end-use markets that some buyers seem to possess. It is in the seller's interest to charge all of its buyers a uniform price; but some buyers, for the various reasons already described, will inevitably negotiate the seller down to a lower price (or price intensity). A low price intensity is a reflection of the buyer's relative bargaining power with respect to the manufacturer. Price intensity thus reflects the overall average price disadvantage or advantage aggregated over a number of transactions.

Service intensity is measured in terms of the relative advantage or disadvantage that some buyers have with respect to the other buyers of the same seller (for the same product). Sellers often offer a different mix of service components to different buyers. The different combinations are driven partly by the purchase elasticities of each buyer and partly by the negotiating power of the buyer. The service intensity dimension, unlike the price intensity dimension, consists of several components, such as delivery time, frequency of sales calls, product assortment, inventory levels and so on. Service intensity, therefore, is an aggregate measure of relative service in comparison to the other buyers.

Based on a measure of these two dimensions, the seller-buyer interaction may be classified into four categories, as shown in figure 6–1:

The seller opportunism category: The seller charges the buyer a relatively high price but offers only a relatively low service intensity. The seller is being opportunistic and is expected to make a relatively higher profit margin on such accounts.

The buyer opportunism category: The buyer in this case is able to get a higher service intensity at a relatively lower price and has clearly taken advantage of his negotiating power. The seller is expected to make a relatively lower profit margin on such accounts.

The transaction orientation category: The exchange between the seller and buyer in this case is quite fair. The buyer is able to negotiate and obtain a lower price, but he also receives a lower service intensity. The profit margin to the seller in this case is expected to be normal. In reality, the profit margin may be a little higher or lower than normal, depending

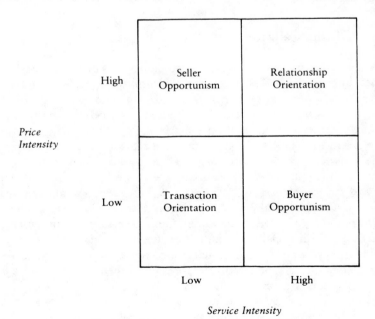

Figure 6–1. Four Categories of Seller-Buyer Interaction

on the seller's strengths in marketing the product as a commodity (low price, low service) rather than as a differentiated product (high price, high service).

The relationship orientation category: The exchange between the seller and buyer in this case is also quite fair. However, in this case, the seller provides a higher service intensity and also charges a correspondingly higher price for the service provided. As in the transaction orientation category, the actual profit margin may be a little higher or lower than normal, depending on the seller's strength in marketing the product either as a commodity or as a differentiated product.

The framework suggested in figure 6–1 is simplistic in some ways. Buyers often buy more than one product. Some products may be routine supply items, while others may have a larger technical component. This is especially true in industrial distribution, where machinery and spare parts almost inevitably go through the same distribution channel. Different products clearly require different service components. Whereas product availability may be an important requirement for spare parts distribution, warranty service may be crucial for capital equipment distribution. The generalized mathematical model incorporating these extensions is presented in the next section.

The Mathematical Model

Basically, a buyer is classified on the two dimensions of price intensity (P_i) and service intensity (S_i). The subscript i identifies the individual buyer. The classification process is repeated for each of the product categories that the buyer receives from the seller. The subscript j is used to identify the various product categories. In effect, we are suggesting a series of mappings (P_j, S_j) for every product j. The classification map that represents the various buyers of a single product $(j = 1)$ is presented in figure 6–2. Every buyer is uniquely located on the map for this product by the two dimensions of price intensity (P_{i1}) and service intensity (S_{i1}). The (P_{i1}, S_{i1}) location is uniquely transformed into (x_{i1}, y_{i1}), which is also a measure of distance, but along two different axes that have a theoretical interpretation. It may be recalled from figure 6–1 that the cells on the diagonal represent fair profits for the seller. Theoretically, this would be represented by a diagonal (called the *equilibrium axis*) through the origin in figure 6–2. The x term measures the perpendicular distance from the equilibrium axis (where the profit norms were expected to be fair). The greater the distance from this axis, the larger the opportunism is. In one case, it is in favor of the supplier; in the other case, it is in favor of the buyer. The y term measures the distance along the equilibrium axis. The distance from the origin along the axis characterizes the increasing differentiation of the product and the associated relationship orientation of the interaction.

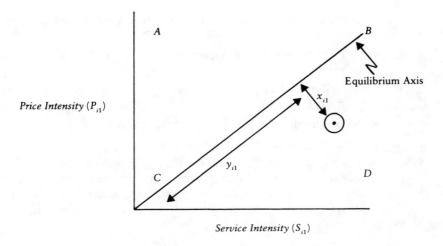

Figure 6–2. The Buyer Classification Map for a Single Product

If the nature of the relationship and the negotiating patterns between the seller and the buyer fit the proposed classification scheme, it is predicted that the seller profitability will be high in the northwest corner marked A in figure 6–2 and low in the southeast corner marked D in the figure. The profits along the equilibrium axis are expected to be fair and normal, although different differentiating strategies will lead to different profitabilities along this axis. The northeast corner marked B in the figure reflects a highly differentiated strategy, while the southwest corner marked C reflects a commodity strategy.

The same principle is applied for each of the other products $j = 2, 3, \ldots, n$. The overall classification map for a single buyer is modeled as a lienar addition of the distances x_{ij} and y_{ij} over each of the j products. The relative importance of each product is captured by a weight parameter. The mathematical equation that captures the foregoing properties is

$$\gamma \left(\sum_{\substack{j=1 \\ x_{ij} \in \phi}}^{n} a_{ij}\, x_{ij} - \sum_{\substack{j=1 \\ x_{ij} \in \psi}}^{n} a_{ij}\, x_{ij} \right) + \theta \sum_{j=1}^{n} a_{ij}\, y_{ij} + \alpha = \pi_{\iota} \tag{6.1}$$

where i = index on accounts;

j = index on products;

a_{ij} = a weighting factor that calculates gross margin on net sales of product j to account i as a proportion of overall gross margin on sales of all products to i; sales revenue is calculated net of all discounts and incentives; $a_{ij} = r_{ij} m_{ij} / \Sigma_{j}\, r_{ij}\, m_{ij}$;

x_{ij} = perpendicular distance to the equilibrium axis for account i for product j;

y_{ij} = distance from origin along the equilibrium axis for account i for product j;

π_i = overall gross margin as a percentage of sales on all products sold to account i;

ϕ = set of all points above the equilibrium axis;

ψ = set of all points below the equilibrium axis;

γ,θ,α = parameters to be estimated: γ may be interpreted as a behavioral parameter that reflects a seller's bargaining style; θ may be interpreted as a strategy parameter that reflects a seller's differentiation efforts; α is merely the regression constant.

Methodology

The mathematical model discussed in the preceding section was parameterized using data collected from a large industrial firm. The implementation methodology consisted of the following steps.

1. A team of executive judges put together a list of services required for each of the products being distributed. The team also arrived at judgmental importance weights for each of the services associated with a product. For example, if a product j required services $q = 1, 2, \ldots, m_j$ to be performed, the judges arrived at β_{qj}, which was the importance weight for service q when distributing product j.

2. The company's marketing services manager held meetings with each of the four regional sales managers. The purpose of each meeting was to fill out a questionnaire for one representative account in each region. This questionnaire was anchored as a reference for the region, and each salesperson was asked to fill out a questionnaire for each of his or her accounts, using the reference questionnaire as a guide. (The sample questionnaire is shown in the chapter appendix.) One such questionnaire was filled out for each account. The final step consisted of a review and a revision by the regional sales managers wherever necessary.

3. Each account was plotted on the two dimensions of service intensity (S_{ij}) and price intensity (P_{ij}). For service intensity:

$$S_{ij} = \sum_{q=1}^{m_j} \beta_{qj} \, s_{qij} \tag{6.2}$$

where q = 1, 2, . . . , m_j, an index for services offered by the seller for product j;

β_{qj} = importance weight for service q in the sale of product j (arrived at by executive judgment);

s_{qij} = level of service q *offered to account i* for product j (obtained from the questionnaire).

The level of price intensity (P_{ij}) was also obtained from the questionnaire. (The questionnaire also gathered other pieces of information, which will be discussed in the next section.)

4. There were as many observations for equation 6.2 as there were accounts. A significant R^2 for equation 6.2 signified the acceptance of our hypotheses.

The statistical results of the study will be presented elsewhere in a subsequent paper. Here, we will discuss the implications of the modeling methodology and results with a special emphasis on managerial decision making.

Implications of the Results

The decision framework for evaluating each buyer account is first explained by examining two accounts, $i = a$ and $i = b$, in the positions shown in figure 6–3. Clearly, it is in the seller's interest to move a toward the equilibrium axis. This can be achieved by means of several paths. Path 1 involves cutting back on both price and service; paths 2 and 3, and many others in between, involve cutting back on service, increasing price, or both; and path 4 involves increasing price and service. However, the key question is whether the account will respond to any of these strategies. That is, how elastic is the account's demand curve to price and service? Besides the elasticity calculation, we must also assess the buying power of the account. What is the importance of our product to the buyer? What opportunities and motivation does the account have for switching to the competition? Is it at all worthwhile to alter either our marketing mix or our buyer relationships to achieve this movement?

If we look at account b in figure 6–3, the implications of the move are obvious. Fundamentally, any move toward the equilibrium axis will involve a loss in gross margin. Should we then make an effort to move this account at all? Is this account satisfied with our product because of its inherent importance and value, or is this account not well informed of the alternative offerings in the marketplace? If the latter, there is a distinct possibility of account migration to the competition. What can we do to retain this account? Should we provide the necessary knowledge and information that might, in fact, increase the accounts negotiating leverage with us?

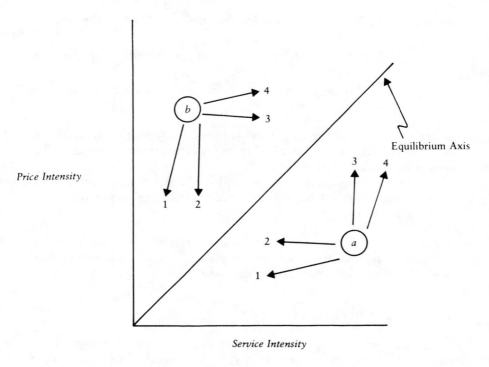

Figure 6–3. Possible Paths for Influencing Account Movement

Our modeling framework identified and confirmed our buyer classification framework, but to answer the many questions regarding each individual account, we had to use the modeling framework along with other inputs on the nature of the seller-buyer relationship gathered from the questionnaire.

A flow diagram such as the one shown in figure 6–4 was used to analyze and evaluate each account. As can be seen from the figure, Strategy 1 is the implementation of a revised price/service mix. The exact nature of the revision will be based on the individual account elasticity, which would be calculated on the basis of the sales manager survey. The implications of the other strategies are not so straightforward:

Strategy 2. The exchange is fair and our profit margins are equal to the norm. Therefore, these are valuable accounts, and our channel management emphasis should be on sharing profits and other benefits between us. Honesty and fairness in negotiation would be helpful and beneficial. The current mix of service and price is about right, and there is no reason to change the mix.

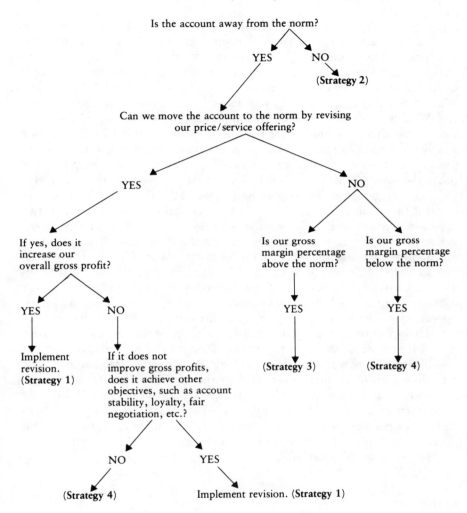

Is the account away from the norm?

YES   NO

(Strategy 2)

Can we move the account to the norm by revising
our price/service offering?

YES   NO

If yes, does it   Is our gross   Is our gross
increase our   margin percentage   margin percentage
overall gross profit?   above the norm?   below the norm?

YES   NO   YES   YES

Implement   If it does not
revision.   improve gross profits,   (Strategy 3)   (Strategy 4)
(Strategy 1) does it achieve other
              objectives, such as account
              stability, loyalty, fair
              negotiation, etc.?

NO   YES

(Strategy 4)   Implement revision. (Strategy 1)

Figure 6–4. Flow Diagram for Evaluating Accounts

Strategy 3. For some reason, this distributor account allows us to earn an above-average gross margin; moreover, this account is not particularly sensitive to our price/service mix. Clearly, then, we should keep the account in its current position and, depending on the intensity of competition, we may want to inform and educate this buyer. Under intense competition, it is quite likely that this account may become sensitive to our price/service offering and thus will require a different strategy. We may even need to add certain special account-specific services, so long as our gross margins are not jeopardized.

Strategy 4. These are probably the toughest accounts to deal with in terms of marketing strategy. Either these accounts are not sensitive to our service/price offerings or, if they are, it does not work to our advantage in terms of overall gross margins. These accounts generate below-average gross profits for us, so we must carefully evaluate the work of retaining each account. We may want to drop some of these accounts. Many of these accounts may wield undue power by virtue of their size and volume buying, in which case we have no alternative in the long run but to improve our bargaining position slowly. We need diplomacy and accommodative negotiations to retain the rest of the accounts. Careful cultivation of the channel relationship may improve the loyalty and service sensitivity of these accounts in the long run.

The foregoing framework was used to analyze 160 accounts of a large industrial firm. These accounts are buying a capital equipment line and two commodity lines from the same seller. Our decision heuristic revised the service/price mix for 25 percent of the accounts, and the other strategy recommendations are being implemented for the other accounts. A small number of the accounts (5 percent) are being considered for cancellation. Besides its value in dissecting the buyer base, the methodology also gave the selling firm a quick grasp of its buyer classification, which was heavily in the buyer-opportunism quadrant. This has enabled the company to focus its long-run marketing plan on creating product differentiation through account servicing.

The purpose of this chapter was to illustrate the feasibility of a buyer classification framework and its subsequent development for decision making regarding each individual buyer. One of the major weaknesses of this approach is its sole reliance on the seller's perception in operationalizing the price intensity and service intensity measures. As noted earlier, the buyer's and seller's perception could vary tremendously; ultimately, the interaction is governed by a joint evaluation, rather than by a one-party evaluation such as that proposed in this chapter.

References

Bonoma, T.V., and Shapiro, B.P. (1983). *Segmenting the Industrial Market.* Lexington, Mass.: Lexington Books.

Brown, J.R., and Frazier, G.L. (1978). "The Application of Channel Power: Its Effects and Connotations." In *Research Frontiers in Marketing: Dialogues and Directions,* ed. Subash C. Jain. Chicago: American Marketing.

Dwyer, F.R. (1980). "Channel-Member Satisfaction: Laboratory Insights." *Journal of Retailing* 56 (Summer):45–65.

Etgar, M. (1978). "Selection of an Effective Channel Control Mix." *Journal of Marketing* 142 (July):53–58.

Gaski, J.F. (1984). "The Theory of Power and Conflict in Channels of Distribution," *Journal of Marketing* 48 (Summer):29.

Hunt, D.S., and Nevin, J.R. (1974). "Power in a Channel of Distribution: Sources and Consequences." *Journal of Marketing* 11 (Spring):186–193.

Lusch, R.F. (1976). "Sources of Power: Their impact on Intrachannel Conflict." *Journal of Marketing Research* 13 (Nov.):382–90.

Moriarty, R.T., and Reibstein, D.J. (1982). "Benefit Segmentation: An Industrial Application." Working paper, Marketing Science Institute, Cambridge, Mass.

Porter, M.E. (1974), "Consumer Behavior, Retailer Power and Market Performance in Consumer Goods Industries." *Review of Economics and Statistics* 56 (Nov.): 419–436.

Rosenberg, L.J., and Stern, L.W. (1971). "Conflict Measurement in the Distribution Channel." *Journal of Marketing Research* 8 (Nov.):437–442.

Shapiro, B.P., and Moriarty, R.T. (1982). "National Account Management: Emerging Insights." Special report, Marketing Science Institute, Cambridge, Mass.

Stern, L.W., and Reve, T. (1980). "Distribution Channels as Political Economies: A Framework for Comparative Analysis." *Journal of Marketing* 44 (July):52–64.

Wilkinson, I.F. (1974). "Researching the Distribution Channels for Consumer and Industrial Goods: The Power Dimension." *Journal of the Market Research Society* 16 (1):12–32.

Williamson, O.E. (1975). *Markets and Hierarchies: Analysis and Antitrust Implications—A Study in Economics of Internal Organization.* New York: Free Press.

Appendix:
Questionnaire Used for Data Collection

Please respond to each product category under a separate column. All questions pertain to your operations in 1983 with respect to this specific account.

Code number of account _____

Total size of account (sales turnover) $ _____

	Product 1	Product 2
1. Your 1983 sales volume.	$	$
2. Your 1983 market share with respect to the competition.		
3. Your 1983 gross margin as a percentage of sales.		
4. Your 1983 net margin as a percentage of sales (gross margin net of direct marketing costs).		
5. As compared to other accounts of your company, what is the price level you are able to charge this particular account? (Make your estimate on a 1 to 10 scale. A score of 1 would mean that this account is able to negotiate a relatively low average price net of all discounts. A score of 10 would mean that this account plays a relatively high average price net of all discounts.)		
6. If you were able to drop prices (from the score you indicated in question 5) by one unit on the 1 to 10 scale, what is your best guess of increase in sales volume?	%	%
7. If you were able to increase prices (from the score you indicated in question 5) by one unit on the 1 to 10 scale, what is your best guess of decrease in sales volume?	%	%

	Product 1	Product 2

8. As compared to other accounts of your company, what is the service level you offer to this particular account for each of the service components listed against each product category? (Make your estimate on a 1 to 10 scale. A score of 1 would mean that you offer a relatively low service level. A score of 10 would mean that you offer a relatively high service level).

9. If you were able to drop service levels uniformly by one unit over all the service components (from the scores you indicated in question 8), what is your best guess of decrease in sales volume?   %   %

10. If you were able to increase service levels uniformly by one unit over all the service components (from the scores you indicated in question 8), what is your best guess of increase in sales volume?   %   %

11. How important or critical is your product for the business activity in which the account is involved? (Use a 1 to 5 scale, in which 1 stands for not at all important and 5 stands for extremely important.)

12. How would you rate the risk of losing this account to competition? (Use a 1 to 5 scale, in which 1 stands for very little risk and 5 stands for extreme risk.)

13. How well informed is this account regarding the competition and their products? (Use a 1 to 5 scale, in which 1 stands for poorly informed and 5 stands for very well informed.)

14. How difficult is it to do business with this account? (Use a 1 to 5 scale, in which 1 stands for not at all difficult and 5 stands for extremely difficult.)

15. How would you generally characterize this account's negotiating strategy? (Enter 1 if tough, 2 if fair, 3 if accommodative.)

16. How would you generally characterize your own negotiating strategy with this account? (Enter 1 if tough, 2 if fair, 3 if accommodative.)

7

Channel Alternatives in the Press Industry: A Comparative Analysis

Guido Cristini

The aim of this chapter is to analyze the structure of the channels of distribution in the daily and periodical press industry, with special reference to the bargaining power relationships that arise between publishers and distributive intermediaries. To assess channel composition as an index of the differing bargaining power positions of producers and distributors for the attainment of channel leadership, the press industries of various countries were compared. Attention was paid to countries such as Great Britain, the Federal Republic of Germany, and France, which have well-established traditions in publishing and in reading habits, and to others, such as Italy, which, though undergoing considerable change, are still lagging behind the aforementioned countries. Differences in market width and in the elasticity of the demand for certain press items and the presence or absence of legal constraints (prices laid down in the daily press sector) are elements that considerably affect the structure and conduct of the supply side. By tackling channel processes through a behavioral approach,[1] this chapter attempts to formulate some interpretative hypotheses concerning the evolution of the power relationships between publishers and distributive intermediaries in the press industry and to offer some indications of the dynamics of development of the industry itself.

Channels of Distribution in the Press Industry: A Functional or a Behavioral Approach?

There are several different theoretical approaches to the relationships that exist between the actors in the product marketing process. I shall refer particularly to Gattorna's (1978) treatment of the state of the art in the distribution channel area. In my view, the approaches referred to in Gattorna's classification as "functional" and "behavioral" are the most likely to provide a clear understanding of the economic interactions between the members of any given channel.[2] Indeed, in the various settings discussed in this chapter (Great Britain,

Germany, France, and Italy), the structure, conduct, and performance of the channels seem to be affected substantially by the role and functions performed by each channel member in the marketing process of daily and periodical press items.

Marketing authors (Mallen, 1972) have pointed out that the main aspect of the functional approach is represented by the performance of marketing functions by different channel members.[3] In this connection, the inherent question that arises relates to the allocation of functions in a definite channel, as assessed on the basis of efficiency. A further question relates to the way in which the different allocation of functions by channel members affects and modifies the channel structure itself.

In particular, according to Mallen (1972), function integration leads to modifications in (1) the number of transactions within a channel, (2) the number of channels used, (3) the type of intermediary that acquires greater weight, and (4) the number of intermediaries that acquire greater importance on each level. Each industry may require marketing functions that differ from those required by each channel intermediary; moreover, the evolution of the market itself or the degree of development of the industry involves changes—sometimes substantial—in the type, quality, and intensity of the functions that the various members are required to fulfill. In regard to the identification of the functions performed by channel members, several authors have suggested more than one classification.[4] However, the sole concern of this chapter is to point out how functions that are normally performed by distributive intermediaries are performed by the producers themselves in the press industry. For instance, if the press industry is compared with the grocery industry, it is readily apparent that in the press industry, the distributive intermediaries, whether wholesalers or retailers, (1) do not undertake any commercial risks (the product remains the property of the publisher until the time of purchase by the reader); (2) do not offer commercial guarantees (the reader does not associate decline in product quality with the image of the newsagent); and (3) play no role in establishing consumer price (which is fixed by the publisher).

Although some aspects of the press industry make it comparable to other industries that are subject to public regulations, in view of the ways in which the structure and the roles performed by channel members undergo change, it may also be compared to other industries that are not subject to external constraints (for example, low-unit-value convenience goods). Indeed, if the phenomenon of channel redefinition is to be grasped to its full extent, due consideration must be paid to the importance of power relationships between channel members (the behavioral approach).

In this connection, Schulz (1971) argues that "conduct of channel members as well as performance of channels are affected considerably by the behavioral interactions among channel members." Schulz also points out that the entire channel process is affected by the amount of market power held by any one of its members and by the type of policy—cooperation or conflict—each member intends to pursue vis-à-vis its partners.

Three factors define the relationships between channel members: (1) power within the channel, (2) conflict or cooperation between members; and (3) leadership. With respect to the power relationship, Moyer (1971) emphasizes market structure (for instance, the number and relevance of sellers and buyers) as the single most important factor. Other authors (Cunningham, 1973) have attempted to measure the effects of modifications in the commercial policy of the producers in an industrial-type approach. In my view, this kind of analysis should be supplemented with a precise assessment of the determining role played by the distributive intermediaries. Economic analysis has shown that changes in the role of the structures and functions of business enterprises eventually affect the power of the producers themselves.[5]

With respect to conflict versus cooperation in the marketing channels, Gattorna (1978) has identified some critical factors underlying possible conflicts between members:

1. Communications, structures, and decision-making processes;
2. Manipulation of channel members by other members of the same channel;
3. Introduction of innovations (including new technology) that are resisted by barriers to change;
4. Denial of legitimate claims for reallocation of power and functions;
5. Differences between channel members in primary business philosophy;
6. The exchange act itself, specifically in terms of reaching agreement on terms of trade.

An important question arises regarding whether conflict within the channel should be considered beneficial or detrimental. I agree with Rosenberg and Stern (1971), who state that "where no conflict exists, there may be situations of complacency in which innovation would not be generated." Channel efficiency, with ensuing reduction of excess profits, obtains where competition exists between the various members; by integrating and disintegrating functions that are usually performed by others, the channel members are able to mutually affect their respective market power. Since a gradual decline in the role of the producer in many sectors is being parallelled by an increase in the role played by the commercial intermediaries—which have taken over functions formerly performed efficiently only by the producer—the full extent of the change affecting the distribution process is readily apparent.[6] Conflict therefore becomes an observable element in all those channels that must also take into account the dynamics of external competition.

Finally, some authors (Little, 1968) consider that channel leadership policies are designed to ease tensions resulting from competition within the channel—as such tensions are considered "unnecessary."[7] This may shed new light on Stern's (1972) statement, that power relationships within the channel result from the "asymmetric interdependence of the members on each other." In other words, the dynamism of the channel (hence, its degree of efficiency) is largely dependent on the bargaining power held, from time to time, by each of the members.

Since the behavioral model is more effective in pointing out the dynamic aspects that characterize relationships among producers, intermediaries, and consumers, it appears particularly suitable for analyzing an industry that is undergoing continuous evolution, such as the press. Furthermore, comparisons between different countries provide support for two separate contentions: (1) the structure of distribution channels varies considerably from country to country; and (2) the higher the stage of development of the industry, the less power is held by the publishers vis-à-vis the intermediaries. It follows that the observed dynamics of competition have favored the channel members placed between production and consumption. (We shall see later *how* this happens.)

The Press Market in Great Britain, the Federal Republic of Germany, France, and Italy

To provide a rough outline of the structure of the distribution channels in the press industry in Great Britain, Germany, France, and Italy, some significant data were collected concerning the relative size of the daily and periodical press markets in these countries. Dailies and periodicals were examined separately, as these products present similar features only in few limited areas. For example, one element that characterizes the daily press sector is higher perishability. A survey on the time at which daily papers are normally bought in Italy showed that approximately 70 percent are sold before 10 A.M.[8] (Since almost all newsagents open at about 6 A.M., most sales are effected in a 4-hour time span.) After 1 P.M, newspaper sales are marginal (approximately 10% of the total in countries where evening papers account for a mere fraction of the market). The periodicals sector is different, although here, too, weeklies have a relatively short life cycle; approximately 62 percent of all purchases of weeklies occur within the first 48 hours of issue.[9]

Success in the industry, therefore, seems to be structurally correlated with speed and effectiveness in planning and in the actual distribution of the products. This explains the importance of obtaining reliable data relative to the flow of printed products that reach consumers through the channels of distribution.

Data regarding the structure of supply in various countries are shown in figure 7–1. However, to identify considerable concentrations in the press industry, thereby determining whether any monopoly positions exist, information concerning the exact definition of shares within the market would be needed. In fact, though conditioned by laws that forbid concentrations in the press industry,[10] some publishing groups are unquestionably market leaders (for example, Axel Springer Verlag in Germany, Hachette in France, Rizzoli and Mondadori in Italy).

Regarding circulation, a significant difference in market width can be observed between Great Britain and Germany on the one hand and France and Italy on the other (see figures 7–2 and 7–3). The gap in readership between Italy and the other European countries is shown clearly in figure 7–4. The data indicate that German and English newspaper readerships are, on average, four times larger than those in Italy, and French readership is twice as large as Italy's. At this stage, it would be useful to identify the three main classes into which the daily press is usually subdivided: national newspapers (which, to borrow a term commonly used in the Anglo-Saxon market, may be referred to as *quality papers*); popular newspapers (which also circulate on a national basis); and local papers. The term *national* should be used with some caution; in most cases, especially in the quality press sector, the term refers to dailies that perform the function of local papers in the larger urban center and circulate throughout the rest of the country. This is perhaps less apparent where one city holds unquestionable preemineence over the others,

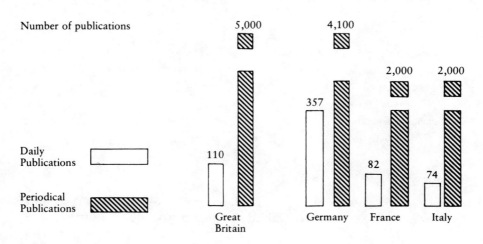

Source: Adapted from data from the Audit Bureau of Circulation (ABC), London; Office de Justification de Diffusion (OJD), Paris; Accertamenti Diffusione Stampa (ADS), Milan; Federazione Italiana Editore Giornali (FIEG), Rome; and Auflaenstatistik (IVW), Munich.

Figure 7–1. Structure of Supply in the Press Industry in Great Britain, Germany, France, and Italy

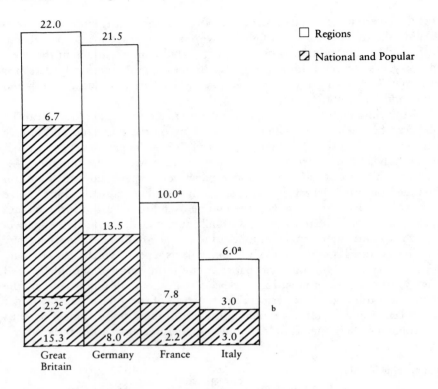

22.0 21.5

6.7

10.0ᵃ

13.5

6.0ᵃ

7.8 3.0

2.2ᶜ

15.3 8.0 2.2 3.0 b

Great Britain Germany France Italy

☐ Regions

▨ National and Popular

Source: Adapted from ABC, OJD, ADS, FIEG, and IVW data.

Note: 1981 data, Sunday papers not included (except as noted). Figures in millions.

ᵃ1983 data.

ᵇNational dailies as a percentage of total.

ᶜNational papers only.

Figure 7–2. Average Circulation of Daily Papers in Great Britain, Germany, France, and Italy

as in Great Britain and France, but it clearly applies to countries such as Italy or Germany, which are characterized by a polycentric urban structure.[11]

If the circulation figures are reconsidered in the light of these remarks, the results obtained provide a less generic explanation of the meaning of Italy's low readership figures in comparison with those of the other countries. In figure 7–2, the data relative to national newspapers point to some kind of homogeneity among the four countries: 2.2 million in Britain, 8.0 million in Germany,[12] 2.2 million in France, and 2.2 million in Italy. The picture is somewhat different if the popular and local papers are taken into account.

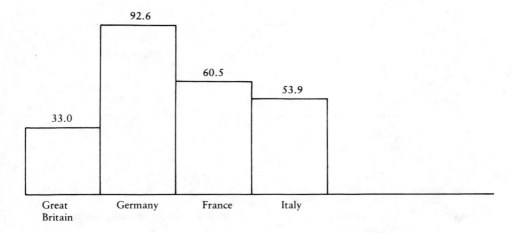

Source: Adapted from ABC, OJD, ADS, FIEG, and IVW data.
Note: 1981 data. Figures in millions.

Figure 7–3. Average Circulation per Issue of Periodicals in Great Britain, Germany, France, and Italy

The popular papers are especially responsible for the wide gap in circulation between Italy and the other countries; the respective readership figures for Italy, France, Germany, and Britain are 3.0 million, 7.8 million, 13.5 million, and 6.7 million copies for the popular papers.

The healthiest segment of the supply market seems to be represented by the local press; over the last decade (as illustrated best by the French case), a substantial increase in the sales figures for local newspapers has been paralleled by a decline in sales of their national counterparts. As will be noted later, in analyzing the structure of the distribution channels, this aspect is significant for a definition and assessment of the relationships that exist between publishers and distributors.

A distinction must also be made between Italy and the other countries with respect to the consumer price of daily papers. In Britain, Germany, and France, the retail price is set by the individual publishers; hence, readership segmentation also occurs on the basis of this variable. In Italy, however, the price is fixed by the authorities.[13] The establishment of a ceiling price results in a considerable constraint on circulation strategies; some of the tools available in the marketing mix remain unused because of their limited effects on a readership that is highly homogeneous.[14] Although the limited segmentation of Italy's press market may also be viewed in this perspective, one should not overlook the fact that the stage of development of its readership in the daily press

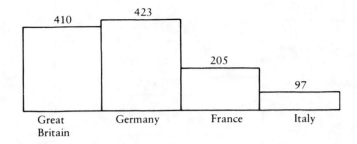

Source: Statistical Yearbook, 1979–80 (New York: United Nations, 1981).
Note: 1977 data.

Figure 7–4. Readership per 1,000 Inhabitants in Great Britain, Germany, France, and Italy

sector is well behind that of the other countries referred to here as well as the vast majority of industrialized countries.[15]

The picture is somewhat different in the periodical press market (see figure 7–3). Although the data were obtained from the relevant boards of certification and therefore do not reflect actual circulation, they may be considered reasonable indexes for the periodicals market.[16] With the notable exception of Germany (with a circulation of 92.6 million copies per number), circulation in the English, French, and Italian markets is fairly homogeneous. This is particularly significant in the case of Italy, where a considerable delay was observed in the daily press sector. This can be partly accounted for by the fact that, as noted earlier, periodicals function as popular newspapers on a weekly basis; thus, periodicals with a sufficiently generic content and an obviously generalized target, both in the lower-medium and the upper-medium tiers, have very wide circulation.

The Structure of Distribution in the Press Industry and Relationships between Channel Members

As noted earlier, the channels of distribution that publishers use to meet the demands of their readership differ from publisher to publisher as well as from country to country. The increasing importance of distribution processes, functions performed by individual intermediaries, and policies regarding the granting of discounts to channel members often entail changes in existing power relationships between publishers and intermediaries. In the press industry in general, there are normally four types of channels, depending on the degree of vertical organization:

1. *Direct channel:* (a) publisher–subscriber via mail and (b) publisher–reader via home delivery;

2. *Short channel:* publisher–newsagent–reader;

3. *Long channel (four stages):* publisher–local distributor–newsagent–reader;

4. *Long channel (five or more stages):* publisher–national distributor–local distributor–newsagent–reader.

It should be noted that not only are these different channels found in the press industry in general but a given publication (daily or periodical) may be distributed in a number of different ways. The differences may depend on the size of the relevant market (national or local), the audience (number of readers per copy sold), the publication's perishability (ranging from evening papers to quarterlies), the degree of efficiency of the intermediary (for example, the mail), the cost of intermediation, and the number of unsold and returned copies.

The channels most commonly employed are the direct channel in both of its modes (mailing to subscribers typically used by periodicals and delivery by newsboys typically used by local dailies) and the long channels, involving all relevant distributive intermediaries (typically used by periodicals and by national and popular dailies).

For a more accurate quantification of the flow of goods sold through the various channels, it would be best to refer to the specific features of each country. This will also enable us to assess the relative weight of each channel member.

In Germany, 40 percent of the periodicals are distributed directly to subscribers (31.5 percent through the mail, 3 percent by the publishing firms themselves, 2.5 percent through readers' clubs); the remaining 60 percent are circulated through long channels (see figure 7–5). National distributors play a considerable role in that their typical customers include small- and medium-sized publishers of periodicals that are unable to see to the distribution of their products directly. The cost of intermediation is considerable, as we shall see later, but this is the only means by which small publishing firms can reach the final sales network. In contrast, local distributors perform functions that are performed by wholesalers in other sectors; that is, within a specific area, they see to the distribution of the products to all the

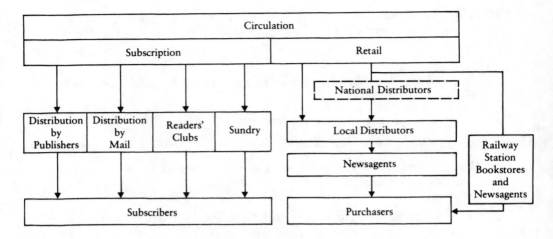

Figure 7–5. The Structure of Periodicals Distribution in Germany

newsagents, they check that returns do not exceed a level that may reasonably be considered average, and they make sure that the newsagents send off the proceeds from sales on time. Local distributors are sometimes bypassed by national distributors, which directly supply newsagents in areas where circulation is particularly wide (this does not seem to occur, however, in Germany).

German daily press subscribers account for about 59 percent of the total (41 percent of the dailies are distributed through retail sales networks); as much as 43 percent of the subscriptions are distributed by the publishing firms themselves (see figure 7–6). The significant role played by home delivery by newsboys (approximately 9.2 million copies per day) is partly due to the wide circulation of local dailies; when a considerable portion of the readership is located in an area near the production plant, publishers find it more profitable to take direct charge of distribution to subscribers, rather than relying on a sales network. (This entails cuts in intermediation costs through drastic reductions in the number of copies returned.)

The distribution structure of the British press is similar to that of the German press (see figure 7–7). The only significant difference concerns daily papers (both national and local), which are distributed to subscribers by newsagents rather than by the publishers (50 percent of the market of both national and local papers is accounted for by subscribers to whom the products are home-delivered). The truly peculiar feature of the British model, however, is that the publishers of national dailies do not acknowledge the

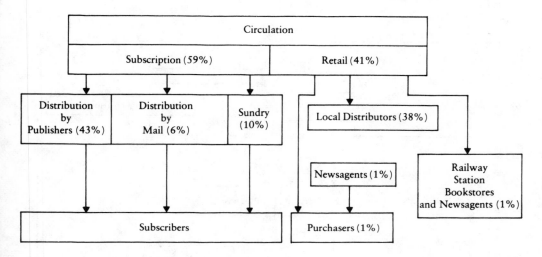

Figure 7–6. The Structure of Daily Press Distribution in Germany

distributor's right to return any unsold goods; that is, the sole responsibility for marketing strategies rests with the intermediaries, as they cannot return any unsold copies to the publishers. Therefore, because local distributors and newsagents must undertake the commercial risks involved, the additional service supplied by the newsagents (home delivery) is aimed at increasing the number of subscribers. This helps them ensure that no copies remain unsold.

The French intermediation structure differs considerably from the British and German structures (see figure 7–8). The NMPPs (Nouvelles Messageries de la Presse Parisienne) are the only channels available to publishers for the distribution of either periodicals or daily newspapers. The NMPPs are established, run, and controlled by the publishers' cooperatives and perform functions that are typically performed by publishing firms; that is, they carry out market research, distribute products, check distributors' payments, see that unsold goods are returned, set distribution premiums, pass on orders to the publishers, and assess the efficiency of the sales network. Even this brief list of the most important functions performed by the NMPPs is sufficient to identify them as the leaders of the entire distributive system. Moreover, because of their virtually monopolistic position in the market, the NMPPs are able to run the entire process without facing any significant conflict. The NMPPs own the large regional warehouses, the Hachette agencies, and the central warehouses. They supply approximately 3,000 local distributors as well as newsagents in large urban centers and in railway stations. In addition to this,

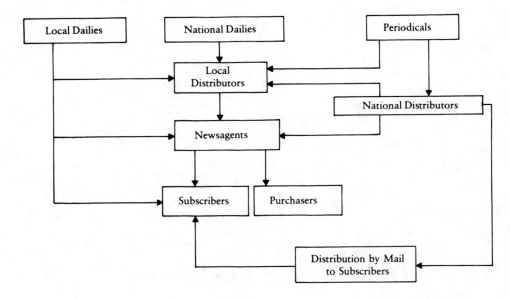

Figure 7–7. The Structure of Periodical and Daily Press Distribution in Great Britain

they are the direct suppliers of all newsagents located in the Paris district. Local newspapers, however, are largely distributed via newsboys; this channel accounts for approximately 30 percent of the publications sold. The remaining 70 percent is handled by local distributors, which supply the final sales network.

Finally, in Italy, press distribution is mainly through long channels (see figure 7–9). In fact, because of the negligible weight of local newspapers, home delivery is virtually nonexistent.[17] What characterizes the Italian model of distribution is the prevailing specialization of the retail network. Unlike other countries, Italy's newsagents have a selection of printed items that is considerable both in width and in depth and that is only partly associated with other products.[18] This means that distribution is particularly difficult for publishers and national distributors, as they have to supply virtually all points of sale, which entails substantial costs for actual distribution.

Long Channels and Direct Channels: Intermediation Margins and Market Power

With respect to long channels, table 7–1 summarizes the data on the local distributors and newsagents in the countries we have been comparing. Considering the foregoing discussion of the functions performed by channel intermediaries

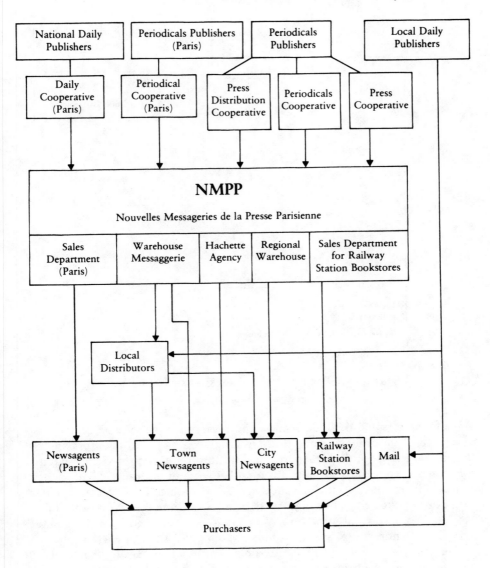

Figure 7–8. The Structure of Periodical and Daily Press Distribution in France

and their importance in the distributive process, considerable differences among the countries are readily noticeable. For example, the French model is characterized by a high number of local distributors (about 3,000), whereas the German model features no more than 83 distributors, supplying 85,000 newsagents.

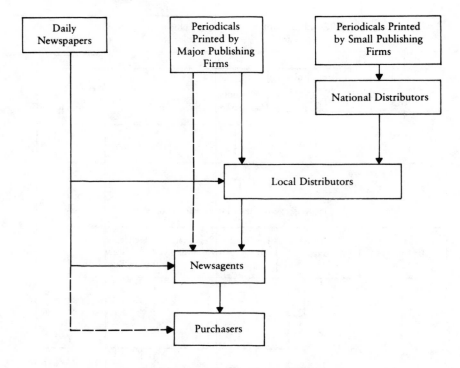

Figure 7–9. The Structure of Press Distribution in Italy

To understand these differences, however, more specific accounts must be given of the structures and of the roles played by the distributors and by the newsagents. For the most part, the distributors are specialized only in Italy; they are considerably less specialized in Britain and in France (that is, their stocks include both printed products and other products).[19] According to data supplied by the British newsagents' associations, printed items account for 40 to 50 percent of total sales. Finally, in Germany, the press network is made up almost entirely (95% of the total) of points of sale whose stocks include products other than press items and only a limited number of publications.[20]

France has such a high number of local distributors because they also act as retailers (newsagents) and, in most cases, they see to the organization and supply of other newsagents located in their areas.

The term *monopoly* may be applied to the German case. Not only do the 83 local distributors perform their activities in a contractual framework defined by sole distribution in given areas, the right to return unsold goods, and forced prices, but two-thirds of their turnover is accounted for by Germany's four most important publishing firms.[21]

Table 7–1
Press Intermediation Market: Number of
Wholesalers (Local Distributors) and
Retailers (Newsagents)

	Number of Local Distributors	*Number of Newsagents*
Great Britain	500	35,000
Germany	83	85,000
France	3,000	40,000
Italy	400	25,000

To point out the elements that characterize long distribution channels in the various countries, tables 7–2 and 7–3 summarize the data on the cost of commercial intermediation in the daily press sector and the periodicals sector, respectively. This information concerning the margins realized by the various classes of intermediaries provides us with some further indications of the bargaining power of channel members.

First, the range of variation of the commercial margins fluctuates between a peak value of 43 percent of the cover price (in France, for periodicals) and a minimum of 25 percent (in Italy, for daily papers and periodicals). Because the gap between the two values is considerable, the causes underlying this situation require a more detailed treatment.

Although British distributors have rather low margins, the newsagents' margins are relatively higher (28 percent and 25 percent, respectively, for daily papers and periodicals). It must be recalled, however, that unsold goods cannot be returned; therefore, the commercial risk is borne entirely by the newsagents.

The cost of wholesale intermediation in Germany (15.6 percent for the daily press and 16 to 30 percent for periodicals) indicates, as noted earlier, the significant weight acquired by local distributors in the intermediation process. In fact, the overall marketing cost is between 36 percent and 50 percent, although a rather low premium is granted to newsagents (18 to 20 percent).

The higher cost of intermediation in France is largely attributable to the presence of the NMPPs (16 to 20 percent, respectively, for dailies and periodicals); the margins gained by other channel members (in France, the long channel includes five stages, not four as in the other countries) are relatively low (5 percent for distributors, 15 percent for newsagents). Recall, however, that the NMPPs perform several functions that are performed by the publishing firms in other countries (for example, computerized returns and direct crediting to the publisher).[22]

Finally, in Italy, the lower cost of commercial intermediation (25 percent for all printed items) can be attributed to the lesser margins of local distributors

Table 7–2

Average Premium of the Distributive Intermediaries in the Daily Newspaper Industry in Great Britain, Germany, France, and Italy (*Percentages*)

	Price	National Distrib. (A)	Local Distrib. (B)	Final Network (C)	A + B + C	Publisher's Margin	Return of Unsold Goods
Great Britain	100	—	8 (10 London)	28 (30 locals)	36	64	No (admit return 2–5)
Germany	100	—	15.6	18	33.6	66.4	Yes
France	100	16 (NMPP)	8	15 (19 Periodicals)	39	61	Yes
Italy	100	—	5	20	25	75	Yes

(5 percent) and newsagents (20 percent). It should be noted that although the publishers and the national distributors are, to some extent, channel leaders— and this is made apparent by the relatively low cost of distribution—they have to make up for the organizational and management inefficiency of the intermediaries by performing functions that entail considerable costs (for example, counting returns and developing suitable policies for promoting given points of sale).

The process of distribution in Italy's press industry is in a less developed stage than that of the other countries considered here. The channel structure itself, with only a marginal presence of the direct (publisher–reader) channel, indicates that the commercial intermediaries have failed to attain a higher level of development. Indeed, whatever objections may be raised regarding the peculiarity of the press industry, in Italy, it is beyond question that the

Table 7–3

Average Premium of the Distributive Intermediaries in the Periodicals Industry in Great Britain, Germany, France, and Italy (*Percentages*)

	Price	National Distrib. (A)	Local Distrib. (B)	Final Network (C)	A + B + C	Publisher's Margin	Return of Unsold Goods
Great Britain	100	—	8	25 (installments 22.5)	33	67	Yes
Germany	100	—	16.1–30	20	36–50	64.50	Yes
France	100	20 (NMPP)	7	16	43	57	Yes
Italy	100	—	5	20	25	75	Yes

Source: CESCOM.

transformation of business enterprises through a redefinition of their role within the channel has resulted in an important change in vertical relationships in many industries. The outcome of this change, from a behavioral point of view, is an increase in the bargaining power of the distributive intermediaries vis-à-vis the producers and, consequently, greater welfare for the whole system.

In view of the marginal role (in terms of power) now played by the business enterprises in Italy's press industry, a future change—at least a partial one—leading to improved channel position and enabling them to increase their bargaining power can easily be predicted. This can be expected in spite of forced prices applied by publishers, for it is clear that although forced prices act as leveling factors on the dynamics of competition between business enterprises (horizontal competition), favoring the less efficient ones, greater integration of the marketing functions by such enterprises eventually enhances the overall weight of commercial intermediation with respect to production, resulting in an increase in their margins. It is revealing, in this connection, that the analysis of distribution channels in more advanced press systems brought to light a structure in which the intermediaries enjoy greater privileges than the publishers; the lesser intermediation margins characterizing the Italian model clearly support our assumption. Not only do wholesalers and retailers, as a whole, have greater bargaining power, but a channel leader can be identified in all channels: a national distributor in France (the NMPP), the local distributors in Germany, and the newsagents—though in a less clear-cut way—in Britain.

In the light of these data, consider the strategies that the publishers develop and implement to undermine the position of the channel intermediaries. As noted earlier, a positive correlation exists between the degree of development of the press industry (which also means larger quantities of goods sold) and the lesser market power of the publishers. Channel alternatives are undoubtedly one of the favorite options available to publishers; the direct channel is both encouraged and preferred in all of the more advanced countries. The data presented in table 7–4 testify to the high degree of development of the direct channel (readers' subscriptions). Despite some differences in the ways actual distribution is carried out, the data indicate that almost 50 percent of all British, German, and French press items bypass the intermediation stages. This is because the publishers of periodicals find the mail system reliable and efficient, and in the daily press sector, home delivery is a way of achieving a high percentage of subscribers. As noted earlier, home delivery fulfills two basic requirements of the publishing firms: (1) to reduce the percentage of unsold copies; and (2) to strengthen readership allegiance to a certain publication. Since the selling price plays an important role in the competitive process in an advanced publishing system, it is readily apparent why subscription is a successful distributive option.[23] Since competition between publishers eventually results in discounts to subscribers, it follows that (1) variable discounts are permitted in all countries and (2) all subscribers enjoy a certain reduction in the subscription price.[24]

Table 7–4
Width of the Subscription Channel (Daily Newspapers and Periodicals) in Great Britain, Germany, France, and Italy
(*Percentages*)

	Daily Papers	Periodicals
Great Britain	50–60[a]	40–50
Germany	55–60	40
France	20–30	N.A.
Italy	1–5	10–15

Source: CESCOM.
Note: Subscriptions (delivery by newsboys and mail) as a percentage of total circulation.
[a]Delivery of newsagents.

Conclusions

The mechanism governing the distribution systems in Great Britain, Germany, and France seems to be driven by competitive dynamics, both within the individual channels and between alternative channels. Moreover, the effects of competition follow two directions: a vertical direction, which involves publishers and commercial intermediaries, and a horizontal one, which involves the various segments within them (including publishing firms).

Comparison of the different competitive frameworks in which the channel members of the press industries in Britain, Germany, and France operate with the Italian model suggests that in spite of its delay because of a number of factors (especially the consumer market), the Italian press industry will, in the long run, adopt models such as those adopted by the more advanced countries. Furthermore, this change will be brought about by the dynamics of competition between the members of different channels for the attainment of channel leadership. Because behavioral factors play a role in determining market power—as noted earlier—any assessment of the structure and evolution of the channels of distribution in the press industry must take into account the competitive policies undertaken by the various channel members.

In reviewing press distribution models in some European countries, our analysis focused on interrelationships between channel members—in an attempt to point out the role played by these phenomena in the development of the industry. In particular, with reference to the elements that define the bargaining position of channel members, it was noted that in all models reviewed, a substantial decline in the market power of the publishers was parallelled by an increase in such power among commercial intermediaries (national distributors in France, local distributors in Germany, and newsagents in

Great Britain). The basis of role reallocation within the channel was seen to stem from growth in the distributive functions performed by the business enterprises (computer-aided assessment and recording of circulation). Publishing firms cope with the progressive reduction of their bargaining power within the long channel by promoting policies aimed at developing the direct channel (publisher–subscriber) in an attempt to obtain the largest possible readership. The fact that about 50 percent of the press items circulating in the advanced countries (Great Britain, Federal Republic of Germany, and France) is accounted for by subscribers is a good indication of the aggressive pricing policies (discounts granted to subscribers) typically undertaken by the publishing firms to gain a steady market share.

In sum, the dynamics of competition between distribution channels have a positive welfare effect on the entire industry. This is best borne out by the speed and efficiency with which deliveries are effected and by the low rates paid by subscribers.

Notes

1. The classification suggested by Gattorna (1978) was adopted. For more details, refer to the next section of this chapter.
2. In his treatment, Gattorna (1978) refers to six models: microeconomic, functional, systems, organizational, institutional, and behavioral.
3. According to the functional model: (1) marketing functions are the various types of job tasks or activities that channel members undertake; (2) these functions can be allocated in different mixes to different channel members; (3) the functional mixes will be patterned in a way that provides the greatest benefit either to the consumer (in the form of lower prices and/or more convenience) or to the channel members with the most power (which depends on market structure); (4) if one or more channel members see an opportunity to change the functional mix of the channel to increase profits, will attempt to do so; and (5) if the attempt is successful, and if the functional mix change is big enough, it will change the institutional arrangement in the channel—that is, the channel structure.
4. In particular, Kotler (1976) points out six main functions: contractual, merchandising, pricing, propaganda, physical distribution, termination. Dommermuth and Andersen (1969) indicate four: transportation, inventory, promotion, transactions. Finally, Davidson (1967) lists six: exchange, buying, selling, transportation, storage, and facilitating.
5. The theoretical contribution made by Lugli (1976) is particularly significant for an assessment of distribution in the convenience goods industry.
6. In the grocery industry, for example, large distribution firms play an important role with respect to manufacturing companies in the commercially advanced countries (such as the United States, France, and Britain).
7. However, Little (1968) does not explain what is meant by "unnecessary."
8. CESCOM (1984).

9. Ibid.

10. These antitrust laws protect the freedom of the press, imposing restrictions on concentration and establishing ceilings for the concentration of published material. In Italy, for instance, this ceiling is set at 25 percent.

11. CESCOM (1984).

12. This figure includes sales of both national and popular newspapers.

13. Increases in cover prices are subject to approval by the CIP (Inter-ministerial Price Board).

14. Some social and economic factors relating to Italy's population during this century (low income, high percentage of illiteracy, limited movement to the towns) have widened the readership gap between Italy and the more developed European countries.

15. According to data supplied by the United Nations (1981), Italy is in twentieth place in average circulation per inhabitant and is preceded not only by all of the more industrialized countries but also by countries such as South Korea, Venezuela, Kuwait, and Puerto Rico.

16. This review refers to periodicals published on a weekly, fortnightly, monthly, and quarterly basis.

17. Home delivery is supplied by few papers, including *La Stampa* and *Il Sole—24 Ore*. These are national papers, that offer this service only to readers located in the same town and district where the production plant is located (Turin and Milan). Even for these papers, home delivery accounts for a very small percentage of the copies sold (7 percent and 2 percent of total sales, respectively).

18. Most specialized newsagents offer a selection of about a thousand publications (both daily papers and periodicals).

19. The goods held in stock by a typical British retailer, for example, include tobacco, confectionery, and press items—hence the names used to refer to these shops: confectionery, tobacconist, and newsagent (CTN).

20. The class that by far exceeds the others in percentage is grocers' shops—about 28,000.

21. The publishing companies are Axel Springer Verlag A.G., Heinrich Bauer Verlag, Gruner, and Jahr and Burda.

22. The NMPPs rely on a centralized electronic data processing service, which enables them to reduce considerably the time required for conveying the goods, counting the copies returned, crediting sales, and sending unsold goods for pulping.

23. During the last few years, many British publishers have launched prize games for their readers (bingo, lotto). As the prizes are sometimes very rich, these policies have succeeded in increasing circulation considerably.

24. In Italy, a 20 percent average discount is granted, although the agreement between the publishers and the newsagents does not set a ceiling on the reductions granted to subscribers.

References

Alderson, W. 1965. *Dynamic Marketing Behavior*. Homewood, Ill.: Irwin.

Boone, L. 1973. *Marketing Channels*. New York: General Learning Press.

Bucklin, L.P. 1967. "The Economic Structure of Channels of Distribution." In B.E. Mallen (ed.), *The Marketing Channel*. New York: Wiley.

CESCOM. 1985. *La distribuzione della stampa in Italia*. Rome: Editorial Statistics.

Cunningham, M. 1973. "Innovation in Sales and Distribution Systems." In *Proceedings*, 11th Marketing Theory Seminar, Strathclyde, Scotland.

Davidson, W. 1967. "Distribution Breakthroughs." In L. Adler (ed.), *Plotting Marketing Strategy: A New Orientation*. London: Business Books.

Dommermuth, W., and Andersen, R. 1969. "Distribution Systems, Firms, Functions and Efficiencies." MSU *Business Topics* (Spring):51–56.

Gattorna, J. 1978. "Channels of Distribution. Conceptualizations: A State of the Art Review." *European Journal of Marketing* 7 12 (7):470–512.

Kotler, P. 1976. *Marketing Management*. Englewood Cliffs, N.J.: Prentice Hall. 1967, 3r edizione italiana, ISEDI.

Little, R. 1968. *Power and Leadership in Marketing Channels*. Denver: American Marketing Association.

Lugli, G. 1976. *Economia della distribuzione commerciale*, Milan: Guiffre.

McCarthy, E.J. 1957. *Basic Marketing: A Managerial Approach*. Homewood, Ill.: Irwin.

Mallen, B.E. 1972. "Conflict and Cooperation in Marketing Channels." In L.E. Boone (ed.), *Management Perspectives in Marketing*. Encino, Calif.: Dickenson Publishing.

Moyer, R. 1971. "A Bargaining Theory of Price." *European Journal of Marketing* 5 (5):161–167.

Rosenberg, L., and Stern, L.W., 1971. "Conflict Measurement in the Distribution Channel," *Journal of Marketing Research* 8(Nov.):437–442.

Schulz, R. 1971. "Laboratory Study of Power Base. Conflict Relationships as Applicable to Distribution Channels." Columbus: Ohio State University.

Stern, L. 1972. "Communicating with Resellers." Columbus: Ohio State University, College of Administrative Science.

U.N. Statistical Yearbook 1979–1980. New York: United Nations, 1981.

8
Counterfeiting—A Worldwide Problem: What Is the Role of Channel Members?

Gary J. Bamossy
Debra L. Scammon

I f imitation is indeed the highest form of flattery, then hundreds of multinational firms representing a broad range of industries and products have much to be flattered about. Conservative estimates of the commercial counterfeiting of consumer and industrial products suggest that the activity is a worldwide phenomenon, with hundreds of millions of dollars in sales revenues being diverted annually through the manufacturing and trafficking of counterfeit goods.

The impacts of counterfeiting are both tangible and intangible. Counterfeiting affects both individual firms and society, and injuries resulting from counterfeiting befall both the corporation whose goods are counterfeited and the consumer who unknowingly purchases counterfeit products. Tangible impacts include the revenues lost by the trademark owner to the counterfeiting manufacturer; intangible impacts include the loss of goodwill and consumer confidence. These microeconomic effects are magnified when lost revenues are translated into lost jobs and dissatisfaction is translated into negative attitudes toward business in general. Indirectly, consumers pay the costs of counterfeiting through higher prices necessitated by corporate expenditures on trademark protection. More directly, they also pay in the form of dissatisfaction with counterfeit products, personal injury from faulty counterfeit products, and confusion regarding avenues for redress.

There is an abundant literature focusing on the legal aspects of counterfeiting (such as trademark and copyright infringement), and the popular press regularly reports incidences of counterfeiting in the marketplace. However, there is considerably less literature reviewing the activity within the channels of distribution through which bogus products reach the marketplace. The empirical studies that have been published are descriptive, focusing either on manufacturer or industry surveys (Kaikati and LaGrace, 1980; U.S.I.T.C., 1984) or on consumer issues (Bamossy and Scammon, 1984). Apart from a few references in testimony before various government agencies as part of lobbying efforts by industries interested in tightening import controls on counterfeit goods, the role that channel members play in the facilitation of or protection from counterfeiting has basically been ignored.

The purposes of this chapter are, first, to define the practices generally included as counterfeiting as well as other similar unfair business practices. Second, we identify and discuss the varied environmental factors that allow the practice of product counterfeiting to thrive in both the United States and world markets. This discussion reviews the political, technological, and economic developments of the past three decades that have strongly influenced counterfeiting activities. Third, the chapter provides a review of the key legislation that has been proposed to combat product counterfeiting. The basic intent and potential impacts of the legislation are reviewed within the United States (the world's most lucrative market for counterfeit goods) and at the multinational level.

Finally, we present implications for channel members of proposed legislative reforms as well as current marketing practices to curtail counterfeiting. The costs and benefits of various actions are examined as they might accrue to various channel members. The chapter concludes by presenting a framework for systematically researching product counterfeiting, with some specific proposals for channels research at the international and national level.

The Scope of Counterfeiting and Why It Thrives

The two most outstanding characteristics of counterfeiting today are its overwhelming financial significance and the international scope of the problem. It has been conservatively estimated that $6 billion to $8 billion of domestic and export sales were lost by U.S. industry as a result of foreign product counterfeiting and copyright or patent infringement of products during 1982 (U.S.I.T.C., 1984). The clothing, recording, and transportation industries report the most severe losses, although counterfeiting and related activities are pervasive across a wide array of consumer and industrial industries.

Counterfeiting and Related Activities

Manufacturers and their distributors often have differences of opinion regarding what activities should be covered by the term *counterfeit product*. A strict definition includes only goods bearing an authorized representation of a trademark that is legally registered for such goods in the country of importation or sale. This definition does not include goods produced or marketed under a protected trademark by the owner of the trademark right or with the owner's consent, nor goods bearing an authorized trademark that are imported or sold in contravention of a commercial arrangement. Manufacturers object to the exclusion of these unfair trade practices from the definition because sales of their products may be severely affected by such practices. Manufacturers would also include "gray market sales" and "passing off" within the definition.

"Gray market sales"—sometimes referred to as diverted goods, parallel sales, or unauthorized sales—are a big problem for some manufacturers. The term refers to goods bearing an authorized trademark that are sold in contravention of a commercial arrangement. Such sales can occur through the legal *production* by a licensee of goods that are then *sold* in markets restricted by the licensing agreement. They can also occur through deliberate unreported overproduction by a licensee that is sold without the knowledge of the trademark holder.

"Passing off"—which includes the use of a similar, but not identical, trademark on a substantially similar product and the use of similar or identical packaging without the trademark—is a problem for some manufacturers. Other unfair practices include copyright infringement, patent infringement, and the unauthorized use of a trademark on a substantially nonsimilar product.

It is difficult to estimate the magnitude of lost sales resulting from these practices. Naturally, estimates of the extent of the problem of counterfeiting are influenced by the breadth of the definition adopted. Most manufacturers make no distinction between outright counterfeit goods and gray market sales when estimating lost revenues. The incidence of these practices varies by industry, however. For example, counterfeiting is a more significant problem for U.S. producers of apparel and footwear than other similar unfair trade practices. However, passing off and patent infringement are important for automobile parts and accessories, drugs and pharmaceuticals, agricultural chemicals, and cosmetics and toiletries. Piracy or copyright infringement is significant for records and tapes, video games, and computer software, as are gray market sales (see table 8–1).

Manufacturers view gray market sales as a significant portion of their losses. Industry efforts to combat foreign counterfeiting increased during 1980–82 from $4.1 million to $12.1 million. During the same period, an *additional* $5.6 million in identification and enforcement costs were expended to combat gray market sales (U.S.I.T.C., 1984).

Counterfeiting has spread into a variety of industries, and the incidence of counterfeiting has increased over the past few years. For U.S. producers, the biggest increases have been in foreign markets and with chemicals, transportation equipment, parts, and accessories, and machinery and electrical products. The industry that has experienced the greatest increase in incidence of counterfeiting in the U.S. market has been tapes and records (see table 8–2).

Market Factors Conducive to Counterfeiting

The worldwide appeal of brand name merchandise means that counterfeiting can exploit brand names, regardless of their national origin, in domestic as well

Table 8–1
Reports of Unfair Trade Practices by Various Industry Sectors

Industry Sector	Gray Market Sales	Trade Dress/ Passing Off	Patent Infringement	Copyright Infringement	Counterfeit Products
Wearing apparel and footwear	6	14	2	5	31
Chemicals and related products	8	18	6	0	25
Transportation equipment, parts, and accessories	3	9	7	4	28
Metal, machinery, and electrical products	3	15	4	3	18
Records and tapes	5	1	1	6	13
Sporting goods	5	3	3	2	10
Miscellaneous manufacturers	6	17	7	9	48

Source: Adapted from United States International Trade Commission, "The Effects of Foreign Product Counterfeiting on U.S. Industry," U.S.I.T.C. Publication 1479, Washington, D.C., 1984, pp. xi and xii.

Note: Entries represent the number of product items reported to be facing competition from sellers using various unfair practices in a survey of U.S. firms conducted by the U.S.I.T.C.

as export markets. Although the United States is the largest single market for foreign counterfeits of U.S. products, the market for counterfeit goods is by no means restricted to the United States. The counterfeiter typically reaps substantial profits with minimal investment in marketing, since the legitimate trademark holder has already undertaken significant marketing effort. Traditionally, the goods most often targeted by counterfeiters have been consumer goods with strong brand name identification and high-priced markups based on these brand names. An examination of the existing conditions in countries that are active *sources* of counterfeit products and in those that are thriving *markets* for counterfeit products suggests some important common characteristics. A country's general level of affluence helps explain the existence of key markets for counterfeit goods. However, some countries, such as Japan and West Germany, have high levels of general affluence and yet are relatively minor markets for counterfeit goods, and other countries with relatively low levels of general affluence serve as both key sources of and markets for counterfeits. Many of these countries are characterized by dualistic economies in which much of the country's wealth and power is concentrated in a small portion of the population. There is typically a burgeoning merchant class that operates highly fragmented channels of distribution, some of which cater exclusively to the tourist segment (for example, Brazil).

The factors common to countries that are primary sources of counterfeits also relate to their economic makeup. Dualistic economies often have a large segment of the population providing cheap semiskilled labor. The production of such goods as fashion apparel and jewelry and watches tends to be labor-

Table 8–2

Reports of Product Counterfeiting in the United States and Abroad by Various Industry Sectors

Industry Sector	U.S. Market		Foreign Markets	
	1980	1982	1980	1982
Wearing apparel and footwear	13	14	16	17
Chemicals and related products	0	0	14	25
Transporation equipment, parts, and accessories	7	10	11	18
Metal, machinery, and electrical products	2	5	8	13
Records and tapes	4	8	5	5
Sporting goods	2	4	4	6
Miscellaneous manufacturers	22	26	16	22

Source: Adapted from United States International Trade Commission, "The Effects of Foreign Product Counterfeiting on U.S. Industry," U.S.I.T.C. Publication 1479, Washington, D.C., 1984, p. xi.

Note: Entries represent the number of product items reported to be experiencing competition from counterfeit products in a survey of U.S. firms conducted by the U.S.I.T.C.

intensive, and many of the newly industrialized countries that are key sources of these counterfeit goods (Taiwan, South Korea, Singapore, Hong Kong) have cheap and abundant sources of labor.

Another necessary ingredient is technological know-how. The use of very standardized technology in the production of products such as records and tapes of popular artists makes entrance into the market relatively inexpensive. The manufacturing sector can produce credible counterfeit labels and products, providing an important source of foreign exchange for many newly industrialized countries.

In addition to the development of highly modern and competitive industrial infrastructures in many developing countries, the rapid diffusion of technological innovation has allowed counterfeiting to move not only into the manufacturing of capital-intensive goods, such as automobile parts, but also into the high-tech arena of computer hardware and software. The firms in such industries are plagued with the problem of protecting newly developed technology at least long enough to recoup the research and development costs required to bring products that utilize the technology to the market. Innovative entrepreneurs can sidestep the original research and development costs and, for a small fraction of the cost, can flood the market with cheap (but often reliable) imitations and undersell the trademark owner. Although estimates of the monetary impact of this "new level" of counterfeiting activity are not yet available, the popular press regularly reports on counterfeit chips and counterfeit brand name personal computers ("Apple Counterattacks," 1982; Chase, 1982; Inman, 1984).

The Role of Channel Members

Counterfeit goods are present in almost all markets, yet the channels through which they reach the market appear to differ around the world. In less developed countries, where channels of distribution are highly fragmented, the trafficking of counterfeit goods appears to be even more commonplace than in developed countries. Wholesalers and distributor/dealers play a key role in both U.S. and foreign markets in supplying the counterfeit products to channel members closer to the final consumer. They sell countefeit products to traditional retailers, such as department stores, discount stores, and small businesses, and to nontraditional retailers, such as street vendors and flea markets. In the U.S. market, manufacturers most often point to discount stores as retailers of counterfeit products. These discount retailers, in turn, cite street vendors and flea markets as the main channels of distribution. In foreign markets, street vendors are most commonly cited, followed by small, independently owned retail outlets (U.S.I.T.C., 1984).

The Legal Environment

There are currently no international agreements to which the United States is a party that treat counterfeiting *specifically,* although a number of agreements do relate to counterfeiting. Chief among these agreements is the Paris Convention on Industrial Property, which allows signatory nations the same protection and legal remedies against infringements of their trademarks as nationals of the country in question. There are some existing laws in the United States as well as some proposals for reform that deal with the problem of counterfeiting. The environment in foreign countries is very diverse, and international agreement on how to proceed against counterfeiters appears slow in coming.

The U.S. Market

Within the United States, the Lanham Act is the principal federal statute relating to counterfeiting. The act provides for civil remedies for trademark infringement and counterfeiting through the federal court system. There are currently no criminal penalties for counterfeiting, a condition that makes counterfeiting a low-risk proposition, particularly when compared to the potential for profits. The current versions of the proposed Trademark Counterfeiting Act would amend the Lanham Act to provide criminal penalties for counterfeiting and enhance the civil relief available. The Senate bill (S. 875), passed on June 28, 1984, establishes criminal penalties of up to five years in prison and fines of up to $250,000 for individuals found guilty of intentionally trafficking in counterfeit goods. In addition to the increased relief from injury provided by S. 875, a proposed House of Representatives bill (H.R. 5929) would give the Federal Trade Commission authority to seek court orders providing for seizure and/or detention of counterfeit goods and would amend the FTC act to make trafficking in counterfeit goods and services an unfair act or practice and an unfair method of competition. The intent of the proposed legislation is to provide stiffer civil penalties (trademark owners could sue for up to treble damages in federal courts) and to introduce criminal penalties for counterfeiters.

Foreign Markets

While U.S. laws are evolving toward stiffer civil and criminal penalties, foreign laws relating to counterfeiting vary with regard to their breadth of coverage and their penalties for violation and therefore with regard to their effectiveness and usefulness. As a practical matter, many developing countries simply do not have specific laws that address product counterfeiting. Those countries that do have anticounterfeiting statutes typically have nominal penalties for violations and very lax attitudes regarding enforcement.

Proposed International Anticounterfeiting Legislation

Because of the tremendous explosion of international counterfeiting activity during the early 1970s, the first large-scale discussions of an anticounterfeiting code took place at the 1973 General Agreement on Tariffs and Trade (GATT) negotiations. Drafts of the code remained on the agenda over the next six years, but the agreements signed by the Tokyo Round negotiators in April 1979 did not include an anticounterfeiting code. The proposed code is still under the auspices of the GATT secretariat. Its basic purpose is to specifically discourage international trade in counterfeit goods, and its adoption would result in greater standardization of laws relating to counterfeiting.

As with many of the negotiated issues in the Tokyo Round, there are differences in perspectives and goals between the developed countries and the developing countries. To date, the developing countries (in which intellectual and industrial property rights are typically not well protected) have prevented adoption of the code. Those countries base their opposition to stronger laws on several arguments: (1) more protection of patents and trademarks would allow multinational firms to keep their technology confidential and monopolize world markets with their exports; (2) stronger protection would mainly serve to increase multinational firms' profits, at the expense of small, local companies; (3) tougher laws would cut into domestic and overseas markets of local producers; and (4) it is immoral to impose restrictions on production and marketing of certain chemicals and drugs that fight human suffering ("Chemical Firm Seeks Technology Protection," 1982).

Developed countries argue for adoption of the code for two basic reasons. First, they suggest that the failure of nations to protect products sufficiently discourages foreign suppliers from introducing new technology in these countries and from transferring it to domestic producers. This argument emphasizes that patents serve to stimulate economic development by providing incentives for innovation within a country and for importation of technology to a country. Second, developed countries argue that by limiting or ignoring trademark protection, the nonparticipating nations undermine the trademark's function of ensuring product quality and reliability—an outcome that is detrimental to all parties ("Chemical Firm Seeks Technology Protection," 1982).

Multilateral negotiation within the GATT framework is a painstakingly slow and cumbersome process, and the adoption of an international anticounterfeiting code is not likely to occur in the near future. In the meanwhile, the United States, Japan, Canada, and the European Community may soon agree to open the code to bilateral adoption in order to overcome the political problems presented by developing countries' opposition to the code. In addition, individual countries are beginning attempts to apply political pressure on nonsignatory nations. For example, a bill currently before the U.S. House of Representatives (H.R. 2447) would deny duty-free trade benefits under the Generalized System of Preferences (GSP) to those developing countries that do not provide adequate protection and enforcement of intellectual and industrial property rights of U.S. firms. Passage of this bill may prove persuasive, as approximately 70 percent of all GSP imports in 1983 came from Taiwan, South Korea, Hong Kong, Mexico, Brazil, and Singapore—countries that have historically provided minimal or no protection for trademarks or property rights (U.S.I.T.C., 1984).

Implications for Channels Members

Legislation at the multinational level will likely continue to be slow in evolving and consequently will continue to have little direct impact on channels of distribution activities. Within the United States, however, pending anticounterfeiting legislation (S.875 and H.R. 2447) will have implications both for channel members inside the United States and for channel members that import to the United States. For the immediate future, practical efforts to deter manufacture and trafficking of counterfeit goods will continue to come from private industry—in the form of covert "sting" operations, legal injunctions wherever possible, and the use of counterfeit-detection techniques such as light beam marked labels, microscopic identity parts, or holograms—and from cooperative efforts between manufacturers and members of their channels of distribution. Both the proposed legal changes and many of the manufacturer-imposed anticounterfeiting activities will place burdens on the various members of the channels of distribution. Both also carry risks and benefits for the manufacturer or trademark owner.

Retailers

The proposed bills before the U.S. Congress would place a good deal of responsiblity for the policing of counterfeiting activities on retailers. Some lobbyists claim that the bills provide for unnecessary search and seizure raids, treble damages, and criminal penalties against retailers—actions that they believe are too harsh and are directed toward the wrong target. Retailers argue that bills placing liability on them for selling counterfeit goods are inequitable, especially since the bills do not distinguish between intentional and unintentional possession or sale of countefeit merchandise or between true counterfeits and gray market sales (U.S.I.T.C., 1984, p. 64).

Even if such provisions in the laws are modified, retailers are apt to find, more and more, that their purchase contracts with manufacturers place responsiblity for detection of counterfeits on them. Retailers should develop strategies for ensuring that counterfeits do not enter their product lines. In the event that they are "caught" with counterfeit merchandise, retailers should consider strategies for proving that the products were acquired unintentionally or unknowingly. Some suggested actions include:

1. Be sure that buyers are well trained, have adequate product knowledge, and are educated about trademarks. Always require written trademark releases and warrants from suppliers stating that their title to the merchandise is good and that there is no infringement of trademark or licensing agremeents.

2. Research new vendors to be sure they are reputable. Otherwise, deal with known suppliers or legitimate goods.

3. Use "competitive shoppers" to detect counterfeits being sold by discounters for much lower prices. If detected, report counterfeiting dealers to the trademark owner.

4. Watch inventory movements closely to be sure that items with expected high turnover are in fact selling up to expectation. When expectations are not met, report shotfall to the trademark owner.

Manufacturers

Manufacturers generally support stronger anticounterfeiting legislation. Stricter civil and criminal penalties, increased surveillance by customs authorities, seizure of counterfeits at points of importation, and financial support to track down counterfeiters are all considered imperative for the control of counterfeiting. In addition to utilizing the protection afforded by registering their trademarks with U.S. and foreign customs authorities, manufacturers use a variety of other methods to curb the problem of counterfeiting. Many manufacturers build in anticounterfeiting devices (usually in labeling); rely on their sales force, distributors, and licensees to monitor counterfeiting in the field; and sponsor campaigns to raise consumer awareness of counterfeiting.

Manufacturers sometimes require that resellers report sales of counterfeit goods by other dealers (wholesalers or retailers). One potentially significant risk to both manufacturer and resellers in such a system is the possibility of an antitrust violation. Whenever manufacturers and their middlemen "conspire" with one another to the disadvantage of someone not included in the conspiracy, such a possibility exists. Generally, however, if the purpose of such a conspiracy is to deal with the problem of some unlawful business practice, such as counterfeiting, the joint action will not be considered a violation.

To control the distribution of their products more tightly, manufacturers can impose restrictions on their wholesalers and retailers in terms of customers, sources of supply, and prices. For example, a manufacturer might require that its wholesalers not sell to discount retailers, that its retailers buy only from authorized dealers, or that its middlemen keep prices above some manufacturer-suggested minimum. Although these restrictions may benefit the manufacturer, they impose costs on the middlemen. A wholesaler that is required not to sell to discounters must know a good deal about the modus operandi of its potential customers to avoid dealing with a discounter. This requires research, which is expensive in terms of both time and money. A retailer that is required to purchase only from authorized dealers may thereby guarantee itself acquisition of authentic products but may forgo price savings available from a "bootlegger" selling authentic products obtained from, for example, a foreign licensee selling in that particular market in violation of its licensing agreement. Middlemen that are asked to maintain their prices on authentic goods facing competition from counterfeits may discover that the manufacturer-suggested price is merely a means for the trademark owner to control supply in the market. Retailers may argue that this amounts to vertical price fixing on the part of the manufacturer.

In the United States and in many foreign markets, such restrictions carry with them the suspicion of potential antitrust violations. United States law currently applies the "rule of reason" when examining most manufacturer-imposed restraints on trade (with the possible exception of resale price maintenance). This implies that such restrictions may be found perfectly acceptable if they are fostered by a legitimate business purpose and do not have adverse net impacts on interbrand and intrabrand competition. Thus, manufacturers that choose tight controls on members of their channels of distribution as a means of combating counterfeiting must be sure to spell out their rationale in detail in a marketing plan, must be sure that the requirements imposed are the least restrictive alternatives available, and must demonstrate that "legitimate" competition will not be adversely affected thereby (Scammon and Sheffet, 1986).

Franchising is one method that offers an opportunity for tighter controls by trademark owners. In most franchise systems, the trademark is the most valuable asset, and its ownership is retained by the franchisor. Franchisees are often closely tied to their franchisors for supplies, merchandise, and operating advice. If they don't buy products directly from the franchisor, they usually buy from other franchisor-approved vendors. The franchisor-franchisee relationship is closer than that between most manufacturers and retailers. The franchisees know their products and are not easily fooled by bogus products. Thus, it is harder for counterfeiters to introduce their products into a franchise distribution system.

A potential problem with franchising that may increase as franchisors move more into foreign markets is the fraudulent registration of a franchisor's trademark by an unscrupulous individual before the legitimate trademark owner is able to do so. In many cases, the individual abroad who beats the legitimate trademark owner to registration has no plans to produce the product but simply seeks to strike some kind of deal with the legitimate owner. To combat this problem, franchisors may want to register their trademarks not only in the countries where they are currently doing business but also in countries where future expansion is contemplated.

Research Questions

In deciding what methods to adopt to combat counterfeiting, legislators, manufacturers, and middlemen (especially nondiscounting retailers) will need to answer several questions. The costs and benefits to society, manufacturers, and resellers of various alternatives must be compared. Some of the following questions of impact could be answered through research.

Effects on Manufacturers

The costs and benefits to the manufacturer of various methods for dealing with the problems of counterfeiting should be evaluated. For example, simple registration of a trademark with a country's customs authority is probably less definitive proof of ownership than packaging or labeling with a detection device, such as glass particles. In addition, once the production process has been established to include the anticounterfeiting device, manufacturing costs may not be significantly higher for the "protected" product. However, for a firm selling in multiple countries and considering expansion to even more, the cost of trademark registration may be quite high. Information could be compiled to estimate the costs associated with trademark registration and packaging changes. Effectiveness could also be monitored.

As another example, the cost to the manufacturer of sponsoring an advertising campaign designed to stimulate consumer awareness of the problem of counterfeiting and to build demand for authentic trademarked products may be too high for one manufacturer to consider. However, if several manufacturers use cooperative advertising or a trade association representing many manufacturers pays for the campaign, it might be affordable. Although such a campaign *might* have a positive impact on the desirability of trademarked products, it might also raise doubts in the minds of consumers, leading to decreased confidence, increased skepticism, and increased returns of unsatisfactory merchandise. These negative impacts may be felt more by retailers than by manufacturers, thus leading to disrupted relationships within the channel of distribution. These impacts could be assessed through survey research prior to initiation of an ad campaign or through monitoring of consumers' attitudes and behavior following a campaign.

Effects on Channel Members

When soliciting the help of retailers and wholesalers in tracking down the sources of counterfeit products, manufacturers must consider the advantages and risks to middlemen in helping them police counterfeiting activity. Manufacturers may want to consider ways to increase the incentives for their middlemen to cooperate with efforts to combat counterfeiting. For example, manufacturers may sponsor advertising campaigns that list all of their authorized dealers in each market area. They might also provide promotional materials to resellers that will identify them to consumers as authorized dealers. In exchange for their assistance in curtailing counterfeiting, middlemen may bargain for exclusive distribution rights within their markets. Such selective distribution may be in the manufacturers' best interests if they are stressing to consumers the need to shop only at reputable stores. Consumer prices and retailer and brand reputation could be determined within various types of channel networks (that is, selective versus intensive distribution) to help predict the impact of various channel decisions.

Anticounterfeiting measures by marketers may increase concentration in distribution. By relying on the product knowledge of their retailers to help keep counterfeits out of the channel of distribution, manufacturers may make it more difficult for legitimate businesses to succeed by increasing barriers to entry by new channel members. Trademark owners that refuse to deal with any but the most reputable retailers may be cutting out smaller or newer retailers that have not yet proved their abilities or their desires to help detect counterfeits. These costs to society should be balanced against the advantages, one of which is likely to be the elimination of channel members that seek out accounts with manufacturers to receive literature and other forms of promotional support, then use these "signs of legitimacy" while also buying and selling counterfeits of those manufacturers' products. Of course, these tradeoffs are not easy to make, nor is there likely to be total agreement on the optimal outcome.

A Framework for Researching Counterfeiting Activities

The development of effective legislation and strategies for dealing with counterfeiting depends largely on improving our understanding of how counterfeit products get into the hands of consumers. Figure 8–1 illustrates the distribution of counterfeit and gray market goods. It can serve as a framework for systematically researching counterfeiting activities within channels of distribution and for predicting the impacts of various proposed solutions to the problems.

Depending on the product category, the lengths of the channels of distribution, and the number of sources for obtaining counterfeit goods, reputable channel members can unknowingly receive counterfeit goods from a variety of suppliers. Figure 8–1 depicts a direct link from the counterfeiter as well as an indirect route from the counterfeiter via other wholesalers. In addition, genuine goods that are, in fact, gray market goods can be distributed to authorized channel members, either directly or via a middleman. Although most authorized channel members do not knowingly carry counterfeit goods, there is clearly a potential for consumers to unknowingly purchase a counterfeit from a reputable channel member. Presumably, such an outcome would be less likely to occur to a customer who patronizes a franchise store.

There are also "unauthorized" channel members who intentionally buy, distribute, and sell counterfeit goods. Here, it seems that channels are likely to be shorter and less formal than authorized channels. Counterfeiting through these unauthorized dealers appears to be more prevalent in underdeveloped countries, where channels of distribution tend to be highly fragmented. With unauthorized dealers handling counterfeit products, there is the possibility that consumers will purchase bogus goods either *unknowingly* or *knowingly*.

This framework provides a structure for examining the pertinent questions of impact and effectiveness raised both by proposed legislative changes and by common marketing practices. The solutions to the problem of counterfeiting should become clearer through investigation of issues discussed in this chapter. Only through understanding counterfeiting as it is perpetrated can effective preventive methods be developed.

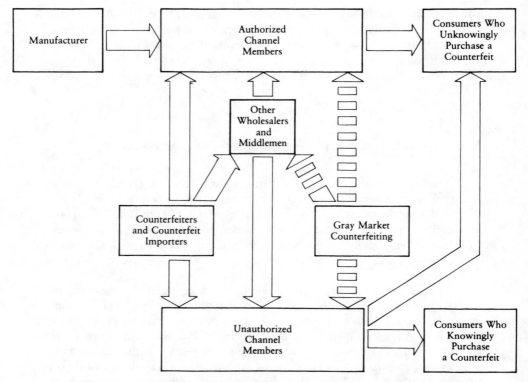

Figure 8–1. Distribution of Counterfeit and Gray Market Goods

References

"Apple Counterattacks the Counterfeiters." *Business Week*, 16 August 1982, p. 82.

Bamossy, G., and Scammon, D.L. (1984). "Product Counterfeiting: Consumer and Manufacturer Beware." In M.B. Holbrook and E.C. Hirschman (eds.), *Advances in Consumer Research*, Vol. XIII. Ann Arbor, Mich.: Association for Consumer Research.

Chase, M. (1982). "Apple Computer Says Small Asian Firms Are Producing Counterfeit Apply II Models." *Wall Street Journal*, March 17, p. 8.

"Chemical Firm Seeks Technology Protection for Licensing in Asia." *Business Asia*, 1982, pp. 121–22.

Inman, Virginia (1984). "Fake Apple Computers Were Smuggled from Taiwan, U.S. Grand Jury Charges." *Wall Street Journal*, February 10, p. 11.

Kaikati, J., and LaGrace, R. (1980). "Beware of International Brand Piracy." *Harvard Business Review*, March–April, p. 52.

Scammon, D.L., and Sheffet, M.J. (1986). "Legal Questions in Channels Modification Decisions." *Journal of Public Policy and Marketing* (forthcoming).

United States International Trade Commission. (1984). "The Effects of Foreign Product Counterfeiting on U.S. Industry." U.S.I.T.C. Publications 1479, Washington, D.C.

Part III
Location Strategy
and Forecasting Demand

9
Shopping Behavior and Optimal Store Locations in Multipurpose Trip Environments

Avijit Ghosh
Sara McLafferty

T he locational plan for store outlets is an important component of successful retail strategies. Location is one of the key determinants of the attractiveness of stores and their long-term profitability. Evaluating and modeling the profitability of retail locations requires an understanding of consumer spatial behavior and its relationship to the spatial organization of firms. These subjects have attracted considerable attention from researchers in a number of disciplines (for a review, see Craig, Ghosh, and McLafferty 1984).

Although retail location models have become increasingly refined and sophisticated (see, for example, Coehlo and Wilson 1976; Jain and Mahajan 1979; Achabal, Gorr, and Mahajan 1982; Ghosh and McLafferty 1982; Ghosh and Craig 1983), they all assume that consumers make only single-purpose shopping trips from a fixed origin. A number of empirical studies (Shepard and Thomas 1980; MacKay 1972; Hanson 1980; O'Kelly 1981), however, have drawn attention to the phenomenon of multipurpose shopping. In multipurpose shopping, consumers bypass their closest store and visit more distant ones in order to buy two or more goods on a single trip. Multipurpose shopping trips represent a rational behavior pattern that reduces the time and cost of shopping (Bacon 1983; Ghosh and McLafferty 1984). One consequence of multipurpose shopping is that store choice decisions will be affected by the presence of neighboring establishments (MacKay 1972). The overall attractiveness of a site is determined not only by its accessibility to travel origins but also by the relative location of other shopping opportunities. In spite of the growing evidence on multipurpose trips, however, only a few studies have attempted to incorporate such behavior in optimal location models (see, for example, McLafferty 1982; O'Kelly 1981).

The purpose of this chapter is to investigate the impact of multipurpose shopping on the spatial organization of retail stores and to present a location allocation model for determining optimal retail locations in the presence of multipurpose shopping. The chapter is organized in two parts. First, we present a model of consumer shopping behavior that determines for each consumer the optimal travel pattern, given the spatial organization of shopping opportunities. In the second part of the chapter, the individual shopping model is used to study the impact of multipurpose trips on the level of competition among stores, and a location allocation model is developed to determine the best locations for new stores.

The Optimal Frequency of Shopping Trips

Underlying any model of retail location are assumptions regarding the spatial behavior of consumers. The optimal location pattern selected by a model is determined by the nature of these assumptions. Existing models of retail location start with the assumption that consumers make only single-purpose trips and that the frequency of trips is independent of the consumer's location in relation to shopping opportunities. Central place models (Christaller 1966; Losch 1954), for example, assume that consumers make a fixed number of single-purpose trips to the nearest available shopping outlet. Although location procedures based on the Huff (1962) model or the multiplicative competitive interaction (MCI) model (Nakanishi and Cooper 1974) allow for visits to more than one store, they, too, consider single-purpose trips only. As noted earlier, such assumptions are empirically unsatisfactory, since a large number of shopping trips are multipurpose trips. A number of studies (Eaton and Lipsey 1982; Mulligan 1983; Kohsaka 1984; McLafferty and Ghosh 1984) have shown that the presence of multipurpose trips may result in a spatial organization of firms that is different from that proposed by classic central place theories. Consequently, it is unsatisfactory from both theoretical and empirical perspectives to compute optimal retail locations without regard for multipurpose trips.

The advantage of incorporating multipurpose trips in retail location models is that it integrates the spatial and temporal aspects of shopping. As Curry (1967) notes: "It is evident in the shopping problem that activities operating in the time domain such as inventory management must have spatial implications" (p. 222). Most researchers, however, have devoted more attention to the spatial aspects of shopping while ignoring the temporal dimension. Only by considering both aspects simultaneously is it possible to fully understand consumer shopping behavior.

A Consumer Shopping Model

To achieve this goal, we propose a model of shopping behavior that determines the optimal frequencies of single-purpose and multipurpose trips for each consumer, based on the assumption that consumers minimize total shopping cost. The model explicitly considers three components of consumer shopping cost: (1) cost of travel; (2) cost of the goods to be purchased; and (3) cost of holding inventory. Together, these costs determine the frequency of shopping trips and the spatial pattern of trips. Although the effect of transport cost on consumer travel is well recognized, inventory costs also influence consumer shopping decisions (Reinhardt 1973; Lentnek, Harwitz, and Narula 1981; Bacon 1983). Inventory costs arise because of the opportunity cost of holding physical inventory and the cost of physical storage. The risks of perishability and spoilage also increase with the size of the inventory and impose an additional cost on the consumer. Although the different components of inventory costs can be identified separately, we use the term *inventory cost* to refer to all costs associated with storing goods.

For expositional clarity, we present our model in terms of a two-level retail hierarchy. The extension to retail systems with more than two levels should be apparent to the reader. Consider a consumer who purchases two goods j and k. We refer to good j, which is more widely available, as the low-order good and to k as a high-order good. During a given planning horizon, the consumer demands D_j units of good j and D_k units of good k. Let t_j be the cost of travel to the nearest source for good j and t_k the cost of travel to the nearest source for good k. The unit price of good j is P_j and that of good k is P_k.

Each good is consumed at a constant rate through time, and there are no random fluctuations in consumption rates. The cost of holding inventory, $I\{.\}$, is a function of the average level of stock held by the consumer. The consumer shopping model can then be written as

$$
\begin{aligned}
\text{Min } TC = \; & N_j T_j + I\{(1 - \alpha)(D_j/2N_j)P_j\}(1 - \alpha) \\
& + N_k T_k + I\{\alpha(D_j/2N_k)P_j\}\alpha + P_j D_j \\
& + I\{(D_k/2N_k)P_k\} + P_k D_k
\end{aligned}
$$

$$
\text{Subject to } N_j = mN_k \tag{9.1}
$$

where N_j and N_k are the number of trips made to place j and k, respectively, α $(0 \leq \alpha \leq 1)$ is the amount of good j bought on multipurpose trips to place k, and m is a nonnegative integer. The constraint that N_j be an integer multiple of N_k follows from the assumption of constant depletion rate and is necessary to ensure that purchases of the two goods on multipurpose trips coincide in time (see also Bacon 1983; Eaton and Lipsey 1982; McLafferty 1982).

To illustrate the implications of the model, consider the example shown in table 9–1. Two columns in the table show the optimal number of trips, level of costs, and the value of α from the shopping model for two different scenarios. The next two columns give the corresponding values when only

Table 9–1
Trip Frequencies and Shopping Costs with and without Multipurpose Trips

	Single-Purpose and Multipurpose Trips		Single-Purpose Trips Only	
	$T_k = 40$	$T_k = 20$	$T_k = 40$	$T_k = 20$
N_j	6.90	6.82	9.13	9.13
N_k	2.30	3.42	2.23	3.16
α	.25	.33	0	0
Travel cost	112.70	88.86	116.58	90.58
Storage cost	114.12	82.89	117.07	90.68
Total travel and storage cost	226.82	171.75	233.65	181.26

Note: Simulation results are based on the following assumptions: $D_j = 200$, $D_k = 40$, $P_j = 10$, $P_k = 40$, $T_j = 3$. The cost of storing inventory is 25 percent of the cost of the good.

single-purpose trips are allowed. As is obvious in the table, the total travel and storage costs are always less in the multipurpose shopping case than in the single-purpose case. When multipurpose trips are permitted, consumers can reduce their travel costs, and thus their shopping costs, by purchasing a portion of the low-order good in conjunction with the high-order good. So long as the mill price of good j at place k is less than the delivered price at place j, there is incentive for a rational consumer to engage in multipurpose shopping (Mulligan 1983). The optimal rate of multipurpose shopping depends on the relative demands for the two goods, their prices, storage cost, and the cost of transportation (Ghosh and McLafferty 1984).

Table 9–1 also shows how the optimal travel pattern and shopping frequency vary with changes in travel costs. When the cost of travel to place k falls from 40 to 20, ceteris paribus, the number of trips to place k increases from 2.3 to 3.4. The increased number of trips to the high-order place provides more opportunity for multipurpose travel and increases the value of α to .333 from .25. The implication is that the optimal shopping pattern and propensity for multipurpose shopping are spatially nonstationary and unique for each consumer. The values of N_j, N_k, and α all depend on the consumer's location relative to shopping opportunities. This finding is in sharp contrast to findings in a number of previous studies of multipurpose shopping (Mulligan 1983, 1984), which assume an exogenously determined, constant rate of multipurpose shopping for all consumers.

Determining Optimal Retail Locations

In this section, we present a location allocation model that uses the consumer shopping model to determine the optimal location pattern of retail outlets in a multipurpose trip environment. Location allocation models have been widely used in retailing (see, for example, Huff 1966; Coehlo and Wilson 1976; Achabal, Gorr, and Mahajan 1982; Ghosh and McLafferty 1984; Ghosh and Craig 1983). Location allocation models systematically evalaute a large number of possible locational configurations and select the one that maximizes the firm's performance. Central to any location allocation model is the procedure for evaluating how a change in location affects the objective function. This depends on the assumption regarding consumer behavior that is embedded in the model. The simplest models assume that people visit their nearest store. An alternative procedure is to use consumer utility functions obtained from revealed preference analysis. The gravity, MCI, and Huff models, for example, have been widely used for this purpose. Since our objective is to incorporate multipurpose trips in the location model, we develop a location allocation procedure in which the consumer shopping model presented in the preceding section is used to determine consumer patronage at different outlets. Thus, embedded in the location allocation procedure is an optimization model for calculating each consumer's optimal shopping itinerary.

To illustrate the model, we use a two-dimensional region consisting of eighty-one customer origins evenly spaced on a grid. Each of these customer origins is uniformly populated by ten consumers. We also assume that these origins are feasible locations for retail outlets. For clarity, we use the index m ($m = 1, 2, \ldots , 81$) to refer to customer origins and n ($n = 1, 2, \ldots , 81$) to refer to these points as potential center locations. The points are numbered consecutively from left to right, top to bottom. We consider a two-level retail hierarchy, with one high-order firm already established in the region. In addition, two low-order firms are in operation. Consider now that a new retail chain that sells the low-order good wishes to enter this market. How many stores should the chain open in this market, and where should these stores be located? This is the problem we address.

In selecting a location strategy, we assume that firms behave rationally and maximize the total expected profits of outlets belonging to the chain. Define as R_n the revenue earned by a low order store located at site n. This value is given by:

$$\sum_{m \in S_n^l} (1 - \alpha_m^*) D_j P_j, \quad \text{if } j \text{ is low-order place}$$

$$\sum_{m \in S_n^l} (1 - \alpha_m^*) D_j P_j + \sum_{m \in S_n^h} \alpha_m^* \ D_j P, \quad \text{if } j \text{ is high-order place} \quad (9.2)$$

where α_m^* is the optimal propensity for multipurpose shopping or consumers at site m. This is found by solving the shopping model (equation 9.1) for each site m. Also, S_n^l is the set of customer origins for which the closest low-order store is at n, and S_n^h is the set of origins for which the closest high-order store is at n.

If C is the profit margin and F is the fixed cost of operating a store, the expected profit for a low-order store at n is

$$\pi_n = R_n C - F \qquad (9.3)$$

If the firm locates p low-order stores, and Y_p is the set of these p locations, the firm's total profit is

$$\pi(Y_p) = \sum_{n \epsilon Y_p} \pi_n \qquad (9.4)$$

The firm's objective is to maximize total profit by selecting the best combination of p locations. Thus, equation 9.4 must be evaluated over all possible sets Y_p to select the one that maximizes the value of $\pi(Y_p)$.

Solution Method

To determine the best configuration of p stores, we use a vertex substitution heuristic fashioned after that of Teitz and Bart (1968). Because of the large size and complexity of the combinatorial problem, it is difficult to use any exact algorithm to solve the location allocation problem described. Although heuristic algorithms do not necessarily determine globally optimal solutions, the vertex substitution procedure has been found to be very robust and efficient for locational problems (Rosing, Hillsman, and Rosing-Vogelar 1979) and finds the near-optimal if not the optimal solution (Achabal, Gorr, and Mahajan 1982). To reduce the possibility of local optimality, each problem is solved with a number of different starting solutions. Our confidence in the heuristic is bolstered by the fact that different starting solutions to the same problem never led to different answers.

To initiate the heuristic algorithm, a set of p locations is chosen randomly. For this set Y_p, the algorithm next solves equation 9.1 to determine the optimal propensity for multiple shopping, α_m^*, for each consumer. Once the rate of multipurpose shopping is calculated, the expected profit for that locational plan can be calculated from equations 9.2 and 9.3. The algorithm then uses a hill-climbing strategy, which systematically exchanges locations that are in the solution with those that are not, in order to find a configuration that increases profit. Whenever a substitution results in an improvement in the objective function, an interchange is made. This process is repeated (see figure 9–1) until a complete round of substitution fails to result in any improvement in the objective function.

Model Illustration

To define the location model, the following parameters must be specified: transportation costs from an origin m to a site n, the cost of holding inventory,

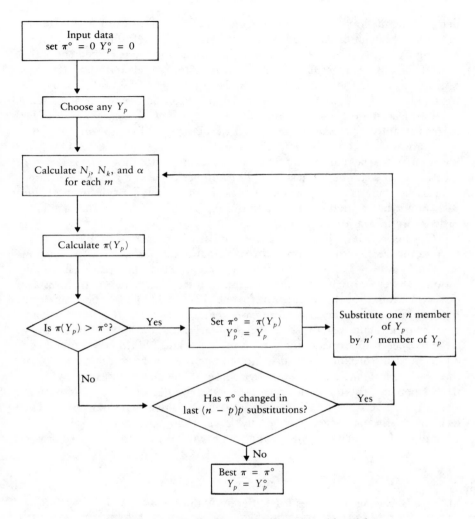

Figure 9–1. The Location Allocation Algorithm

the demand for the two goods and their prices, and the profit margin and fixed costs of outlets. For the purpose of this illustration, we make the following assumptions: The cost of transportation from a node m to a site n is $(d_{mn} + 1.0) * 1.5$ when n is a low-order store and $(d_{mn} + 1.0) * 8.0$ when high-order goods are purchased at site n (d_{mn} is the Euclidean distance between two nodes m and n). The additional cost of travel to a high-order store reflects the additional shopping time required at such stores. There is no extra travel cost for purchasing the low-order good on a multipurpose trip. The demand for the low-order good is 200 units at a retail price of $10. The demand for the high order good, which sells for $40, is 40 units. The cost of holding a unit in inventory for the entire planning horizon is 25 percent of the cost of the unit. Furthermore, the net profit margin of each outlet is 50 percent of sales, and the fixed cost of operating a store is $50,000. Finally, we assume that no more than one low-order store can be opened at any site.

In the scenario chosen for our illustration, we assume that a high-order store is established at site 41 (the center of the region). In addition, two low-order stores operated by a competitor are located at sites 41 and 12. Our firm wishes to enter the market and find the best locations for new stores given the location of the competitor's stores. The number of new stores to be located (*p*) can vary and is an important component of the retailer's decision. Table 9–2 shows the optimal locations and the expected level of sales for each low-order store for various values of *p*.

One approach to determining the number of stores to open in the market is to compare the cost of operating an additional outlet with the gain in revenue. Table 9–3 allows us to assess directly the marginal profits from additional stores (shown in the last column of the table). When two stores are opened by the firm, the total profit for the chain is $259,167. The increased revenue from adding another store more than compensates for the additional cost, as profits increase to $272,583. Similarly, it is more profitable for the store to open four stores in the area than three. The additional revenue from adding a fifth store, however, does not compenste for the incremental cost of the new outlet. Although the market share of the chain increases by more than 4 percent, there is a net decrease in the chain's total profit. Note that even in the five-store case, each outlet has a positive expected profit. The level of profit, however, is generally lower than that in the *p* = 4 case. Overall profits are less because some of the sales of the fifth store are drawn

Table 9–2
Optimal Store Locations and Sales for Different Values of *p*

	p = 2 Location	Sales	*p* = 3 Location	Sales	*p* = 4 Location	Sales	*p* = 5 Location	Sales
Existing stores	41	$642,340	41	$603,000	41	$587,800	41	$553,670
	12	259,330	12	171,830	12	84,330	12	44,330
New stores	49	325,000	22	151,830	11	125,000	11	118,330
	42	393,330	42	368,330	23	216,670	42	280,000
			49	325,000	49	298,330	68	304,330
					52	307,870	40	116,670
							13	152,670

Table 9–3
Market Shares and Profits for Different Values of p

Value of p	Market Share	Total Profit
2	44.3%	$259,167
3	52.2	272,583
4	58.5	273,833
5	63.1	261,000

from the market areas of the other stores belonging to the chain. As a result, the net increment in sales is small and is not enough to compensate for the cost of opening the new store.

The best locations for the four outlets for the chain are shown in table 9–2 and figure 9–2. Given the locations of the two existing low-order stores at sites 12 and 41, the best sites for the chain are at sites 11, 23, 49, and 52. The outlet at site 11 directly competes with the existing outlet at site 12 and captures a portion of site 12's patronage from the northeast sector of the region. The other optimal sites are positioned to compete with the agglomerated store at site 41. The performance of these stores is very sensitive to their location relative to the store at the agglomerated place. On the one hand, it is desirable to locate in close proximity to the agglomerated store to cut into its market area. This favors clustering of stores, as in the classic Hotelling (1929) model. There is a countervailing force, however. If the new stores locate too close to the agglomerated site, the average distance to low-order centers increases for the customer. This may result in an increased propensity for multipurpose shopping and thus reduced sales for the new stores. Similarly, the relative distances between the new stores also have an impact on the profitability of the stores. A clustered location pattern reduces accessibility to the market as a whole and thus decreases the competitive advantage of the chain by encouraging more multipurpose shopping or shopping at competing stores. The location allocation model systematically considers these trade-offs in choosing the optimal locational configuration for the chain.

The optimal frequency of single-purpose and multipurpose trips and the amount of multipurpose shopping are shown in figures 9–3 and 9–4. Consumers at demand node 41, being closest to both types of stores, make the maximum number of trips: 5.55 multipurpose trips and 5.55 single-purpose trips. Thus, they purchase 50 percent of their requirement for the low-order good on multipurpose trips. The optimal frequency of travel and rate of multipurpose shopping shows a significant amount of spatial variation. Consumers at nodes neighboring site 41, for example, make only about four multipurpose and four single-purpose trips. The marginal increase in travel costs results in a reduced number of trips. As one moves further away from

```
*      *      *      *      *      *      *      *      *
*     11     12     13     *      *      *      *      *
*      *      *     22     23     *      *      *      *
*      *      *      *      *      *      *      *      *
*      *      *     40     41     42     *      *      *
*      *      *     49     *      *     52      *      *
*      *      *      *      *      *      *      *      *
*      *      *      *     68      *      *      *      *
*      *      *      *      *      *      *      *      *
```

Note: In the 9 × 9 grid network used for the simulations, nodes are numbered from left to right and from top to bottom. Only the nodes appearing in table 9–2 are numbered here.

Figure 9–2. The Spatial Network and Optimal Locations

the high-order place, the number of multipurpose trips and the amount of multipurpose shopping decrease. Consumers at nodes 1, 2, and 3, for example, purchase only 25 percent of the low-order good on multipurpose trips and make just over six trips to their closest low-order place and over two trips to the high-order place. The trip patterns are also affected by the distance to

Single-Purpose Trips

6.02	6.23	6.64	6.94	4.75	4.71	4.59	4.41	4.21
6.32	11.12	9.52	7.71	5.25	5.19	5.00	4.73	4.45
6.70	7.29	5.38	5.91	8.94	5.91	5.53	5.09	4.66
4.71	5.27	3.06	3.57	3.92	3.57	3.06	5.30	4.76
4.87	5.43	6.27	3.92	5.55	3.92	6.17	5.31	4.77
4.78	5.27	5.91	10.05	3.92	7.00	11.45	7.71	4.68
4.62	5.00	5.44	5.91	6.27	5.99	5.38	4.91	4.53
4.41	4.70	5.00	5.27	5.43	5.30	4.97	4.64	4.35
4.20	4.41	4.62	4.78	4.87	4.80	4.60	4.38	4.15

Multipurpose Trips

2.01	2.11	2.21	2.31	2.37	2.35	2.29	2.21	2.11
2.11	2.22	2.38	2.57	2.63	2.60	2.50	2.37	2.23
2.23	2.43	2.69	2.96	2.98	2.96	2.77	2.55	2.33
2.35	2.64	3.06	3.57	3.92	3.57	3.06	2.65	2.38
2.43	2.71	3.13	3.92	5.55	3.92	3.09	2.65	2.39
2.39	2.64	2.96	3.35	3.92	3.50	2.86	2.57	2.34
2.31	2.50	2.72	2.96	3.13	3.00	2.69	2.45	2.27
2.21	2.35	2.50	2.64	2.71	2.65	2.49	2.32	2.18
2.10	2.21	2.31	2.39	2.43	2.40	2.30	2.19	2.08

Note: The frequency of trips made by consumers is presented at each of the demand nodes in the 9 × 9 grid network. The nodes are numbered from left to right and from top to bottom.

Figure 9–3. Frequency of Trips

0.25	0.25	0.25	0.25	0.33	0.33	0.33	0.33	0.33
0.25	0.17	0.20	0.25	0.33	0.33	0.33	0.33	0.33
0.25	0.25	0.33	0.33	0.25	0.33	0.33	0.33	0.33
0.33	0.33	0.50	0.50	0.50	0.50	0.50	0.33	0.33
0.33	0.33	0.33	0.50	0.50	0.50	0.33	0.33	0.33
0.33	0.33	0.33	0.25	0.50	0.33	0.20	0.25	0.33
0.33	0.33	0.33	0.33	0.33	0.33	0.33	0.33	0.33
0.33	0.33	0.33	0.33	0.33	0.33	0.33	0.33	0.33
0.33	0.33	0.33	0.33	0.33	0.33	0.33	0.33	0.33

Note: The optimal value of α is presented for each node in the 9×9 network. The nodes are numbered from left to right and from top to bottom.

Figure 9–4. Optimal Level of Multipurpose Shopping

the nearest store. Consumers in the northeast corner of the region, because of their proximity to the two stores at nodes 11 and 12, generally make more single-purpose trips than consumers in the southern part of the region. Thus, the optimal travel patterns are determined by the relative distances to the low- and high-order places.

As can be seen in table 9–2, the low-order store located at site 41 has substantially higher sales and profits than the other low-order stores. In the $p = 4$ case, for example, the low-order store at site 41 has sales of $587,800, compared to average sales of $206,440 for the other low-order outlets. This store, besides selling to consumers from its own market area, benefits from multipurpose shopping by other consumers. All consumers in the region patronize the low-order store at site 41 to some extent. Thus, the benefit of agglomeration depends on the level of multipurpose shopping in the region.

To explore the phenomenon of agglomeration more fully, consider the situation in which there is no existing low-order store at site 41. The optimal locations for the chain's outlets and their sales are shown in table 9–4. The chain locates one store at site 41 to benefit from agglomeration with the high-order firm. This store has sales of $851,000. This is substantially greater than the average sales of $190,940 for the other low-order stores belonging to the chain. The total profit for the chain in this scenario is $511,916— substantially greater than the $273,833 expected in the previous case. In fact, the profit for the store at site 41 itself is $375,500.

The monetary advantage of the agglomerated low-order firm is due to multipurpose shopping. The high-order store, therefore, may claim part of this excess revenue in the form of rental subsidies or side payments. When there is more than one high-order store, the comparative benefit of agglomeration with any one of them depends on their ability to attract customers and promote multipurpose shopping. The amount of payment any high-order store can negotiate depends on its ability to generate sales for the

Table 9–4
Optimal Locations When Existing Firms Are
Unagglomerated ($p = 4$)

	Location	Sales
Existing stores	52	$ 43,500
	12	152,670
New stores	41	851,000
	44	211,830
	11	141,670
	61	219,330

agglomerated low-order store. This phenomenon of rental subsidy for high-order stores is often observed in regional shopping malls, where large "anchor" stores pay significantly lower rents than smaller stores, which are attracted by the drawing power of the large stores.

Conclusions

In this chapter, we have developed a model of consumer shopping behavior and optimal retail locations in multipurpose trip environments. Most existing models start with the assumption of single-purpose trips from fixed origins. Given that many shopping trips are multipurpose, it is important to incorporate such behavior in retail location models. We first presented a consumer shopping model that determines the optimal frequency and spatial pattern of single-purpose as well as multipurpose trips. Simulation analyses using the model indicate that consumers' optimal travel patterns are always nonstationary. In particular, the frequencies of single-purpose and multipurpose trips and the propensity for multipurpose shopping depend on the consumer's location relative to shopping opportunities. In this way, the model explicitly considers the important relationship between spatial structure and spatial behavior.

In the second part of the chapter, we developed a location allocation model that simultaneously determines optimal consumer shopping patterns and retail locations. The model allows a number of important theoretical contributions. It provides a theoretical rationale for the agglomeration of stores selling low-order goods with high-order stores. Such agglomerated stores invariably generate greater revenues that their nonagglomerated counterparts. This leads to the development of a hierarchical spatial organization of retail outlets (see also Eaton and Lipsey 1982) in which high-order places sell both high- and low-order goods. It is important to note that this hierarchy is deduced from the behavioral postulates of the model, rather than being exogenously specified, as in the theories of Christaller (1966) and Losch (1954). The precise characteristics of the hierarchy depend on demand, price and cost conditions, and the spatial behavior of competing firms. Although our findings are preliminary at this stage, unraveling such relationships, which lie at the heart of retail location theory, is the ultimate goal.

References

Achabal, D.; Gorr, W.L.; and Mahajan, V. (1982). "MULTILOC: A Multiple Store Location Decision Model." *Journal of Retailing* 58 (2):5–25.

Bacon, R. (1983). "A Model of the Frequency of Consumer Purchase Patterns: A Contribution to the Theory of Retail Locations." In Franco Angeli (ed.), *Economics of Distribution: Proceedings of the Second International Conference on the Economics of Distribution*. Milan, Italy: CESCOM.

Christaller, W. (1966). *Central Places in Southern Germany* (Trans. C.W. Baskin). Englewood Cliffs, N.J.: Prentice-Hall.

Craig, C.S.; Ghosh, A.; and McLafferty, S. (1984). "Models of the Retail Location Process: A Review." *Journal of Retailing* 60 (1):5–36.

Coehlo, J.D., and Wilson, A.G. (1976). "The Optimal Location and Size of Retail Centers." *Regional Studies* 10:413–21.

Curry, L. (1967). "Central Places in the Random Spatial Economy." *Journal of Regional Science* 7:217–38.

Eaton, C., and Lipsey, R. (1982). "An Economic Theory of Central Places." *Economic Journal* 92:56–72.

Ghosh, A., and Craig, C.S. (1983). "Formulating Retail Location Strategy in a Changing Environment." *Journal of Marketing* 47:56–68.

Ghosh, A., and McLafferty, S. (1982). "Locating Stores in Uncertain Environments: A Scenario Planning Approach." *Journal of Retailing* 58 (Winter):5–22.

———. (1984). "A Model of Consumer Propensity for Multipurpose Shopping." *Geographical Analysis* 16:244–49.

Hanson, S. (1980). "Spatial Diversification and Multipurpose Travel: Implications for Choice Theory." *Geographical Analysis* 12:245–57.

Hotelling, H. (1929). Stability in Competition." *Economic Journal* 39:41–57.

Huff, D. (1962). "Determination of Intra-Urban Retail Trade Area." Los Angeles: University of California, Real Estate Research Program.

———. (1966) "A Programmed Solution for Approximating an Optimal Retail Location." *Land Economics* 42:294–305.

Jain, A.K., and Mahajan, V. (1979). "Evaluating the Competitive Environment in Retailing Using Multiplicative Competitive Interactive Models." In J. Seth (ed.), *Research in Marketing*. Greenwich, Conn.: JAI Press, 217–35.

Kohsaka, H. (1984). "An Optimization of the Central Place System in terms of the Multipurpose Shopping Trip." *Geographical Analysis* 16:250–69.

Lentnek, B.; Harwitz, M.; and Narula, S. (1981). "Spatial Choice in Consumer Behavior: Towards a Contextual Theory of Demand." *Economic Geography* 57:362–73.

Losch, A. (1954). *The Economics of Location*. New Haven, Conn.: Yale University Press.

MacKay, D. (1972). "A Microanalytic Approach to Store Location Analysis." *Journal of Marketing Research* 9:134–40.

McLafferty, S. (1982). "Locating Services to Minimize Consumer Travel with Multipurpose Trips." Paper presented at the International Conference on Improving Geographical Accessibility to Rural Services, Bangalore, India, August 1982.

McLafferty, S., and Ghosh, A. (1984). "A Simulation Model of Spatial Competition with Multipurpose Trips." *Modeling and Simulation* 15 (1):477–82.

Mulligan, G. (1983). "Consumer Demand with Multipurpose Shopping Behavior." *Geographical Analysis* 15:76–80.

———. (1984). "Central Place Populations: Some Implications of Consumer Shopping Behavior." *Annals of the Association of American Geographers* 74:44–56.

Nakanishi, M., and Cooper, L.G. (1974). "Parameter Estimates for Multiplicative Interactive Choice Models: Least Squares Approach." *Journal of Marketing Research* 11:303–11.

O'Kelly, M. (1981). "A Model of Demand for Retail Facilities Incorporating Multistop, Multipurpose Trips." *Geographical Analysis* 13:134–48.

———. (1983). "Multipurpose Shopping Trips and the Size of Retail Facilities." *Annals of the Association of American Geographers* 73:231–39.

Reinhardt, P.G. (1973). "A Theory of Household Grocery Inventory Holdings." *Kyklos* 26:497–511.

Rosing, K.; Hillsman, E.; and Rosing-Vogelar, H. (1979). "A Note on Comparing Optimal and Heuristic Solutions to the P-Median Problem." *Geographical Analysis* 11:86–89.

Shepard, I.D., and Thomas, C.J. (1980). "Urban Consumer Behavior." In J.A. Dawson (ed.), *Retail Geography*. London: Croom Helm.

Teitz, M.B., and Bart, P. (1968). "Heuristic Methods for Estimating the Generalized Vertex Median of a Weighted Graph." *Operations Research* 16:955–61.

White, R.W. (1977). "Dynamic Central Place Theory: Results of a Simulation Approach." *Geographical Analysis* 9:226–43.

10

Locational Interdependency: The Impact of Change on Retail Images

John P. Dickson

R etailers have long considered a store's physical environment to be one of the most important determinants of the success or failure of a firm. Although price, merchandise mix, and promotional strategies are fairly easy for competitiors to match, the physical environment is not; therefore, it can give a retailer a differential advantage. Similarly, the image customers and potential customers have of a retailer—including, in part, its physical environment—is considered to be extremely important to store loyalty and creating a differential advantage (Bellinger et al. 1976).

The literature on physical environment, though extensive, tends to fall into two broad categories: (1) evaluating sites in terms of market potential (Kerin and Harvey 1975; Ghosh and Craig 1983; Nevin and Houston 1980) and (2) designing and evaluating store layouts ("What Makes a Good Store Layout" 1976; Curhan 1973). Research on image analysis also tends to fall into two major categories: (1) defining image and the components of image (Dickson and Albaum 1977; Kelly and Stephenson 1967; Kunkel and Berry 1968; Lindquist 1974–75) and (2) the methodological problems of measuring image (Doyle and Fenwick 1974–75; Marks 1976).

Relatively few studies have looked at the interaction between a store's physical environment and its image during a period of dynamic change in the competitive environment. What happens to a store's image when a change is made in its location and physical layout? What is the impact of such a change on its competitors' images?

Unfortunately, most studies that deal with image consistency focus on similar stores at one point in time (Hirschman et al. 1978) or on the issue of instrument reliability (Dickson and Albaum 1977; Hawkins et al. 1976–77). The first types of studies are static evaluations of environment. The second types try to pick very stable environments so that the researcher can minimize the effects of the environment and therefore better test the reliability of the instrument. However, the retailer is much more interested in such questions as "Is my image improving over time?" or "What impact are my competitors' strategies having on my image?"

One recently published article by Arnold et al. (1983) provides an important new direction in the study of attributes that affect retail patronage decisions over time. Using a multinomial logit model, the researchers evaluated determinant attributes in retail patronage decisions over a 6-year period. Although they reported many interesting findings, the nature of the study did not permit evaluation of what affects individual store images. Rather, the study focused on what consumers reported to be the determinant attributes in their evaluation of food stores in general. No specific store was evaluated at any point in time or over time.

The Purpose of This Study

The purpose of this study is to consider the dynamics of retail images over time during a period when one competitor changes its physical environment (location, store design, and layout). What happens to a store's image when the firm relocates its physical plant but stays in the same community and uses the same products, advertising media, personnel, and pricing strategies? Will its customers rate its image more favorably? What will happen to the underlying structure of how consumers evaluate its image? Will this remain stable regardless of an improvement in the store's overall image? What will happen to its competitors' images? To address these questions, the following research objectives were developed:

Objective 1: To determine the underlying factor structures of two competitive supermarkets and then assess the stability of their factor structures before and after the relocation of one of the two stores.

Objective 2: To determine whether consumers' attitudes regarding a supermarket will move in the desired direction after a locational change that involves a substantial change in its physical plant.

Objective 3: To determine whether consumers' attitudes regarding the supermarket's major competitor change as a result of the move. It was hypothesized that the change would be negative, as one of the competitive alternatives would suddenly become more favorable (Festinger 1957; Helson 1964; and Tversky and Kahneman 1981).

Two supermarkets were selected in Cheney, Washington, a small, suburban town on the outskirts of Spokane. One store, Safeway, is a member of a large chain of supermarkets represented throughout the western United States. The other store, Ranch Thrift, is a member of a large regional buying cooperative. Ranch Thrift was the store that was going through the move. As is commonly done, the semantic differential was selected as a measurement technique to collect image data for the study (Kelly and Stephenson 1967; Marks 1976). The scales for the semantic differentials that were used to study the retail stores were selected from those previously developed by Dickson and Albaum (1977) for use under similar situations. The twenty-four scales were randomly ordered on the questionnaire in terms of both polarity and vertical position on the page. The typical 7-point scale was used. The instrument was administered to respondents by personal interview. The presentation order of the questionnaires for the two stores was rotated to control for order bias; in other words, half the respondents were presented with the Safeway questionnaire first, half with the Ranch Thrift questionnaire.

Respondents were interviewed at two time periods. The first group of respondents was interviewed 3 months before Ranch Thrift moved, and then a second group of respondents was interviewed 3 months after the move. In both cases, a probability sample of respondents was selected from within a 3-mile radius of the two stores. The geographic area from which the respondents were selected was the same for both stores, as the stores were sited four blocks apart. After the move, Ranch Thrift was only four blocks from its original location. In the first time period, 108 respondents rated Safeway and 95 rated Ranch Thrift. In the second time period, 109 respondents rated each store. The stores were competitive; Safeway had about 10,000 square feet of sales area, and Ranch Thrift had about 7,000 square feet in its old location and about 11,000 square feet in its new location. Ranch Thrift retained the same employees in the new location, as well as adding some additional part-time help. Both stores continued using the same advertising media and pricing strategies over the 6 months. Ranch Thrift's product mix was maintained, with no new major product lines or departments being added.

Analyses and Results

Factor Structure Stability

The semantic differential responses for both stores were factor-analyzed before and after Ranch Thrift changed locations. The principal component factoring method was used, and the main diagonal elements of the correlation matrix were replaced with the squared multiple correlation between a given variable and the rest of the variables in the matrix. Next, the resulting factor matrix was orthogonally rotated using the Varimax procedure. The number of factors extracted was determined by the eigenvalue of the image covariance matrix, and factors with eigenvalues greater than 1.0 were retained. The factor structures are presented in tables 10–1 and 10–2.

Table 10–1 shows the factor structures for Safeway before and after Ranch Thrift changed locations. Factor I was identified as "store environment," as indicated by the high loadings on such scales as "neat," "attractive store,"

Table 10–1
Rotated Factor Structures—Safeway

	Time Period 1 Factors			Time Period 2 Factors		
	I	*II*	*III*	*I*	*II*	*III*
Factor I: store environment						
1. Well-spaced merchandise	.59	.03	.35	.68	.10	.21
2. Bright store	.42	.34	.09	.55	.14	.18
3. Well-organized layout	.50	.20	.06	.45	.14	.05
4. Pleasant store to shop in	.52	.32	.33	.54	.38	.22
5. Attractive store	.60	.29	.30	.71	.14	.11
6. Big selection of products	.59	.10	.01	.46	.35	.29
7. Neat	.81	.12	.19	.62	.20	.12
8. Spacious shopping	.61	.33	.04	.75	.04	.03
9. Clean	.61	.14	.16	.58	.27	.15
10. Good displays	.50	.42	.16	.60	.16	.33
Factor II: service personnel						
11. Helpful salesmen	.29	.59	.37	.13	.65	.19
12. Good service	.27	.66	.18	.23	.79	.12
13. Friendly personnel	.24	.71	.30	.19	.85	.07
14. Easy to return purchases	.20	.50	.21	.18	.49	.29
15. Fast checkout	.13	.66	.12	.42	.45	.27
Factor III: product price promotion						
16. High-quality products	.34	.13	.33	.25	.04	.55
17. Low prices	.05	.35	.47	.03	.22	.37
18. Good sales on products	.12	.13	.71	.10	.19	.59
19. Good buys on products	.12	.18	.91	.14	.30	.78
20. Reasonable prices for value	.23	.23	.67	.05	.09	.62
21. Good specials	.19	.33	.63	.24	.13	.75
Outliers						
22. Ads frequently seen by you	.15	.49	.22	.08	.14	.28
23. Convenient location	.23	.13	.35	.04	.36	.45
24. Easy to find items you want	.40	.22	.29	.14	.01	.22

and "spacious shopping." Factor II had high loadings on "good service," "friendly personnel," and "fast checkout" and was labeled "service personnel." The high loading of .91 on scale 19 ("good buys on products") helped identify Factor III as "product price promotion." These factors are similar to the ones reported by Dickson and Albaum (1977). Columns 4, 5, and 6 contain the factor loadings for Safeway after Ranch Thrift changed location. When the before and after loadings are compared, the factor structures of the store images, as indicated by the loadings, appear to be very similar.

Table 10–2 shows the factor loadings for Ranch Thrift before and after it moved. Once again, high loadings on such scales as "attractive store," "well-spaced merchandise," "bright store," "heat," and "spacious shopping" led to the identification of Factor I as "store envioronment." Factor II was identified as "service pesonnel" because of high loadings on such scales as "Helpful salesmen,"

Table 10–2
Rotated Factor Structures—Ranch Thrift

	Before-Move Factors			After-Move Factors		
	I	II	III	I	II	III
Factor I: store environment						
1. Well-spaced merchandise	.59	.10	.13	.38	.23	.33
2. Bright store	.63	.10	.02	.50	.13	.08
3. Well-organized layout	.42	.14	.46	.46	.20	.24
4. Pleasant store to shop in	.54	.42	.41	.43	.25	.51
5. Attractive store	.85	.03	.13	.67	.25	.32
6. Big selection of products	.72	.06	.23	.46	.44	.26
7. Neat	.66	.31	.33	.82	.11	.19
8. Spacious shopping	.71	.01	.14	.56	.38	.06
9. Clean	.49	.38	.43	.81	.06	.28
10. Good displays	.57	.28	.37	.40	.57	.28
Factor II: service personnel						
11. Helpful salesmen	.00	.73	.22	.51	.43	.15
12. Good service	.01	.68	.11	.27	.72	.11
13. Friendly personnel	.05	.76	.25	.42	.68	.19
14. Easy to return purchases	.02	.58	.42	.19	.52	.29
15. Fast checkout	.19	.42	.10	.03	.67	.28
Factor III: product price promotion						
16. Low prices	.15	.06	.57	.01	.15	.56
17. Good sales on products	.20	.28	.57	.19	.29	.55
18. Good buys on products	.25	.34	.61	.17	.21	.74
19. Reasonable prices for value	.20	.18	.55	.12	.24	.72
20. Good specials	.03	.26	.65	.22	.26	.68
Outliers						
21. Ads frequently seen by you	.04	.31	.19	.11	.08	.47
22. High-quality products	.34	.29	.13	.23	.26	.38
23. Easy to find items you want	.16	.17	.55	.18	.39	.27
24. Convenient location	.15	.50	.05	.32	.21	.05

"good service," "friendly personnel," and "easy to return purchases." High loadings on such scales as "good specials," "good sales on products," and "reasonable prices for value" led to the identification of Factor III as "product price promotion." In this case, the factor structures before and after the move appear to be less similar than Safeway's are. Several scales for both stores were labeled "outliers," in that they were not closely aligned with any of the three factors extracted.

Are the factor loading patterns for Ranch Thrift before and after it changed location similar? Does the Safeway structure remain stable over time? Determining the extent to which factors obtained in different samples with fixed variables are related has been problematic for factor analysts. Harmon (1976) and Tucker (1951) discuss the problem and suggest an index described as the coefficient of congruence. Recently, Ahmavaara's (1954) approach for comparing factor structures has become more widely used (Anderson et al. 1976) and more easily calculated (Veldman, 1967). Ahmavaara suggested comparing factor structures by transformation analysis, wherein one factor matrix is arbitrarily specified as a reference matrix and then the other matrix is rotated so that it conforms as closely as possible to the reference matrix. The degree of correspondence among factor structures is revealed by inspecting angles between factor axes. The cosines are interpreted in much the same fashion as correlation coefficients. Using this technique, the before and after factor structures for each store were compared; the results are presented in table 10–3. Cosine values above .90 indicate substantial congruence between factors. As can be seen in the table, the factor structures are similar in all cases. These findings are consistent with the comparisons analyzed using Tucker's (1951) coefficient of congruence.

Regardless of whether the factor structures are compared by visual inspection or by mathematical analysis, the conclusion is the same. The underlying structures by which respondents judged the two stores over time and through a marked store environmental change remained remarkably stable. Evidently, there is a sort of "bedrock" by which people judge the stores. Although perceptions of how the stores rate on individual scale items (for example, neat versus messy) may vary over time, the relationships among the scale items remain relatively stable.

Image Shift

To address the second and third objectives, the data were summarized and means were computed for each semantic differential scale for both stores before and

Table 10–3
Relationships among Factor Structures Before and After Move:
Cosine Matrix

After Before	Safeway		
	Factor I	Factor II	Factor III
Factor I	.991	−.098	.093
Factor II	.098	.995	.004
Factor III	−.093	.005	.996

After Before	Ranch Thrift		
	Factor I	Factor II	Factor III
Factor I	.999	.034	−.013
Factor II	−.034	.998	.046
Factor III	.015	−.045	.999

after Ranch Thrift changed locations. Low scores (near 1) are more favorable than high scores (near 5). The results are presented in table 10–4 and in figure 10–1. The critical element in deciding to move was the desire by Ranch Thrift's management to improve consumers' image of the store's physical environment. Thus, management spent a great deal of time, effort, thought, and money trying to improve the physical features of the new store and its new site. It was hoped that this effort would be reflected in an improved image.

As can be seen in the table and the figure, Ranch Thrift improved its image on an overall basis as well as on a significant number of individual scales— as indicated by the twelve positive changes in the thirteen scales that changed significantly, Ranch Thift improved its image. The one negative change was location, as might be expected, since customers had to change driving habits to shop at the new location. The new location was also a little more remote

Table 10–4
Image Before and After Move
(average scores)

	Ranch Thrift			Safeway		
	Before (N = 97)	*After* (N = 109)	*D*	*Before* (N = 108)	*After* (N = 109)	*D*
1. Well-spaced merchandise	4.60	2.31*	+	3.36	3.88*	–
2. Bright store	4.22	2.53*	+	3.08	3.47	–
3. Well-organized layout	4.25	2.45*	+	3.15	3.54	–
4. Pleasant store to shop in	3.35	2.18*	+	2.73	3.11	–
5. Attractive store	4.11	1.87*	+	2.97	3.33	–
6. Big selection of products	4.29	2.62*	+	3.10	3.38	–
7. Neat	3.60	1.79*	+	2.78	3.09	–
8. Spacious shopping	4.83	2.10*	+	3.37	4.13*	–
9. Clean	3.42	1.76*	+	2.38	2.76*	–
10. Good displays	3.91	2.69*	+	3.28	3.46	–
11. Helpful salesmen	2.85	2.62	+	2.94	3.13	–
12. Good service	2.71	2.77	–	3.25	3.24	
13. Friendly personnel	2.47	2.49		2.95	2.81	+
14. Easy to return purchases	3.30	3.30		3.25	3.16	+
15. Fast checkout	3.06	2.90	+	3.72	3.99	–
16. Low prices	4.41	4.41		4.41	4.04	+
17. Good sales on products	3.29	3.19	+	3.13	3.33	–
18. Good buys on products	3.36	3.51	–	3.20	3.28	–
19. Reasonable prices for value	3.72	3.46	+	2.37	2.55	–
20. Good specials	3.27	3.07	+	3.12	3.23	–
21. High-quality products	3.43	3.07	+	3.05	3.31	–
22. Ads frequently seen by you	3.41	2.43*	+	3.13	2.41*	+
23. Easy to find items you want	4.05	3.30*	+	3.63	3.29	+
24. Convenient location	2.88	3.35*	–	2.78	2.40*	+
Average	3.62	2.76*	+	3.12	3.26	–

*Significant at α = .05.

D = Direction of shift: + = positive; – = negative.

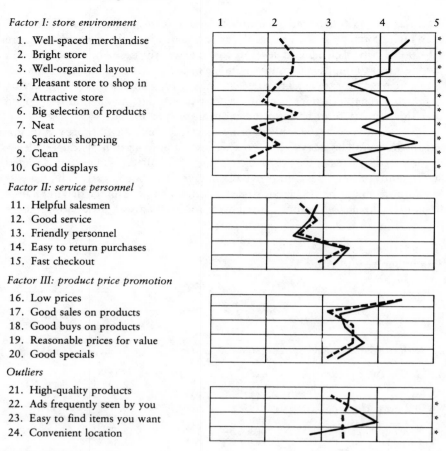

	1	2	3	4	5

Factor I: store environment

 1. Well-spaced merchandise
 2. Bright store
 3. Well-organized layout
 4. Pleasant store to shop in
 5. Attractive store
 6. Big selection of products
 7. Neat
 8. Spacious shopping
 9. Clean
10. Good displays

Factor II: service personnel

11. Helpful salesmen
12. Good service
13. Friendly personnel
14. Easy to return purchases
15. Fast checkout

Factor III: product price promotion

16. Low prices
17. Good sales on products
18. Good buys on products
19. Reasonable prices for value
20. Good specials

Outliers

21. High-quality products
22. Ads frequently seen by you
23. Easy to find items you want
24. Convenient location

*Significant at $\alpha = .05$.
Solid line = before; broken line = after.

Figure 10–1. Ranch Thrift Image Before and After Move

from the population center of the town. Equally interesting is the fact that all ten of the scales associated with the factor labeled "store environment" improved significantly. Finally, the overall image, as measured by the average shift, improved significantly.

Another indicator of the broad impact of the location change on consumers' attitudes can be seen by examining the direction of the shifts in image. It was predicted that most shifts would be favorable (D = positive in table 10–4) with the exception of location. The averages on nineteen scales moved in the predicted direction, two did not, and three remained unchanged. Using the Sign test (Siegel 1956), it was determined that having such a large number of positive changes is significant at $\alpha = .001$. Thus, it would appear that the improvement in the shopping environment was generalized to the other factors, as would be expected (Howard 1981).

Although Safeway did not exhibit a significant shift in its overall image, a significant number (five) of the mean scores changed on individual scales. In fact, there was a generally negative shift in Safeway's image. Evidently, the improvement in Ranch Thrift caused a decrease in the appeal of Safeway to the respondents, as would be expected according to adaptation-level theory (Helson 1964). In analyzing the direction of the Shift (D), the averages on seventeen scales shifted in a negative direction and six shifted in a positive direction. Taking into account the location prediction (Safeway's location would now appear more convenient until new driving habits developed), eighteen shifts were in the hypothesized direction. The probability of such an extreme number of shifts is significant at $\alpha = .005$, again using the Sign test.

Although there were fewer significant shifts on individual scales for Safeway than for Ranch Thrift, the number of shifts was significant, as was the direction. One simply would not expect eighteen out of twenty-four scale means to shift in the predicted direction by chance alone. It would appear that the improvement in Ranch Thrift's image damaged the image of Safeway, even though Safeway's management did not alter its marketing strategy or shopping environment.

Summary and Conclusions

The objective of this chapter was to examine the image shift of retail stores over time during a period of store relocation. May (1973) and Ghosh and Craig (1983) have suggested that image research could be helpful in site selection and evaluation for new stores. The research reported here has shown that image research can be equally valuable for existing stores that are changing locations or for existing stores whose major competitors are changing locations.

In contrast to the underlying factor structure of the two stores, their image profile—as measured by mean scores—changed dynamically over time. Importantly, the shift in image was consistent with the direction one would expect. The change in location and layout dramatically improved people's image of Ranch Thrift's physical environment and, to a lesser degree, their overall image of the store. These findings should be encouraging to retail managers and researchers alike, in that the results indicate that image structure composition can be dealt with as a relatively stable marketing variable. Such stability provides for an environment in which management can develop longer-term marketing strategies based on image profiles and researchers can increase their confidence in the reliability of the factors identified in factor analysis of retail image studies. Similarly, image profile analysis appears to be fairly predictable, which should lend confidence to the use of image analysis in making managerial decisions based on such research.

The importance of locational interdependency has been of interest in research ranging from Hotelling's (1929) original work to the more contemporary works by Ghosh and Craig (1983) and Teitz (1968). Although such research has been very fruitful, it has concentrated on the complexities and dynamics of competitive environments as they affect location decisions. Retail image has been treated primarily as an input into locational decisions or models and has simply been added, for instance, as an additional variable in a gravitational model (Stanley and Sewall 1976). In this chapter, image has been treated as a function of the total store environment, and the importance of this relationship to the competitive environment has been demonstrated. In essence, retail managers must take into consideration the actions of their competitors in a dynamic market if they are to understand the shifts in their customers' image of their store. It is quite apparent that developing a desirable image and then remaining static is not enough for survival. As the marketing environment changes, so must the strategies of all the competitors.

References

Ahmavaara, Y. (1954). *Transformation Analysis of Factorial Data.* Helsinki: Finnish Academy of Science.

Anderson, W.T, Jr.; Sharpe, Louis; and Golden, Linda. (1976). "Promotional Implications of Heterophily and Referent Influence." *Proceedings: AMA, 39 educators conference*, 572–76.

Arnold, S.J.; Oum, T.H.; and Tigert, D.J. (1983). "Determinant Attributes in Retail Patronage: Seasonal Temporal, Regional, and International Comparisons." *Journal of Marketing Research* 20 (May):149–57.

Bellinger, D.N.; Steinberg, E.; and Stanton, W.W. (1976). "The Congruence of Store Image and Self Image as It Relates to Store Image." *Journal of Retailing* 52 (Spring):17–32.

Curhan, R.C. (1973). "Shelf Space Allocation and Profit Maximization in Mass Retailing." *Journal of Marketing* 37 (July):54–60.

Dickson, John, and Albaum, Gerald. (1977). "A Method for Developing Tailormade Semantic Differentials for Specific Marketing Content Areas." *Journal of Marketing Research* 14 (February):87–91.

Doyle, Peter, and Fenwick, Ian. (1974–75). "How Store Image Affects Shopping Habits in Grocery Chains." *Journal of Retailing* 50 (Winter):39–52.

Festinger, L. (1957). *A Theory of Cognitive Dissonance.* Stanford, Calif.: Stanford University Press.

Ghosh, A., and Craig, C.S. (1983). "Formulating Retail Location Strategy in a Changing Environment." *Journal of Marketing* 47 (Summer):56–68.

Harmon, Harry H. (1976). *Modern Factor Analysis.* Chicago: University of Chicago Press.

Hawkins, D.; Albaum, Gerald; and Best, Roger. (1976–77). "Reliability of Retail Store Images as Measured by the Staple Scale." *Journal of Retailing* 52 (Winter):31–38.

Helson, H. (1964). "Current Trends and Issues in Adaptation-Level Theory." *American Psychologist* 19 (January):26–38.

Hirschman, Elizabeth C.; Greensburg, Barnett; and Robertson, Dan H. (1978). "The Intermarket Reliability of Retail Image Research: An Empirical Examination." *Journal of Retailing* 54 (Spring):3–12.

Hotelling, H. (1929). "Stability in Competition." *Economic Journal* 39 (March):41–57.

Howard, John A. (1981). "Learning and Consumer Behavior," in H.H. Kassarjian and T.S. Robertson (eds.), *Perspectives in Consumer Behavior*, 3rd ed. Dallas: Scott Foresman, 96–103.

Kelly, R.F., and Stephenson, R. (1967). "The Semantic Differential: An Information Source for Designing Retail Patronage Appeals." *Journal of Marketing* 31 (October):43–47.

Kerin, R.A., and Harvey, Michael. (1975). "Evaluation of Retail Store Locations Through Probability Analysis." *Journal of Small Business Management* 13 (January):41–45.

Kunkel, J.H., and Berry, Leonard. (1968). "A Behavioral Conception of Retail Image." *Journal of Marketing* 32 (October):22.

Lindquist, Jay D. (1974–75). "Meaning of Image: A Survey of Empirical and Hypothetical Evidence." *Journal of Retailing* 50 (Winter):29–38.

Marks, Ronald. (1976). "Operationalizing the Concept of Store Image." *Journal of Retailing* 52 (Fall):37–46.

May, Eleanor. (1973). "Management Applications of Retail Image Research." A Marketing Science Institute Working Paper, September, 25–62.

Nevin, J.R., and Houston, M.J. (1980). "Image as a Component of Attractiveness to Intraurban Shopping Areas." *Journal of Retailing* 56 (Spring):77–93.

Siegel, Sidney. (1956). *Nonparametric Statistics for the Behavioral Sciences*. New York: McGraw-Hill, 68–75.

Stanley, T.J., and Sewall, M.A. (1976). "Image Inputs to a Probabilistic Model: Predicting Retail Potential." *Journal of Marketing* 40 (July):48–53.

Teitz, M.B. (1968). "Locational Strategies for Competitive Systems." *Journal of Regional Science* 8 (Winter):135–46.

Tucker, L.R.A. (1951). "A Method for Synthesis of Factor Analytic Studies." Personnel Research Section Report #984. Washington, D.C.: U.S. Department of the Army.

Tversky, Amos, and Kahneman, Daniel. (1981). "The Framing of Decisions and the Psychology of Choice." *Science* 211 (January):453–58.

Veldman, Donald J. (1967). *Fortran Programming for the Behavioral Sciences*. New York: Holt, Rinehart and Winston, 236–45.

"What Makes a Good Store Layout?" *Progressive Grocer* (January 1976):68–73.

11

Increasing the Efficiency of Forecasting Seasonal Demand for Individual Products

J. Patrick Kelly
Michael D. Geurts

There has been a great increase in interest in sales forecasting in recent years, and significant improvements have been made in forecasting methodology. Exponential smoothing models were popularized by Brown in 1963, Autoregressive Integrated Moving-Average (ARIMA) models were popularized by Box and Jenkins in 1970, and methods of combining forecasts were developed by Newbold and Granger in 1974. The development of these models has resulted in an increased ability to forecast sales accurately. Most of the studies in forecasting and development of forecasting models have used data from manufacturers. Very little research has been conducted on retail sales forecasting. When research has been directed toward retail sales forecasting, it has focused on predicting sales levels by market area, store totals, or department totals, rather than on individual products or stock-keeping units (SKUs).

Many retailers have been satisfied with using last year's sales figures plus some type of fixed percentage increase as a forecast for next year's sales levels. Sales are typically forecast in dollars, which is useful for planning purposes, but buyers must buy in units. During periods of relatively high inflation, higher dollar amounts may actually cause the same amount of units or fewer units to be purchased to achieve the higher sales levels with inflated dollars.

Ordering specific quantities by unit presents a number of problems for retailers. Many buyers look to the quantities purchased last year and again add a fixed percentage increase. Some items may have sold out before demand diminished, whereas other items may have remained in stock at the end of a selling season, requiring markdowns. Without accurate record keeping of the actual quantities remaining in stock or of when items sold out, the buyer cannot make accurate judgments about the next quantity to order. Another

The authors express appreciation to the Skaggs Institute of Retail Management at Brigham Young University for its funding of the study reported here.

problem is the frequent turnover in buyers of specific products, requiring a new trial-and-error process each year in ordering specific units. Finally, it is easy for merchandise managers to control the buying levels by placing dollar limits on the open-to-buy figure, but it is much more difficult to control the correct purchasing of units to maximize sales potential without becoming dangerously overstocked. The aggregate sales of a one-month period, in dollars, are made up of the selling of many individual units.

The Retailer's Needs for Sales Forecasts

Sales and inventory management requires a forecast of sales. Accurate sales forecasts can help management select appropriate levels of aggregate inventory investment and can provide valuable input to the company's financial and operating planning systems.

The open-to-buy and the complete inventory planning sequence begin with a forecast of sales. Typically, retailers operate on a monthly open-to-buy, stated in dollars. Recently, retailers have attempted to move toward a week-of-supply basis instead of the longer monthly planning sequence. This approach can use units as well as dollar totals in the forecasting process.

Retailers have developed buffer mechanisms that they can use to ease some of the pain of poor forecasts. Individual orders from suppliers are often partitioned into multiple deliveries, the dates of which can be advanced or delayed depending on actual demand. If a retailer overforecasts, resulting in an overbought situation, the store can run promotions or mark merchandise down in price until the overstocked condition is corrected. If management underbuys, it can either expedite a new order or try to substitute other merchandise. The latter strategy is usually not acceptable to the customers who originally demanded the out-of-stock merchandise. The important point for the retailer, however, is that despite such buffers, inaccurate forecasts impose additional burdens in the form of out-of-pocket and opportunity costs, customer goodwill, and poor performance at merchandising levels. The need to mark down merchandise leads directly to lower gross margins and may place the operating profits at unacceptable levels.

One cost that has become increasingly important is the inventory carrying cost. Historically, this cost has been a small part of the total cost of operating a retail firm. However, in the late 1970s and early 1980s, the situation changed dramatically. Many retailers finance inventories with short-term bank loans; therefore, when prime interest rates reached 21.5 percent, and loans to retailers were even higher, inventory carrying costs became a substantial portion of the total cost of store operations. In many cases, interest rates (and hence carrying costs) are several times what stores had been paying earlier.

Unique Problems of Forecasting and Buying
Seasonal Merchandise

The buying function at the retail level is based solely on projected sales during a future time period. Commitments for future delivery are made on projections of future sales. Planning takes place with future projections from one day to 10 to 11 months, or longer. The ability to forecast sales accurately at a 10-month future time period is more critical, and the chances of error are greater than they are when predicting tomorrow's sales and ordering more or less than one day's needs.

A unique problem arises in the ordering of seasonal merchandise—that is, products that have a very short selling season and lose a great deal of value on a specific date. For example, Mother's Day cards, Easter baskets, Halloween costumes, and Christmas ornaments all decline in value the day after the holiday occurs. The demand for the product increases up to the day of the event, then drops to zero or declines substantially, requiring that the price of each item be lowered substantially to sell any remaining products.

Typically, quantities ordered and delivery schedules for seasonal goods are arranged for the entire selling season, because reorders are impossible. For example, it would not be useful to find that not enough Christmas decorations had been ordered just 7 days before Christmas; that is too late for reordering.

The ordering process (ability to predict future sales) is much more critical for seasonal items than it is for staple or basic merchandise that is sold throughout the year. Valentine candy and Christmas decorations are ordered in a number of styles, sizes, and colors. If a retailer is sold out of one size of candy, the customer may select another size. However, the most undesirable situation for the out-of-stock retailer is when the customer goes to another store to make the purchase.

There appear to be two very basic yet totally different approaches to buying and merchandising of seasonal items. One is a supply-side orientation: which says We had a great year because we sold all of a seasonal product that was purchased. This type of sales forecasting is self-fulfilling: We planned to sell $10,000 worth of an item, so we bought $10,000 worth and, sure enough, that's how much we sold. No consideration is given to an out-of-stock situation on a date far in advance of declining demand.

The second approach involves buying to match the demand side of sales potential. A retailer using this approach buys to fulfill total consumer demand for each seasonal product. This retailer may have some merchandise left at the end of the selling season, whereas the supply-side retailer will be out of stock before the end of the season. The demand-side retailer has a different philosophy about selling items at reduced prices after the normal selling season. Selling at half price after the period of higher demand is not a problem, because full demand potential was achieved. The supply-side retailer does not want any remaining stock to dispose of at the end of the selling season. Very tight buying controls are placed on the supply-side retailer. Inventories are tightly controlled, and rewards are based on having no carryover, rather than on achieving a level of sales or gross margin potential, as is the case with the demand-side approach. Of course, in the ideal situation, all demand is satisfied with no carryover. Improved efficiency in forecasting can help make this ideal situation a reality.

Prior Research on Forecasting Retail Store Sales

Forecasting of department store sales can be classified into two categories: (1) forecasting new store sales for site selection analysis and (2) forecasting existing store sales for inventory, financial control, and budgeting purposes. Several studies have been devoted to market size and site selection forecasting, but the published research on forecasting existing retail department store sales is very limited. In an effort to forecast retail supermarket sales, White and Ellis (1971) built an econometric model that forecasted with an average error of 12.04 percent. Schmidt (1979) forecasted total retail sales for the state of Nebraska as a planning tool for retail sales tax collection. He contrasted Box-Jenkins and regression methods and found a Box-Jenkins technique, with an average error of 3.02 percent, to be the best. To our knowledge, little or no research has been conducted on forecasting seasonal demand for individual SKUs.

Objectives of This Research

The objectives of the research reported in this chapter are twofold. The first objective is to develop models for forecasting sales of seasonal products by unit for a single retail store. The second is to test the forecasted sales against actual sales to determine the accuracy of alternative models used to forecast individual unit sales.

Methodology

A large retail drug/discount chain agreed to cooperate in the study by providing sales data on approximately fifty different seasonal Christmas items. The data were provided for the two previous years for stores of the same size. All products used in this study had remained in stock during both of the past two years. The data were obtained as part of a major research effort into the daily sales rates of a wide range of seasonal products. The product categories and numbers of SKUs used in this study were as follows

1. Boxed christmas cards (15)
2. Ribbons and bows (10)
3. Folding gift boxes (8)
4. Christmas wrapping paper (12)
5. Tags and seals (4)

Four different sales forecasts were made for each SKU: an econometric model, a smoothing model, an averaging of the two models, and a subjective figure based on expert judgment. The models and subjective approach were developed in our earlier forecasting research.

The models showed that very accurate forecasts of retail sales could be made for total sales by region, store, and department on a monthly basis (Geurts and Kelly, 1983). One very interesting finding of our prior research was the adjustment of retail sales figures for inflation. Adjusted sales figures show very little growth in retail sales over the past 12 years in the United States. If sales are further adjusted for population growth, the sales levels are actually flat (see figure 11–1). The implication of this finding is that U.S. retail

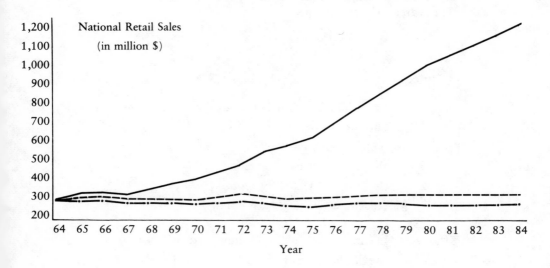

Figure 11–1. Gross National Retail Sales (1964–84)

sales are a function of population and inflation. This explains the accuracy (2.4 percent average error) with which we were able to forecast retail sales using exponential smoothing (Geurts and Kelly, 1983)—one of the approaches used in forecasting sales of Christmas-related merchandise in this chapter. In general, the model is

$$\hat{x}_{t+1} = x_t + \alpha x_t + \beta x_t$$

where $\hat{x}_{t+1}$ = the forecast of sales of the product during the next Christmas period;

x_t = sales during last year's Christmas period (this must be adjusted for stockouts when they occurred);

α = the average inflation rate;

β = the percentage of population growth from last year to this year and last. Thus, with 10 percent population growth, if population last year was 1 million, it will be 1.1 million next year.

A second model was also considered, since exponential smoothing proved to be so accurate in the prior study. An exponential model was used, with the following degrees of smoothing:

Once: $\hat{X}_{t+1} = \hat{t} + 1[\alpha(X_t/\hat{t}) + (1 - \alpha)(S^1X_{t-1})]$

Twice: $\hat{X}_{t+1} = \hat{t} + 1[(S^1X_t)D_1 + (S^2X_{t-1})D_2]$

Thrice: $\hat{X}_{t+1} = \hat{t} + 1[(S^1X_t)T_1 + (S^2X_t)T_2 + (S^3X_t)T_3]$

where α = smoothing weighting constant (takes on values of 0 to 1);

X_t = current sales;

$\hat{X}_{t+1}$ = next month's sales;

$\hat{t}$ = the seasonal factor for month t;

$\hat{t} + 1$ = the seasonal factor for month $t + 1$;

S^1X_t = current smoothing statistic if $S^1X_t = \alpha(X_t/\hat{t})$ $+ (1 - \alpha)(S^1X_{t-1})$;

S^1X_{t-1} = last month's single smoothing statistic

S^2X_t = the double smooth statistic: $S^1X_t + [1 - \alpha] = S^2X_t$;

S^3X_t = the triple smooth statistic: $S^2X_t + [1 - \alpha] = S^3X_{t-1}$;

Since there is no seasonality, $\hat{t}$ is dropped from the formula. The double smoothing model, with $\alpha = .4$, was used according to the criteria outlined by Brown (1963). Also, 1.1 times last year's sales was used as the double smooth statistic S^2X_t.

The third method of forecasting was to average the forecasts from the first two methods, and the fourth forecast was an expert judgment provided by the retail firm's buyer and the principal researcher.

A number of research controls existed that are worthy of mention. First, the same amount of space for each product existed for all three years. The advertising and price reduction sequences were almost identical, and approximately the same quantities were on display in each of the three years of the test.

Results

The four forecasts for 1984 are presented by product category in tables 11–1 through 11–5. These tables also contain the actual sales data by product for 1982 and 1983, which were the year's data points used for the 1984 forecast. The two prior sales years were used to create the other four projected sales figures. For simplicity, the actual product descriptions have been replaced with sequential numbers. Tables 11–1 through 11–5 also contain the percent error for each of the forecasted sales figures for the 1984 data.

Sales of various products varied widely, as can be seen in the tables. Sales in 1983 ranged from a low of 12 units for product 2-1 (ribbons and bows) to a high of 910 units of product 2-8 (also ribbons and bows). Some of the products are color-coordinated and somewhat complementary. For example, as more blue wrapping paper is sold, one might expect the sales of blue ribbons and bows to increase also. These complementary characteristics were considered in the subjective projections, but they were not included in the econometric and smoothing models.

Sales of some products increased substantially from 1982 to 1983, while other products declined in unit sales. Such variation further complicates the forecasting practice of adding a fixed percentge increase in units to all products, as some retailers do. Some of the products that declined in sales involved a licensed character that has declined in popularity during the past three to four years.

Each of the four models was compared with the actual sales for 1984. The error figures were totaled for each of the product categories, and the grand error totals for all five product groups can be found at the bottom of table 11–5. The econometric model had an error for all products of .71 percent. Since this is less than 1 percent, it represents an extremely accurate forecast. The smoothing model had an error of almost 16 percent. The averaged forecast had an error of over 8 percent, and the subjective judgment resulted in an error of almost 3 percent. Thus, it appears that retail sales can best be forecasted using an econometric modeling approach. The judgmental model appears to be second best, followed by an averaging of smoothing and econometric modeling. The smoothing model performed poorest of all four approaches.

Table 11-1
Actual and Forecasted Sales for Boxed Christmas Cards

Product Number	Actual Sales			Econometric Forecast	Percent Error
	1982	1983	1984		
1-1	96	164	99	173	74.75
1-2	78	130	142	137	-3.52
1-3	101	101	166	106	-36.14
1-4	107	130	110	137	24.55
1-5	93	134	188	141	-21.67
1-6	107	143	215	151	-29.77
1-7	94	85	124	90	-27.42
1-8	129	145	207	153	-26.09
1-9	92	67	78	71	-8.97
1-10	93	49	50	52	4.00
1-11	23	21	57	22	-61.40
1-12	55	63	50	66	32.00
1-13	50	26	82	27	-67.07
1-14	27	88	77	93	20.78
1-15	43	44	51	46	-9.80
Total/ Average	1188	1390	1688	1465	-13.21

Table 11-2
Actual and Forecasted Sales for Ribbons and Bows

Product Number	Actual Sales			Econometric Forecast	Percent Error
	1982	1983	1984		
2-1	37	12	20	13	-35.00
2-2	35	49	18	52	188.89
2-3	45	37	42	39	-7.14
2-4	45	26	38	27	-28.95
2-5	45	34	41	36	-12.20
2-6	42	19	55	20	-63.64
2-7	84	55	66	60	-9.09
2-8	969	910	1277	958	-24.98
2-9	98	56	83	59	-28.92
2-10	545	706	678	743	9.59
Total/ Average	1945	1984	2318	2007	-13.42

Smoothing Forecast	Percent Error	Average of Forecasts	Percent Error	Subjective Forecast	Percent Error
110	11.11	141	42.42	148	49.49
89	− 37.32	113	− 20.42	96	− 32.39
101	− 39.16	103	110.00	110	− 33.73
112	1.82	124	12.73	140	27.27
102	− 43.33	121	− 32.78	120	− 33.33
115	− 46.51	133	− 38.14	130	− 39.53
92	− 25.81	91	− 26.61	96	− 22.58
132	− 36.23	142	− 31.40	144	− 30.43
87	11.54	79	1.28	98	25.64
84	68.00	68	36.00	92	84.00
23	− 59.65	23	− 59.65	25	− 56.14
57	14.00	61	22.00	70	40.00
45	− 45.12	36	− 56.10	50	− 39.02
40	− 48.05	67	− 12.99	76	− 1.38
43	− 15.69	45	− 11.76	49	− 3.92
1232	− 27.01	1347	− 20.20	1444	− 14.45

Smoothing Forecast	Percent Error	Average of Forecasts	Percent Error	Subjective Forecast	Percent Error
32	60.00	22	10.00	30	50.00
38	111.11	45	150.00	32	77.78
43	2.38	41	− 2.38	45	7.14
41	7.89	34	− 10.53	45	18.42
43	4.88	40	− 2.44	50	21.95
37	− 32.73	28	− 49.09	42	− 23.64
78	18.18	69	4.55	84	27.27
957	− 25.06	958	− 24.98	1012	− 20.75
89	7.23	74	− 10.84	96	15.66
579	− 14.60	661	− 2.51	630	− 7.08
1937	− 16.44	1972	− 14.93	2066	− 10.87

Table 11–3
Actual and Forecasted Sales for Folding Boxes

Product	Actual Sales			Econometric	Percent
Number	*1982*	*1983*	*1984*	Forecast	Error
3–1	41	44	15	46	206.67
3–2	22	52	29	55	89.66
3–3	87	61	29	64	120.69
3–4	41	89	61	94	54.10
3–5	179	186	175	196	12.00
3–6	67	47	27	49	81.48
3–7	83	30	39	32	– 17.95
3–8	37	24	29	25	– 13.79
Total/ Average	557	533	404	561	38.86

Table 11–4
Actual and Forecasted Sales for Wrapping Paper

Product	Actual Sales			Econometric	Percent
Number	*1982*	*1983*	*1984*	Forecast	Error
4–1	106	123	154	138	– 15.58
4–2	88	169	135	178	31.85
4–3	103	106	106	112	5.66
4–4	163	107	136	113	– 16.91
4–5	50	117	50	123	146.00
4–6	92	124	193	131	– 32.12
4–7	67	131	98	138	40.82
4–8	101	143	124	151	21.77
4–9	109	164	111	173	– 55.86
4–10	63	212	118	223	88.98
4–11	88	151	115	159	38.26
4–12	106	195	161	205	27.33
Total/ Average	1136	1742	1501	1836	22.32

Smoothing Forecast	Percent Error	Average of Forecasts	Percent Error	Subjective Forecast	Percent Error
42	180.00	44	193.33	48	220.00
28	− 3.45	42	44.83	36	24.14
82	182.76	73	151.72	90	210.34
51	− 16.39	72	18.03	65	6.56
180	2.86	188	7.43	190	8.57
63	133.33	56	107.41	75	177.78
72	84.62	52	33.33	60	53.85
34	17.24	29	0.00	48	65.52
552	36.63	556	37.62	612	51.49

Smoothing Forecast	Percent Error	Average of Forecasts	Percent Error	Subjective Forecast	Percent Error
110	− 28.57	120	− 22.08	130	− 15.58
105	− 22.22	141	4.44	160	18.52
104	− 1.89	108	1.89	110	3.77
151	11.03	132	− 2.94	170	25.00
64	28.00	93	86.00	90	80.00
99	− 48.70	115	− 40.41	120	− 37.82
81	− 17.35	109	11.22	115	17.35
110	− 11.29	138	4.84	130	4.84
121	9.01	147	32.43	156	40.54
94	− 20.34	158	33.90	156	32.20
101	− 12.17	130	13.04	144	25.22
125	− 22.36	165	2.48	156	− 3.11
1265	− 15.72	1548	3.13	1637	9.06

Table 11–5
Actual and Forecasted Sales for Tags and Seals

Product Number	Actual Sales			Econometric Forecast	Percent Error
	1982	*1983*	*1984*		
5–1	28	37	43	39	−9.30
5–2	31	50	63	53	−15.87
5–3	19	17	21	18	−14.29
5–4	22	37	23	39	69.57
Total/ Average	100	141	150	149	−0.67
Total/ Average, All Products	4926	5710	6061	6018	−0.71

One limitation of this research was the use of only two data points to create the forecasts. The greater the number of data, the greater the likelihood of accuracy in the forecasting approaches. The data were also product-specific and store-specific. Therefore, the results can be considered generalizable to other similar retail stores and similar product categories. However, because the data came from seasonal merchandise sales with very specific selling seasons, the results may not be generalizable to basic merchandise that is always in stock.

Smoothing Forecast	Percent Error	Average of Forecasts	Percent Error	Subjective Forecast	Percent Error
30	− 30.23	35	− 18.60	36	− 16.28
35	− 44.44	44	− 30.16	48	− 23.81
19	− 9.52	19	− 9.52	20	− 4.76
25	8.70	32	39.13	36	56.52
109	− 75.50516	130	− 13.33	140	− 6.67
5095	− 15.94	5553	− 8.38	5899	− 2.67

References

Box, George E.P., and Jenkins, Givilynn M. *Time Series Analysis Forecasting and Control*, rev. ed. San Francisco: Holden-Day, 1976.

Brown, Robert Goodell. *Smoothing, Forecasting and Prediction of Discrete Time Series*. Englewood Cliffs, N.J.: Prentice-Hall, 1963.

Geurts, Michael D., and Kelly, J. Patrick. "No Adjustment Need to Get Accurate Department Forecasts," *Journal of Business Forecasting* 2 (Fall 1983):16–18.

Makridakis, S., and Hibon, M. "Accuracy of Forecasting: An Empirical Investigation." *Journal of the Royal Statistical Society, Series A* 142 (Part 2, 1979): 97–125.

Newbold, P., and Granger, C.W.J. "Experience with Forecasting Univariate Time Series and the Combination of Forecasts." *The Journal of the Royal Statistical Society, Series A* 137 (Part 2, 1974):131–65.

Schmidt, J.R. "Forecasting State Retail Sales: Econometric vs. Time Series Models," *Annals of Regional Science* 13 (November 1979):91–101.

White, L.A., and Ellis, J.B. "A System Construct for Evaluating Retail Market Locations," *Journal of Marketing Research* 8 (February 1971):43–46.

Index

About the Contributors

Gary J. Bamossy is Universitaire Docent Marketing in the Faculty of Economics at the Vrije Universiteit, Amsterdam, The Netherlands. He has a Ph.D. in marketing from the University of Utah (1983). His research interests are in marketing for public and nonprofit organizations, and his publications appear in research annuals and journals such as *Advances in Nonprofit Marketing* (The JAI Press), *The Journal of Cultural Economics, Empirical Studies in the Arts,* and various proceedings of the Association for Consumer Research. In addition to his faculty appointment, Dr. Bamossy is also active as an occasional consultant to the Dutch Ministry of Welfare Health and Culture and to service organizations in both the public and private sectors of the economy.

William S. Comanor is a professor and chairman of the Department of Economics at the University of California, Santa Barbara. A graduate of Haverford College, he received his Ph.D. in economics from Harvard University. Prior to joining the faculty of the University of California, he taught at both Harvard University and Stanford University and was also Fulbright Visiting Lecturer at the University of Tokyo. Professor Comanor has also served as special economic assistant to the assistant attorney general for antitrust in the U.S. Department of Justice and as director of the Bureau of Economics at the Federal Trade Commission. He is the author of over sixty articles and papers on various subjects in economics. He is also the author of two books, including *Advertising and Market Power* (coauthored with Thomas A. Wilson), which was published by Harvard University Press in 1974.

John S. Chard is a lecturer in economics at Exeter University. He received the B.A. from Manchester University and the M.Sc. from the London School of Economics. He specializes in industrial organization and has carried out research, sponsored by the Office of Fair Trading in the United Kingdom, into the economic effects of vertical restraints. He has published several articles about industrial and competition policies in journals such as *Journal of World Trade Law, European Law Review, European Economic Review,* and *The Antitrust Bulletin.*

Guido Cristini is a research fellow at the Department of Business Administration of Bocconi University, Milan, and he teaches at IFOR, a business school in Milan. He graduated from Bocconi University. He specializes in retail studies, his contributions on this subject include a book on the distribution of the press and articles on innovative forms in retailing, retail brands, and horizontal integration in distribution, published in *Commercio*, an Italian academic journal.

John P. Dickson is the dean of the School of Business and Public Administration at the University of Puget Sound. He received his B.A. from Colorado College, his M.B.A. from Indiana University, and his Ph.D. in marketing from the University of Oregon. He has taught at numerous universities, including Indiana University, University of Connecticut, University of Washington, and Dunedin University in New Zealand. He is coauthor of *Statistical Decision Models for Management*, and his publications have appeared in journals such as *Journal of Marketing Research, Journal of Retailing, Public Opinion Quarterly,* and *Journal of Advertising Research*. He has consulted with firms such as 3M, Campbell Soup Inc., Unilever International, G.D. Searle, and Weyerhaeuser. Prior to becoming the dean in 1985, he was the George Frederick Jewett Distinguished Professor at the University of Puget Sound.

Michael D. Geurts is a professor of business management in the Graduate School of Management at Brigham Young University. He has published work in such areas as shrinkage, price perception, space allocation, and forecasting in such journals as *Management Science, Journal of Marketing Research, Retail Control, International Journal of Retailing*, and *Journal of Retailing*. He consults for such companies as AT&T Communications, Boeing, British Petroleum, Valtec, Godfather's Pizza, and Hewlett Packard.

Avijit Ghosh is an associate professor of marketing at New York University's School of Business. He received his Ph.D. from the University of Iowa. His research interests are in marketing strategy and the spatial aspects of marketing activities. His publications have appeared in journals such as *Journal of Marketing Research, Journal of Marketing, Journal of Retailing, Journal of Business Research, Geographical Analysis,* and *Urban Studies*. He is currently the editor of *Journal of Retailing*.

J. Patrick Kelly is the K Mart Professor of Marketing at Wayne State University. He served at Brigham Young University for eight years, and prior to 1977 he was associate professor of marketing at Virginia Commonwealth University in Richmond. He received his B.S. degree from Brigham Young University in 1965, his M.B.A. degree from the University of Utah in 1966, and his Ph.D. degree from the University of Illinois in 1972. He is an active consultant to a wide variety of national firms. His empirical research has been extensive in the areas of instore signing, retail store productivity, retail store sales forecasting, retailing of services, and marketing strategies for the photographic industry. His recent research efforts have been presented at several national practitioner conferences. Publication of this research has appeared in *Journal of Business Forecasting, Business, Journal of Retailing, Management Accounting, Journal of Marketing,* and *Journal of Advertising.*

John B. Kirkwood is assistant director for evaluation in the Bureau of Competition of the Federal Trade Commission. He received an undergraduate degree in economics from Yale University and a law degree and a master's degree in public policy from Harvard University. After practicing antitrust law with a Washington, D.C., law firm, he joined the Federal Trade Commission in 1977, where he has been responsible for various aspects of policy planning, including development of case selection criteria, administration of the Hart-Scott-Rodino pre-merger notification program, and preparation of reports and policy recommendations on predatory pricing, collusive practices, and other major antitrust enforcement issues. In addition, he has represented the Bureau of Competition at seminars and symposia and published articles in legal, economic, and public policy journals.

Sara McLafferty is an assistant professor of geography at Columbia University. She received her Ph.D. from the University of Iowa. Her research interests are spatial analyses of private and public services with special emphasis on health care. She is the author of a number of papers published in such journals as the *Annals of the Association of American Geographers, Urban Studies, Political Geography Quarterly, Social Science and Medicine, Geographical Analysis,* and *Journal of Retailing.*

V. Kasturi Rangan is an assistant professor of marketing at the Graduate School of Business, Harvard University. He has a B.Tech. in engineering from the Indian Institute of Technology, an M.B.A. from the Indian Institute of Management, and a Ph.D. from Northwestern University. Professor Rangan has had several years of experience in sales and distribution management of consumer and industrial products. His current research interests are in industrial marketing and distribution channels. Professor Rangan's publications have appeared in *Management Science* and *Harvard Business Review.*

Torger Reve is professor of organization science and chairman of the Department of Organization Science at the Norwegian School of Economics and Business Administration, Bergen, Norway. he received a B.A. from Gustavus

Adolphus College, Minnesota, and an M.B.A. and an M.S. (behavioral science) from the Norwegian School of Economics and Business Administration. He has a Ph.D. in marketing from Northwestern University, and he has done postdoctoral work in organization theory at Stanford University. His publications have appeared in the *Journal of Marketing, Journal of Marketing Research, Academy of Management Review*, and many European Journals.

Patrick Rey is administrator of the Institut National de la Statistique et des Etudes Economiques (INSEE). He is currently teaching at Ecole Nationale de l'Administration Economique (ENSAE) and Ecole des Hautes Etudes en Sciences Sociales (EHESS). He graduated from Ecole Polytechnique and ENSAE. He has coauthored several papers on vertical constraints.

Debra L. Scammon is a professor of marketing in the Department of Marketing, College of Business, University of Utah, where she teaches a variety of courses on consumer behavior, advertising and promotion, marketing law, and marketing for health professionals. She graduated with a Ph.D. in marketing from the University of California, Los Angeles, Graduate School of Management, with minor areas in marketing law and social psychology. Dr. Scammon has been in-house marketing and advertising consultant to the Federal Trade Commission and also has consulted on a presidential task force to evaluate agency regulation. She has published extensively in the area of marketing law, with articles appearing in *Journal of Marketing, Journal of Consumer Research,* and *Journal of Advertising*. Dr. Scammon is also on the editorial review boards for several of these journals.

Louis W. Stern is John D. Gray Distinguished Professor of Marketing in the J.L. Kellogg Graduate School of Management at Northwestern University. He received an A.B. in economics from Harvard College, an M.B.A. from the University of Pennsylvania, and a Ph.D. in marketing from Northwestern University. Prior to joining the faculty of Northwestern University, he taught at The Ohio State University. He also taught at the University of California at Berkeley, the Hernstein Institute in Vienna, and the Norwegian School of Economics and Business Administration in Bergen. From 1983 to 1985, he was executive director of the Marketing Science Institute. Cambridge, Massachusetts. He also served as the Thomas Henry Carroll Ford Foundation Visiting Professor at Harvard Business School during 1984–85. His research efforts have centered on the behavioral dimensions of interorganizational relations and on public policy issues. His articles have appeared in a wide variety of marketing, legal, and behavioral science journals. Among the books he has coauthored are *Legal Aspects of Marketing Strategy: Antitrust and Consumer Protection Issues* (Prentice-Hall, 1984) and *Marketing Channels* (Prentice-Hall, 2nd ed., 1982). He has served as a consultant to numerous business firms and to the Federal Trade Commission.

Jean Tirole is an associate professor of economics at M.I.T., where he specializes in industrial organization, regulation, and the theory of the firm. He has engineering degrees from Ecole Polytechnique, Paris, and Ecole des Ponts et Chaussees, Paris; a "doctorate de troisieme cycle" in decision mathematics from the University of Paris 9, and a Ph.D. in economics from M.I.T. From 1981 to 1984 he taught at the Ecole des Ponts et Chaussees. His publications have appeared in journals such as *Econometrica, Review of Economic Studies, Journal of Economic Theory, Rand Journal of Economics, American Economic Review,* and *Journal of Political Economy.*

About the Editors

Luca Pellegrini is a lecturer in the Department of Business Administration at the Bocconi University, Milan. He graduated from the University of Venice and received his M.Sc. in economics from the London School of Economics, where he is completing his Ph.D. He has published a book on the effectiveness of public intervention by Italian regional authorities, contributed to three more books, and published several articles in Italian academic journals. He is deputy director at CESCOM, the Centre for Retail Studies, Bocconi University.

Srinivas K. Reddy is an assistant professor of marketing at New York University's Graduate School of Business Administration. He received his Ph.D. from Columbia University. His research interests are international marketing and advertising research. His publications have appeared in *Journal of Marketing, Multivariate Behavioral Research, Journal of International Business Studies,* and *Advances in International Marketing.* He is on the editorial board of *Journal of Retailing* .